Rodney Needham is a Fellow of All Souls College, Oxford. His recent books include *Circumstantial Deliveries* and *Against the Tranquility of Axioms*, both published by the University of California Press, and *Symbolic Classification*, *Primordial Characters*, and *Reconnaissances*.

EXEMPLARS

Rodney Needham

Exemplars

University of California Press

Berkeley   Los Angeles   London

University of California Press
Berkeley and Los Angeles, California
University of California Press, Ltd.
London, England
© 1985 by
The Regents of the University of California
Printed in the United States of America

1 2 3 4 5 6 7 8 9

LIBRARY OF CONGRESS CATALOGING IN PUBLICATION DATA

Needham, Rodney.
  Exemplars.

  Includes bibliographies and index.
  1. Methodology—History—Addresses, essays, lectures.
I. Title.
BD241.N39   1985   001.1'092'2   83-24326
ISBN 0-520-05200-5

For my Mother
Mary Elizabeth Needham

Contents

Illustrations

Preface

History is philosophy from examples.

Thucydides (attrib. by pseudo-Dionysius of Halicarnassus)

The exemplary personages who are arrayed, and in certain instances arraigned, in the sequence of studies constituting the present volume mark a span of two and a half thousand years, from Archilochus in the seventh century B.C. down to Castaneda in the latter part of the twentieth century A.D. Under this merely temporal aspect they trace out a history of a kind, though not a history in an ordinary sense. What they might be said to compose is a history of ideas without history.

The ambiguity of this phrase is apposite to the undertaking. It can be read as meaning that relations of effective succession are not established; the ideas in question are chronologically distributed, as in a history, but they are not causally linked. Or the assertion can be taken to mean that the ideas have individually no history: they are perennial concerns or inclinations in the mental life of men at any period. These contrasting interpretations are equally apt descriptions of the present work, both in its mode of exposition and in its general argument, and each reinforces the other.

The ideational topics considered, whether abstract concepts or subliminal proclivities, include symbolic archetypes, moral relativism, opposition, innate ideas, criteria of cogency, analogical classification, principles of semantic action, jural/mystical diarchy, and intellectual integrity. The men who here exemplify such deep matters in their writings make up a remarkable variety of human types. The company includes a poet (also a mercenary infantryman) and a sea captain, a repentant impostor and a scientific mystic, three philosophers of divergent persuasions, a historian of Indo-European civilization, and an anthropologist of cultic renown. Their publications are correspondingly varied, yet throughout them there recur common ideas, images, and associations that are already familiar from the comparative analysis of collective representations and social forms. As exemplars, they speak not just for themselves but in testimony to characteristic features of thought and imagination to which men of any period are naturally inclined.

In a previous book, *Against the Tranquility of Axioms*, the suggestion has been made that there are advantages in being ready to suspend an exclusive reliance on the procedures of traditional argumentation, and that revealing changes of aspect can be had by resort instead to aphorisms, maxims, paradigms, and metaphor (Needham 1983, chap. 1). In *Exemplars*, a complementary contention is that there are further advantages to be had from suspending the traditional concentration on social facts, and from considering instead the examples presented by individuals. However far-separated in time, or contrasted in other respects, they too demonstrate that certain steady constituents of human response can be discerned by the criteria of comparativism, and that this can be done by the study of individual representations as well as by the analysis of social facts. Considered methodologically, the exemplars pondered here furnish a new and distinct validation of the efficacy of comparative analysis.

The immediate interest of the present work is likely to be found, however, not so much in considerations of theory or method as in the idiosyncratic characters, thoughts, and values of the personages themselves. It is possible that not every reader will be as familiar with Archilochus as with Locke, and perhaps not many will be equally acquainted with Sextus Empiricus and Psalmanaazaar and Swedenborg. Knox and Dumézil, three centuries apart, yet concur on the structure of absolutism; Wittgenstein has unexpected things to say about a stock topic in anthropology; and even Castaneda is shown to conceal more that is enigmatic than has been suspected. Whatever the intellectual gains to be secured by studying these curiously impressive personages as exemplars, each of them makes a distinct impact that conveys its own humane quality and moral instruction.

R. N.

All Souls College, Oxford
Hilary Term, 1983

Acknowledgments

The essays that make up this book were composed, and delivered as lectures for the University of Oxford, within the walls of All Souls College. I am deeply obligated and most grateful to the Warden and Fellows of All Souls for the inestimable privilege of the fellowship, support, and ambience that the College has accorded me. I am indebted to the Codrington Library and its staff; also most especially to Mr. J. S. G. Simmons, sometime Fellow and Librarian, for unfailing and authoritative scholarly advice over the years.

Most of the study on which the essays are based was made in the Bodleian Library, Oxford, and the work could hardly have been carried through without the magnificent resources of that great institution and the assistance of all grades among its staff.

The essay on Archilochus (chap. 1) was in its original form a contribution to a Festschrift in honor of Guy Davenport. The present version differs very considerably from what was then submitted; the Festschrift, at what I gather was the modest initiative of the honorand, was never published. The piece on Knox (chap. 3) was a response to an invitation to take part in a commemorative volume, intended for publication in Sri Lanka in 1981, to celebrate the tercentenary of Knox's *Historical Relation of the Island of Ceylon*; it too has not been published. The defense of Dumézil (chap. 8) was written for a collaborative work dedicated to him, and it has appeared, with some divergencies, as "Dumézil et le domaine du comparativisme" in *Georges Dumézil*, ed. Jacques Bonnet (Paris: Centre Georges Pompidou/Pandora Editions, 1981), pp. 283–91.

In relation to the essay on George Psalmanaazaar (chap. 5), my accumulated thanks are due to many persons: the Governing Body of Christ Church, Oxford, and the staff of its library, for the kind loan of a copy of the second edition of the *Description of Formosa* and for making inquiries about the author's stay in that college in 1704; Mr. Alan D. Sterenberg (Reference Division, British Library) for help with dates of publication; Mr. I. K. McGilchrist (All Souls) for literary advice; and Messrs. D. J. Molian and P. Robinson for direction to ancillary works. The photographic plates illustrating chapter 5 are reproduced by permission of the Bodleian Library, Oxford, from George Psalmanaazaar, *Memoirs* (shelfmark: 8° Jur. Z. 132; frontispiece) and *Description of Formosa* (shelfmark: 8° J. 23. Linc.; fig 1 at p. 173, fig. 2 opp. p. 174, fig. 5 after p. 224, fig. 8 after p. 226); © Bodleian Library, Oxford, U.K.

No authentic representation of Archilochus has survived (Richter 1965, 1:17, 18, 66–68; cf. figs. 231–42). The drawing that accompanies chap. 1 is the work of Guy Davenport, and I am warmly grateful to him for permission to reproduce it. He drew it originally for his translation *Carmina Archilochi* (University of California Press, 1964), where it was printed in reverse. Here it appears with "Archilochus" in his true attitude: facing to proper right, and right-handed; also, the swastika is displayed under its auspicious aspect. The portrait of Knox was done by P. Trampon about 1708; it is reproduced by arrangement with the National Maritime Museum, London. The painting of Swedenborg is by Per Krafft the Elder; it is in Gripsholm Castle, Sweden, and is reproduced by arrangement with the Svenska Porträttarkiv, Nationalmuseum, Stockholm.

Professor T. H. Irwin (Cornell University) generously lent his aid in seeking the exact source of the epigraph, usually attributed to Dionysius of Halicarnassus, that here introduces *Exemplars*. Mr. E. L. Hussey (All Souls) was helpful on points of translation in the explication of certain fragments of Archilochus, and I have adopted his rendering of the passage from

Heraclitus that serves as epigraph to chapter 1. Professor G. Peiris (University of Sri Lanka) suggested interpretations of phrases in Sinhalese as related by Robert Knox. For information on Eugen Herrigel (Conspectus; cf. chap. 9) I am obliged to Dr. Momoko Takemi (Keio University, Tokyo), Mrs. Yoko Fujita Horise (Linacre College, Oxford), Mr. Daniel P. Simon (Director, Berlin Document Center), and Dr. Andreas Jakob (Archiv der Friedrich-Alexander-Universität, Erlangen). Mrs. Chihoko Moran was so kind as to translate from Japanese for me.

Most of the parts of this book have been delivered, at one stage or another in their composition, as lectures, away from Oxford, at: the meetings of the American Anthropological Association held in December 1980 at Washington, D.C.; the University of Minnesota, the University of Illinois, Indiana University, the University of Uppsala, the State University of New York at Stony Brook, New York University, Yale University, Williams College, Dartmouth College, and the University of New Hampshire.

Among many persons to whom I am very grateful for invitations, hospitality, and other kind attentions, the following are offered my best thanks: the North American Committee of the Royal Anthropological Institute; S. F. Gudeman, M. Penn; C. E. Cunningham; I. Karp, J. H. Vaughan; A. Jacobson-Widding, C. Corlin, O. Hjern; T. O. Beidelman, A. Weiner; W. Arens, L. C. Faron, D. B. Hicks; J. F. M. Middleton; G. Feeley-Harnik; R. M. Green, H. H. Penner, H. S. Alverson, K. M. Endicott; and R. E. Downs. I should like also to record my special gratification at having been invited by Dartmouth College to deliver the tenth annual Orr Lectures on Culture and Religion.

Conspectus

Great examples grow thin, and to be fetched from the past world. Simplicity flies
away, and iniquity comes at long strides upon us.   Sir Thomas Browne

Dr. Johnson defined an exemplar as "a pattern; an example to
be imitated." But when he came to the adjective "exemplary"
he was more prudent. The word retained the sense of "such
as may deserve to be proposed to imitation," but it was also
supplied with the qualifier: "such as may give warning to
others" (Johnson 1755, s.vv.).

The essays that make up the text in the chapters that follow
are marked by both of these opposed characters. Although
most of the personages studied are admirable, not all of them
deserve imitation; in some instances, or under various aspects, certain among them are exemplary in that they serve as
warnings. To these contrasted senses of what it is to be an
exemplar, the Oxford dictionary subjoins: "an archetype,
whether real or ideal." This too is a sense that can appro-
priately be kept in mind when estimating the lessons to be
learned from the exemplary subjects considered.

The exemplars are presented candidly and for the most
part sympathetically; within the scope of the interests that
circumscribe the investigations, each speaks in his own terms.
As for the theoretical connections that can be made among
them, on one or another ground of similarity, these also can
be left to propose themselves. (The parallel allusions to my
own writings are intended to help make such connections,

both by concatenation and by tracing lines of common interest throughout the topics of the book.) Not all of the persons adduced are given equal space, however, or an equally minute scrutiny; some are taken to be more instructive than others, or else they are more likely to be unfamiliar to the reader, and they benefit accordingly from longer treatment. Also, the reasons for which they are found interesting are of different kinds. It may be helpful, therefore, to introduce the exemplars with a few informal phrases before they are put more stiffly on parade.

1. Archilochus appears to us in what Davenport calls the "tattered vision" provided by some three hundred fragments, many of them hardly to be construed, yet the extraordinary form of his mind is still discernible; "not all poets can be so broken and still compel attention" (1964:xiv). Disintegrated as are most of his writings that have come down to us, they call repeatedly for scholarly glosses and amplifications. Not all of these, as we shall see, are persuasive or even readily justifiable. This leaves the way open to reconstruction, extending so far as poetic license, and it is an instance of this that is examined in chapter 1.

The licensee is Davenport, himself a poet, and the interest of the essay below lies in the comparative considerations that are brought to bear in an attempt to trace the implications of the addenda that he happened to make. There is no pretense, in this examination, at a conclusive analysis; what the essay is meant to display is one possible response, on the part of a comparativist, to the imaginative provocation offered by a poetic interpretation. It serves also to introduce, in a wholly nontechnical setting, certain ideas that will be found to recur in the course of the rest of the book. From a scientific point of view, expressible in analytical propositions, these features are central to the entire enterprise; but a reader who does not much care about such abstractions, or who has not previously encountered Archilochus, will have something to gain from even this incidental contact with an exceedingly remarkable man. What an exemplar indeed have we here, in a hard-bitten campaigner who after "the hot work of slaughtering, / Among the dry racket of the javelins" (trans. Davenport, fr. 42) could write the sardonic lines "In the hospitality of war / We left them their dead / As a gift to remember us by" (fr. 184); who could pragmatically dismiss, when he abandoned his shield in battle (flouting the contemptuous charge of *ripsaspis*, shield-discarder) in order to save his skin, the epic claims of heroic values (fr. 79); and who bequeathed over the millennia the apothegm "Fox knows many / Hedgehog one / Solid trick" (fr. 183).

2. The fundamental interest of the skeptical maneuvers of Sextus Empiricus lies in the direct appeal made by the arguments about moral relativism. It is a moving experience to read the *Outlines of Pyrrhonism* and to feel at one with men, two millennia ago, who with resolution and ingenuity faced an ineluctable problem of conscience.

It is chastening, also, to appreciate that the Skeptics already had a technique of analysis and a method of comparison that were not only adequate to their particular purposes but are essentially identical with modern practices. Where they failed in their argument, this was on a point of logic that they were as capable of identifying as we are. That they did not in fact do so provides a historical lesson about the prejudicial power of theory, but, far from persuading us of subsequent progress achieved, it deepens our apprehension about our own vulnerability on the same score. They were, moreover, the first systematic comparativists in the field of social facts; and they initiated a style of explicating human conduct that was not again to be effectively exploited until the Enlightenment.

Today, after the demise of so many antique certitudes, their philosophical stance acquires new force and pertinence (cf. Needham 1981:10–11), and the attraction of their sane example proffers a tested means of coming to terms with the quandaries of human experience.

3. When Robert Knox's *Historical Relation of Ceylon* was first published, in 1681, the work carried a commendation of its great truth and integrity by Sir Christopher Wren, sometime Fellow of All Souls but for all that hardly so knowledgeable about Ceylon as he was genial in astronomy and architecture. Nevertheless, the book does contain an abundance of reliable detail, and as an early classic of ethnography it deserves much lasting praise.

In the matter of the author's own integrity, however, there is a lesson to be drawn from the morality of his age. Knox was a captive of a Ceylonese king, Raja Singha, for twenty years. He did not languish in a dungeon, nor was he shackled, but he was none the less effectively kept a prisoner in the kingdom until at long last he made his escape and was taken off the island. When he returned to England he was given command of a ship; and with this grand liberty he at once turned slave-runner. He was a devout Christian, and repeatedly in his book he offers thanks to God for having delivered him from captivity.

This moral opportunism is instructive in its own way, and so also is the apparent fact that Knox's character in this regard did not impair the integrity of his ethnographic reports. It is these that permit a comparativist to discern a recognizable structure in the absolute social forms of seventeenth-century Ceylon. This structure is expressed, moreover, in a familiar idiom of purity and pollution, and a crucial opposition of ranks is declared by allusion to incest, a practice paradoxically ascribed to both king and beggars. As for the outcome of the analysis, a main theoretical aspect is that the data compose the structural pattern that is isolated not by dint of modern concepts exclusively but by reason of a correspondence between analytical notions and the order that is intrinsic to the collective representations themselves.

4. Locke is famous for his contention that the human mind is at its beginning a *tabula rasa* or, in a less well-known phrase, an empty cabinet.

Not everybody who is familiar with the former tag is as familiar with the argumentative setting from which it is taken. A fair portion of chapter 4, accordingly, is devoted to first expounding the main lines of Locke's position and of the opposed view that he was arguing against. More could surely be made of the fact that the idea of a *tabula rasa* was not a fixed dogma in Locke's thought, and that elsewhere he made concessions to the possible existence of innate ideas. However, the point of the essay is not to offer yet another exposition of his ideas on this topic, or to attempt a definitive and comprehensive account of his thought. The intention behind the initial concentration on Locke's *Essay* is to adduce a classic historical example of a powerful case against innate ideas before proceeding to an alternative, if not precisely contrary, argument in favor of primary factors of experience. Prominent among these factors is the operation of condensation which eventuates in paradigmatic (or exemplary) scenes.

It may be worth special stress in advance, in this connection, that condensation is already well recognized and accepted as a means to the economy by which, in rational and cognitive regards, we cope with experience and order our mental lives. What is proposed below is that this same operation is responsible also for a psychic economy in the field of semantic perceptions, and that the products have a relatively steady character as paradigmatic scenes. It is these phenomena in particular which, as imaginative and affective forms of representation, connect with what we are surely not wrong in calling our real lives.

5. It is one of the tragedies of literary biography (almost comparable with the destruction of Lichtenberg's *Sudelbücher* G and H) that James Boswell did not meet Dr. Johnson until thirteen days after the death of the latter's friend and drinking companion George Psalmanaazaar. It would have been quite fascinating, as well as materially informative, to read what Boswell's scavenger brain would have made of this erstwhile "Formosan," and what he could have recorded of the exchanges between the literary doctor and the publisher's hack.

There are many indications in the sources that we do command that Psalmanaazaar, as a young man, was found most impressive by men of the world who were not easily imposed upon; and this was not just because of his supposed exotic origins, but by reason of his outstanding gifts of quickness, intelligence, knowledge, and much else that was admirable, combined with an air of sincerity and what was evidently a considerable personal appeal. Even when, in retrospect, we can recognize him for the thorough impostor that he then was, still he continues to make a remarkable impact of character.

In many ways he was undoubtedly a great man, and it is not hard to appreciate that in his years of reclusive contrition he should have attracted the company and the deep admiration of Dr. Johnson. While much of his subsequent fame rests on his scandalous success as a fake ethnographer, even in this he remains an exemplar whose flawed achievement carries its lessons, as will be seen, into our own day.

6. The approach to the essay on Swedenborg may acquire direction from a short statement of why it was first undertaken.

In the analysis of symbolic classification, in connection especially with the study of prescriptive systems, the notion of "correspondence" easily proposed itself. A typical proposition was that the symbolic order (the values of right and left, masculine and feminine goods, and so forth) corresponded to the social order (categories of persons, modes of alliance, and so on). Then there was a different kind of proposition, intended this time to be explanatory rather than merely correlational, to the effect that the constituent relations of a prescriptive system corresponded to fundamental properties of the human mind. Clearly the notion of correspondence was theoretically crucial, to the extent at any rate that the propositions in question were sustainable, but it was not itself patently clear. The uses to which other writers had put it did not make it much clearer, and ordinary dictionaries did not decisively clarify the operation of conceiving or establishing a correspondence. On the whole, it seemed a fairly rough and ready term, and not a precise concept such as the analyses demanded.

In due course the philosophical vocabulary of Lalande (1951:192–93, s.v. Correspondance) was found to supply a brief logical definition and also, far more consequentially, an entry on the Theory of Correspondences. This, while not all that helpful in itself, especially since it relied fundamentally on the obscure concept of analogy (cf. Needham 1980, chap. 2), stated that "correspondence," in this context, had been used in particular by Swedenborg. In the end, as will be seen, a lengthy examination of Swedenborg's writings did nothing much to sort out the useful application of the concept of correspondence itself. But the inquiry did lead to a fascinating attempt to come to terms with Swedenborg's mystical doctrine; and this venture, in a field where the idiosyncratic and the imaginative could be presumed to reign, had in the end a surprisingly systematic outcome. On the way to this result it was discovered, against expectation, that the resources of comparativism provided the grounds for an effective analysis; and this analysis, conversely, proved to support—on the basis of mystical materials—the postulation of characteristic features of thought and imagination that otherwise found expression in social facts.

This finding, itself formulable as a correspondence, has
weighty implications for the study of modes of apprehension
and their systematic interrelations. If there is to be a distinct
model of the human mind, derived from the comparative
analysis of representations, then the case of Swedenborg
makes a crucially significant contribution.

7. The two most radically instructive sources for the critical comprehension of ritual are "Doctor Brodie's Report" by
Borges (1976) and "Remarks on Frazer's *Golden Bough*" by
Wittgenstein (1967b; 1979).

This assertion, dealing as it does in superlatives, is no more
extreme than its form announces; and such judgments are
common currency, after all, among social anthropologists.
The difference in this instance is that neither of the exemplars
named has achieved such a degree of commendation, or for
that matter even recognition, in the writings of those who
propound theories about ritual. The topic of ritual is very
prominent in modern anthropological writings, yet the two
short pieces just cited (adding up to no more than twenty-
seven pages between them) are, in general, accorded no place
at all in what is by now an extensive and professionally prestigious literature.

The essay that follows as chapter 7 offers a number of remarks on Wittgenstein's ideas about ritual. (Borges, who is
adduced incidentally at other places in the present work, is
not taken up here; cf. Needham 1981:53–55.) These remarks
do not compose a systematic argument, let alone an integral
theory; they can be seen instead as samples of thinking about
"ritual" in response to the incitements of Wittgenstein's
thought and power of imagination. There is no suggestion
that the responses are in every instance decisive, or that they

are comprehensive; but they are intended to serve rather as occasions for further reflection, in the mind of the reader, on Wittgenstein's perturbing questions.

If there is a general conclusion toward which the present responses lead, it is in essential agreement with that of Whitehead: "My main thesis is that a social system is kept together by the blind force of instinctive actions, and of instinctive emotions clustered around habits and prejudices" (1958:68–69). We need not take the attribute of "instinctive" to the letter, and today, over fifty years after the thesis was first propounded, we should doubtless settle on some more defensible epithet, but Whitehead's general contention is none the less compelling. A modern exemplar of a similar persuasion is Samuel Beckett (cf. Needham 1978:70; 1981:109), and the outlook on ritual that is sketched out in the chapter below has much in common also with his austere paradigm *Le Dépeupleur* (1970).

Just as Beckett's stringent account cannot well be read merely as a literary exercise, so too Wittgenstein's remarks on *The Golden Bough* are not just detached academic speculations, but they evoke a sense of deep seriousness about understanding social forms.

8. The essay on Dumézil is in many ways relatively straightforward, as well as conveniently concise. The reader who is not familiar with Dumézil's ideas, expounded as these are in a very extensive literature in French, will need to grasp only two basic notions.

The first is that archaic Indo-European society is held to have been inspired by an ideology of three social "functions"; these can be roughly indicated as those of priest, warrior, and farmer. The second notion is that sovereignty was partitioned between the first and second functions, which conjointly exercised a form of diarchy combining the mystical with the jural. The Indo-European representation of sovereignty is the

subject of Dumézil's *Mitra-Varuṇa* (1948), a little monograph
that is one of the most attractive and suasive studies of a great
civilization. The principle of diarchy that it isolates is not,
however, peculiar to the Indo-European tradition alone, and
the validity of the concept can also be demonstrated by a
comparison among non–Indo-European societies. This is the
central argument of chapter 8 below, but there are in addition
underlying contentions that have an even more general
interest.

Some of these guiding ideas have to do with characteristic
features of thought and imagery established by comparative
analysis and such as provide a new basis of proof for Dumézil's thesis. But of more consequence, in the end, are the considerations of temperament that imbue and probably form
the ideas of scholars. Borges has already pointed out that
"reason and conviction differ so much that the gravest objections to any philosophical doctrine usually pre-exist in the
work that declares it" (1968:71 n. 3); so this hazard can be
foreseen and, with sufficient critical acumen and self-control,
can be guarded against. What is even more significant, and
immeasurably more insidious, is the temperamental inclination toward boldness or toward prudence that will color an
entire theory and also the opposition to it.

This powerful source of division of opinion is a particularly unmanageable factor, for writers are unequally aware of
its influence, and the more they are aware the more they real-
ize in advance that ultimately it may render both themselves
and their critics impervious to argument. Nevertheless, the
unevadable confrontation of views, as for instance between
Dumézil and his critics, is conventionally and necessarily carried on in accordance with the canons and criteria of strictly
detached argumentation. This makes the issue all the more
awkward and frustrating, beyond what any argument would
need to be if it were really conducted according to considerations of fact and logic alone. Nor does the temperamental di-

vide separate only boldness from prudence, but also idealists from realists, romantics from classicalists, transcendentalists from positivists, the atheistic from the religious, and so on through an interminable range of ideational dimensions and opposed stances.

Whether anything can be done to overcome such divisions is an open question, and the likely answer is not encouraging, but in any event a careful estimation of the factor of temperament is inseparable from a truly rational resolution of adversarial ideas.

9. Carlos Castaneda, the subject of the concluding essay, is undeniably an exemplar of a kind. His great popular success makes his ethnographic saga of Don Juan a consummate test case for the principles, values, and methods that he exemplifies. No more than this need be said here on his particular account, but something may well be noted as to the exposition of the argument.

The essay develops through a sequence of changes of aspect. In this it resembles the Kwakiutl artifact that is known as a transformation mask. This is worn by a dancer who, at the high point of a performance that enacts a myth, pulls on strings which open the mask; slowly the parts (usually there are four sections, sometimes two) separate on hinges, revealing within them another being who also belongs to the myth. This is the basic form of the mask, and the transformation is effected by the disclosure of the inner character, suspended in the center of the parted sections (Hawthorn 1967:59, 319); for instance, the mask of a wolf opens to reveal a man (fig. 454), a raven opens also to reveal a man (figs. 455, 457), a wolf opens to reveal an eagle (fig. 458). With this single transformation the revelation is accomplished. But there exists a yet more ingenious type of this mask. With this construction the outer mask opens to reveal another character inside—and then this second mask in turn is opened to reveal a third. Thus in one example a bullhead opens to display a raven, and the raven itself opens to disclose a third mask representing a human face (Waite 1966:271; fig. 1 illustrates Coll. AMNH No. 16/8942). This revelatory sequence is exactly paralleled by the analysis of Castaneda's presentation of the hidden teachings of Don Juan.

It will be discovered in the course of this inquiry that Eugen Herrigel (analogue to the raven in the triple mask just mentioned) occupies a central position. There are certain more particular details about this secondary exemplar that ought to be on record and that may well be kept in mind as chapter 9 develops.

The first has to do with his command of the Japanese language. An article by Yukio Takeda, "Shahō Hen," on how to shoot with the bow (Tokyo: Yuzan Kaku Publishing Company, n.d. [ca. 1969/71]) reports that in the spring of 1929, a few months before Herrigel left Japan in the August of that year, Tohoku University sponsored an archery demonstration which was made the occasion of a farewell address by Herrigel after more than five years as a professor at that institution. The address, which is described as having been difficult and as philosophical or religious in character (cf. in chap. 9 the enigmatic discourse of Kenzo Awa), was delivered by Herrigel in German; it was translated into Japanese by Professor Sōzō Komachiya.

The second matter has far deeper, and sinister, implications. When Herrigel had completed his training in Zen in the art of archery, and was about to depart from Japan to return to Germany, he was enjoined by his master never to give up his "spiritual archery." It was impressed upon him that archery was "a profound and far-reaching contest of the archer with himself," and that he had become a different person in the course of his years of instruction, so that when he got back to Germany he would "see with other eyes and measure with other measures" (Herrigel 1953:89–90). The vision that he had thus been vouchsafed was the enlightenment of Zen, a way characterized by detachment, harmony, and tranquility. The actual consequence, a few years after he had assumed the position of professor of philosophy at the University of Erlangen, was that Herrigel voluntarily joined the Nazis. He applied for membership of the National Socialist party on 5 December 1937, and under N.S.D.A.P. Anordnung 18/37 he was made a member of the Party (no. 5 499 332) with effect from 1 May 1937.

After the war, a denazification tribunal found that, whereas he had at first been a supporter of the Nazis, he had later withdrawn his inner allegiance. Nevertheless, many had viewed his academic lectures on Japan, and one on National Socialist philosophy, as Nazi doctrine. The tribunal decided however that by his general conduct he had shown that in his inner self he had not been influenced in any way by National Socialism and its ideas. Yet notwithstanding this assumption in Herrigel's favor, and certain other positive aspects of his case, the tribunal concluded, to its regret, that, since his resistance to the Nazis did not satisfy the requirements of the law, it was unable to accede to Herrigel's petition for exoneration. It is not reported to have taken into account his spiritual conversion to Zen.

1

Archilochus and the Intimation of Archetypes

Latent structure is master of obvious structure.   Heraclitus

I

Towards the middle of the seventh century B.C., arguably between 645 and 640, a man of Naxos ominously nicknamed
"Crow" silenced the first individual poetic voice of the west.
He was to be expelled from the temple of Apollo for this
deed, and when he protested that he had killed his victim in
a fair fight, or as an act of war, the priestess nevertheless
obdurately drove him out for having slain a servitor of the
Muses.

Archilochus, the deceased poet (and mercenary soldier),
was probably born at the end of the eighth century or in the
beginning of the seventh, and when he was struck down by
Crow he was perhaps approaching sixty years of age. The
fame of his works, however, handsomely survived him; he is
mentioned by ancient authors from Heraclitus in the sixth
century B.C. to the Church Fathers in the sixth century A.D.
After the revival of learning in Europe the surviving fragments of the writings of Archilochus were published in ten
principal editions between 1560 and 1958 (Lasserre and Bonnard 1958:cxix). Yet for all his fame in antiquity, and the influence he exerted on other poets of the ancient world, "he
has had very little impact upon the modern literary world

outside the field of classical scholarship" (Rankin 1977:95).
Thus when Guy Davenport first published his translations of
the fragments, to be collected under the title *Carmina Archilochi* (1964), it was widely supposed that "Archilochus" was
the invention of the translator, "a new and ingenious American poet" (Kenner, in Davenport 1964:vii). Others assumed
that the translation, which Davenport represented as being as
"literal" as he could manage, was at least very free (xvii).

In the view of one scholarly critic, Davenport's translation
has skillfully caught the mood of Archilochus (Anon. 1965).
According to Rankin, on the other hand, it is very effectively
couched in "vigorously American epigrams" (1977:95), and
this idiom helps to impart "a most important element of immediacy and life"; the translator is held to have brought to
realization "his obviously deeply-felt desire to interpret poetry by poetry, and as poetry." In this way the English version
becomes "an act of literary creation in its own right," and as
such it is found to be "undoubtedly a success" (96).

Here we approach a matter that calls for comparative analysis, and that may be posited by reference to images and
ideas and organizing principles in civilizations other than that
of ancient Greece.

II

Davenport renders one fragment, no. 144 in his ordering
(1964:52), as follows:

> Fortune is like a wife:
> Fire in her right hand,
> Water in her left.

The first line is not in the text but has been supplied after Plutarch, *Life of Demetrius*, who compares Fortune with "the

Plate 1. "Archilochus" (Courtesy Guy Davenport)

woman in Archilochus" (cf. Edmonds 1931:147, fr. 93). Davenport says in his note to this item: "We don't know what symbolism, if any, Archilochus had in mind" (101).

To a comparativist, however, the fragment is very striking, for here we have a fundamental paradigm of symbolic classification, namely:

fire : water :: right : left

Fire and water are elements accorded a special importance in metaphysics since antiquity, while right and left have a relational significance in symbolism that has been universally expressed by mankind (Needham 1973a).

When Davenport's translation appeared, this fragment at once stood out by its inherent interest in these respects. Beidelman, for example, was much struck by it, and to the extent that he soon adopted it as an apposite epigraph to an article of his on sexual symbolism in Africa (Beidelman 1964). But a subsequent check of the Loeb and the Budé editions of Archilochus, together with the assistance of a scan of the text by a classicist, was disconcerting. Edmonds has "water in the one hand, the wily one, and fire in the other" (1931:147, fr. 93). Lasserre and Bonnard, reading as subject "La bête rusée," the wily animal, have "d'une patte portait l'eau et de l'autre le feu" (1958:64, fr. 225), carried the water with one paw and the fire with the other. There is nothing about right and left. The words are not in the Greek.

Edmonds does not gloss the phrase. Bonnard makes it follow another fragment (no. 224), about a monkey and a fox. In the words of Edmonds the relevant lines are:

I will tell thee and thine a fable: The Ape parted from the other beasts and was walking alone in the borderland, when the crafty Fox met him with cunning in his heart.

The translation by Bonnard, rendered into English, goes:

The monkey, excluded from the society of the animals, went away on his own in search of a deserted place. The cunning fox, thinking to play one of his usual tricks, approached him.

It is here that Bonnard introduces the water/fire fragment that is our present subject. In Edmonds, the fable and this fragment are separated, as fr. 89 and fr. 93 respectively, with no significant connections of sense in the intervening fragments. There is no canonical order to the fragments, however, so this contrast does not argue against the postulated connection, but it does emphasize that the sequence in question has to be deliberately made.

The story that links the two fragments can easily be reconstituted, says Bonnard, by reference to two of Aesop's fables. The monkey, an ousted candidate for royalty (cf. Epode V), seeks solitude; the fox, intending to play one of his tricks, accompanies him. The fox "symbolically carries water and fire" (65, commentaire). Bonnard does not state what precisely is symbolic about this; that is, he does not explain why water and fire should be taken as symbols or, if that is what they are, what they are supposed to symbolize. What he writes is: "quoiqu'il [sc. le renard] prétende laver la plaie de son ami, il en cuira au singe de l'écouter"; that is, although he [the fox] offers to solace his friend, the monkey will pay for it if he listens to him. This makes the affair look indeed like a piece of practical trickery, hardly symbolic. For that matter, Bonnard concedes parenthetically that the attribution of the fable fragment to Epode V and its interpretation remain uncertain. And in any case there is no equivalent in the Greek to "la bête," the animal; this noun is supplied, and reflects merely the translator's presumption that the fragment is in fact connected with Aesop's tales, and so too does the rendering of the Greek for "hand" as "patte," paw.

With this much cleared up, let us look again at the water/ fire fragment. Taken literally, word by word, it reads: "In the one hand water carried she, being full of tricky thoughts, and in the other, fire" (trans. E. L. Hussey). The feminine subject corresponds to the gender of "the woman in Archilochus" and of the noun (fox) in the fable.

Davenport in his turn translates the fable fragment separately (as his fr. 197), and then, after a separation marked by a plain rule, continues as part of the same fragment with: "Water in one hand, fire in the other" (1964:68), with no mention of left and right. His note on this fragment indicates only the concordance with Lasserre and Bonnard, frs. 224– 25, 227–29. He offers no interpretation and he does not comment on his repetition, in different words and in a different order, of one and the same fragment about water and fire, for there is only one equivalent passage in the Greek (cf. also Diehl 1952:38, fr. 86).

It is for classical scholars to debate such matters as a possible connection between the fable fragment and Aesop, and hence the plausibility of Bonnard's interpretation of that concerning water and fire, but in any event the outcome of that issue is not the real problem. The crucial point is that the specifications "right" and "left" in Davenport's fr. 144 have no textual basis. Without the explicit lateral symbolism the analogical scheme is gone, and with it the apparently fundamental interest of the lines as he renders them.

Now Davenport did not adopt the lateral specifications from any translator among his predecessors, and he certainly did not mistranslate as "right" and "left" any other words in the Greek text. There is no indication, either, that he was taking into account what might be argued to have been a traditional association in ancient Greece between fire and right, water and left. The conclusion is plain that he simply supplied the adjectives. This may have been the exercise of poetic license (as also in the reversed order of the substantives), yet the effect was that, with apparent significance, he allocated fire to the right and water to the left.

III

The question then is: How did it come about that Davenport arrived at a pair of associations which can strike a comparativist as being so clearly apposite?

The epithet does not mean that we can assert, as an ethnographic generalization, that these associations hold so universally or preponderantly that they will obtain in the Greek case also. It is an elementary observation in the study of dual symbolic classification that homologies depend upon context (Needham 1973a:xxv–xxx). Thus $a : b :: c : d$ (in which a and c are homologues, likewise b and d) may in a different setting, or when viewed under a different aspect, become transformed into $a : b :: d : c$, so that the homologies are reversed (cf. Needham 1980, chap. 2). Even within one tradition, then, fire may be associated with the right in one context and with the left in another. But if this much is conceded as a premise in the analysis of symbolic classification, we have to explain in what sense a certain association, such as fire with the right, can be regarded as strikingly "apposite."

A response that might be sustained is that fire and the right, and also water and the left, tend respectively to be associated by virtue of deeper and more abstract properties which are not made explicit by discrete words or images. Reversed homologies would then be seen as secondary phenomena, the results of common manipulations by which subliminal constants were adapted to circumstantial variables. The association of fire with right, for instance, could then be taken as intrinsic in some regard or other but yet be subject on occasion to a disjunction in favor of an association of fire with left.

An example can be taken from another great and literate civilization, that of classical India. Bosch, writing about the attributes in the pairs of hands of divine images, says that generally speaking hot or luminous objects (among others) are held in the right hands, whereas cool and dark objects are held in the left, but that in both the Hindu and the Buddhist pantheons this symbolic system has repeatedly been discarded (Bosch 1960:220). Thus in one of the most famous and impressive of Indian icons, that of Śiva Naṭarāja, whereas the back right hand holds a drum, the left holds a ball of fire: "Creation arises from the drum: . . . from fire proceeds destruction" (Banerjea 1956:473; see also Coomaraswamy 1957:69, 71; Kramrisch 1981:439–40; and especially O'Flaherty 1973:376, s.v. "fire/water balance"). It is the destructive aspect of fire in this instance that explains the assignment to the left.

If, however, fire is contended nevertheless to have an intrinsic connection with the right, we have to intimate, even if we cannot precisely define or demonstrate, the latent connections that are taken to be basic or primary. Notoriously, though, this can hardly be done convincingly, since the proof is perpetually liable to subversion by uncertainties of criteria and context. Let us therefore contemplate a possible line of argument by stating first that in western thought there is a continuous metaphysical tradition, traceable from the contemporaries of Archilochus down to the European alchemists of the seventeenth century, in which a standard analogy associates hot, male, and the right together in opposition to cold, female, and the left (cf. Lloyd 1964, 1973; Bachelard 1942, 1949). This is not at all an isolated or idiosyncratic doctrine, and these sets of associations have repeatedly been encountered in other societies far separated from the Indo-European in history and over the earth's surface. We need not attempt to say why this should be the case, for even to the extent that the symbolic complex in question is conceded to be stable overall it is open to an endless variety of explanations. The one thing that can be asserted fairly firmly, nevertheless, is that an explanation is not likely to be found by derivation from some other opposition of particular terms.

For instance, early Greek symbolism of the kind, and that of other traditions as well, can be related to the opposition active/passive. Fire is conceived as active, water as passive; the right hand is strong and takes the initiative, the left is weak and lends support. So through these connections one might see both fire and the right as active in opposition to water and the left as passive. But the opposition active/passive is itself underlain, according to a fashionable idea traceable to Freud, by another: the active is phallic and the passive vaginal, so that by this view the more basic opposition is sexual ("Ramming belly against belly / Thigh riding against thigh"; Davenport, fr. 96) and the original symbolism genital. The choice between these alternative explanations is not to be decided by comparison or by some other empirical test, and of course they are not the only ones. The explanations, like the questions, are not given but are products of ingenuity and hence in principle inexhaustible.

An additional candidate, for instance, is the possibility that the opposition of abstractions (active/passive) and that of organs (penis/vagina) are in their several natures symbolic representations of an archetypal mode of apperception which itself is neither conceptual nor sensory. Under this obscure guise the analogical oppositions fire/water and right/left can be viewed as what Bachelard has called "images naturelles" (1942:247), natural images, given directly by nature and following at once the forces of nature and the forces of our own nature.

IV

These are grandly enigmatic themes to take up in response to two epithets supplied by "literary creation" or poetic license, and we may at this point leave the present reflections on them to fend for themselves so far as they are capable. But not without shielding them in advance from one likely objection.

We have been dealing with the apparently symbolic allocation of two elements, fire and water, to the right and left hands. The woman in Davenport's version of the fragment of Archilochus has, as we all have by nature, only two hands. So the chances are equal and obvious that Davenport, in assigning the elements to the right and left hands respectively, should have made either the particular associations that he did make or else the contrary. He might have interpreted Archilochus as having meant "Fire in her left hand, water in her right." He might have done so, but he did not.

Those who may assume that this is merely a statistical accident, a fifty-fifty business, have no problem. Or perhaps, let us instead conceive, they suffer from the dread affliction that Wittgenstein (1967c, sec. 456) called loss of problems—and then "everything seems quite simple to them."

2

Skepticism and Forms of Life

Ein Zweifel ohne Ende ist nicht einmal ein Zweifel.   Wittgenstein

I

It is inevitable that those who commit themselves to the comparative study of social facts shall find themselves committed also to an attitude of mind towards the forms of life by which human experience is framed.

A distinctive feature of these forms is that they are objects of value and conveyers of meaning, and it is only by a deliberate effort of abstraction that we can divest of their humane significance the ideas, sentiments, and customs that we compare. Every form of life is morally didactic, in that it presents an alternative, and perhaps a challenge, to our own; and we cannot remain indifferent to the contrast. The concepts of formal analysis (such as symmetry or transitivity) procure a technical detachment, but in the end even they rely for their efficacy on a translation back into the immediate concerns of other human beings. The question, then, is whether there is a correspondence between the method of comparison adopted and the analyst's attitude of mind with regard to the intrinsic character of what is compared.

One famous precept enjoins us to observe in the face of social facts the attitude appropriate to things; another tells us that we shall never understand social phenomena unless we empathize. In principle, a choice between these opposed injunctions might be made on the basis of their relative scientific usefulness; but neither has carried the day against the other, and the likelihood is that a decision between the two approaches is not to be provided by their respective uses. Instead, the adoption of any particular method probably depends on considerations which are prior to questions of scientific utility. Among these factors there will almost certainly be the attitude of mind which we first put in question; but of course this attitude itself could not have been formed independently of any acquaintance with social facts. We are led the more forcefully, therefore, to consider what may be the connection between the study of social facts and our response to them.

The point of the question can be sharpened if we ask ourselves whether we have anything to learn, in the conduct of our lives, from other traditions; and then, if this is admitted, whether it is feasible for us to modify our own standards in accordance with exotic models. Certainly it is frequently reported by observers that a given people are admirable for their courage or their independence or their resignation; but typically such commendations focus on qualities which are reckoned in the christianized West to be commendable already. If these qualities accompany actions which are not so easily found admirable, such as infanticide or funerary mutilation or slavery, the ordinary recourse is to exculpate the people under study by contending that the actions are comprehensible in the circumstances or are in some other way not to be judged by our standards. This tactic is decent enough, as we might say, in its intention but it scarcely takes seriously the moral example that is contrasted with our own norms. If we are to profit from the comparison, it is surely necessary to consider the alien culture as a whole—which is already a methodological rule in other contexts—and not to pick and choose among its distinctive features according to our predilections. And, naturally, if we are so sure of the worth of our own forms of life, and can be so unhesitating in the rejection of other forms, there is no prospect of moral improvement in making the comparison in the first place. Yet we do not have sufficient justification to be so sure as all that. History shows that moral concepts, at least as they apply to particular modes of conduct, are liable to perpetual change; and ethical theories argue, indecisively, for very different conceptions of just institutions and the virtuous life.

We are left, then, confronting an extensive array of contrasting forms of life, and we have to decide what shall be our response to them. This is necessarily a moral issue. It is not merely that we cannot remain indifferent to the implications of the contrasts they pose, but that we are obliged to take a stand which will have consequences in the appreciation of our own lives. Otherwise, we should be like the solipsist who contended that only his self was real yet carried on his ordinary life by the easy acceptance that other selves exist, or the pragmatist who argued that only practical consequences determine significance or truth yet in his actual decisions was guided nevertheless by transcendental canons. This would be to reduce comparativism, under its humane aspect, to an academic routine; and if I say that this would be reprehensible, the reaction is another way of emphasizing that the question is a genuinely moral issue and hence not to be shirked.

This is a disquieting case to be in, and the disquiet is itself a mark of the moral. How then is quietude to be attained? I take it that any form of dogmatism is to be excluded in advance, if only because that would rule out argument, thus making an end to the issue without settling it. Moreover, even the dogmatist is for ever being disquieted; for he is tormented by what he thinks naturally bad, and he falls into other perturbations when he is in possession of the good but dreads the consequences of change. For our part, we have to contend with the dogmatist, as we have also to try to accommodate ourselves to the variegation of the social facts which argue against any dogma. We have to choose—an act which is essential to the moral—and we do so in the hope of finding quietude.

In phrasing the matter in these terms—perturbation, dogmatism, quietude—I have adopted the idiom of men who deliberately confronted our problem more than two millennia ago. These were the Skeptics, and my representation of the issue is taken from the *Outlines of Pyrrhonism* by the compiler of their doctrines, Sextus Empiricus (ca. A.D. 200). In what follows I want to introduce the Skeptics, as the first methodical comparativists, into the history of social anthropology, and then to draw out some of the implications of their precepts for our own predicament.

II

It is a received idea that Herodotus (fifth century B.C.), "the father of history," was also the founder of anthropology. Kroeber has stressed that half of the nine books of Herodotus are devoted to pure ethnology; and Goldenweiser has traced back to him a concern with the classification of races.

But the dominant characteristic of Herodotus, in the present perspective, is that he was a descriptive ethnographer. He traveled widely, and in his accounts of other peoples he distinguished conscientiously between what he saw with his own eyes and what he was told. But he did not make a systematic comparison of social facts for the sake of drawing general conclusions. This was a task that was to be undertaken by the Skeptics, and not for the main part on the strength of their own experiences but by reliance upon published accounts of the customs of foreign peoples.

Skepticism is traced back to the practical doctrine associated with the name of Pyrrho of Elis (ca. 360–275 B.C.).

R. G. Bury, translator of Sextus Empiricus, thinks we may
fairly assume that the causes which led to the skepticism of
Pyrrho were twofold: first, the intellectual confusion result-
ing from the number of conflicting philosophical doctrines
and rival schools; second, the political confusion and social
chaos which spread through the Hellenic world after the
death of Alexander—"together with the new insight into
strange habits and customs which was given by the opening
up of the East" (Bury 1933:xxxi). Pyrrho himself accompanied Alexander the Great to India, where he remained as a
member of his suite for some time, and it is said that he was
influenced by the philosophical ideas of India (Brochard
1887:53; cf. Patrick 1899:82).

After some four hundred years, a period in which Skepticism is reckoned as having passed through three stages of development, the school came to a culmination in the empirical
recension of which Sextus Empiricus was the spokesman.
Sextus, a Greek physician who lived circa A.D. 160–210, is
generally estimated to have been mainly a compiler, with a
special interest in the history of ideas, and there is probably
little original in his writings. Three works by him have survived: "Outlines of Pyrrhonism," "Against the Dogmatists,"
and "Against the Schoolmasters." Among these it is the "Outlines" that I wish to discuss, primarily because it is a clear general account of Skepticism and is admirably comprehensive.

Skepticism, says Sextus (translated by Bury, 1933), is an
ability or a mental attitude which opposes appearances to
judgments in any way whatsoever, with the result that we are
brought first to a state of mental suspense and then to a state
of unperturbedness (I. 8). The kind of "suspense" in question
is a state of mental rest by virtue of which we neither deny
nor affirm anything (I. 10). The original cause of skepticism
is "the hope of attaining quietude," and to this end the main
basic principle of the Skeptic system is that of opposing to
every proposition an equal proposition, for as a consequence

of this we cease to dogmatize (I. 12). Thus the end sought by the Skeptic is quietude in respect of matters of opinion and moderate feeling in respect of things unavoidable (I. 25). These desirable states are the consequences of an empirical realization. The Skeptics, unable to gain quietude by rational decision, suspended judgment and found that quietude, as if by chance, followed upon their suspense, "even as a shadow follows its substance" (I. 29).

There are different ways of producing this effect by, in general, "setting things in opposition." The tradition among the older Skeptics was that there were ten Modes (otherwise known as "arguments" or "positions") by which suspension of judgment is brought about (I. 36). We need not consider most of these, but for the present purpose we shall concentrate on the tenth (Sextus is careful to add that the order in which the modes are taken up is without prejudice), namely that which is based on "the disciplines and customs and laws, the legendary beliefs and the dogmatic convictions" (I. 37–38). This mode is later described as being mainly concerned with ethics, as it is based on "rules of conduct, habits, laws, legendary beliefs, and dogmatic conceptions" (I. 145). Each of these components is defined; for example, "a habit or custom (the terms are equivalent) is the joint adoption of a certain kind of action by a number of men, the transgressor of which is not actually punished" (I. 146). Each of these components is opposed now to itself and now to each of the others. For example, habit is opposed to habit in this way: some of the Ethiopians tattoo their children, but "we" do not (I. 148). The "we" in the comparison, as in others in the "Outlines," are the Greeks, and the reference is to the laws or customs of Athens especially (cf. Sextus 1933:460 n. *b*). Similarly, law is opposed to law: among the Romans a man who renounces his father's property does not pay his father's debts, whereas among the Rhodians he always pays them. Rule of conduct is opposed to rule of conduct, as when that of the

Laconians is opposed to that of the Italians. Legendary belief is opposed to legendary belief, as when in one story the father of men and gods is alleged to be Zeus, whereas in another he is Oceanos. And dogmatic conception is opposed to dogmatic conception when some say that the soul is mortal while others say that it is immortal. Next, each of the components distinguished is opposed to "the other things" (I. 152). For example, among the Persians it is the habit [for men] to indulge in intercourse with males, but among the Romans it is forbidden by law to do so. In this way, rule of conduct is opposed to law, legendary belief, and dogmatic conception; habit is opposed to rule of conduct, law, legendary belief, and dogmatic conception; law is opposed to legendary beliefs; legendary beliefs are opposed to dogmatic conceptions.

The point I wish to stress is that each of these "antitheses" (I. 163) is illustrated by examples taken from the ethnography of the day. The argument that the Skeptics make by means of the tenth mode is that, since so much divergency is shown to exist in objects (in this case, social forms), "we shall not be able to state what character belongs to the object in respect of its real essence, but only what belongs to it in respect of this particular rule of conduct, or law, or habit and so on. . . ." Hence, Sextus concludes, because of this mode also "we are compelled to suspend judgment regarding the real nature of external objects" (I. 163), that is, the ethical value of social facts. In other words, comparative ethnography is drawn upon in the relative estimation of forms of life.

A strikingly commendable aspect of this method is the carefulness with which it is prosecuted. The fundamental procedure is stipulated as the setting of things in opposition, and the things in question are defined; then examples of these things from different societies are compared, first among things of a kind and then severally among things of different kinds in varied combinations. The conclusion arrived at is definite, and it is the expression of a methodical and empirical relativism. The cogency of the argument is a separate matter, and I shall take that up after an account of the major deployment, in the "Outlines," of the skeptical analysis of social facts.

III

Central to the undertaking is the question whether anything is naturally good or naturally evil.

This is an issue that Sextus takes up in Book III of the "Outlines," beginning with Chapter XXI, "Concerning the Ethical Division of Philosophy." In the succeeding chapters, after the usual definition of the terms of the argument, Sextus considers whether anything is by nature good, bad, or indifferent. His intention is to show that none of the so-called "goods" of life moves all men as being good (III. 179). Likewise, in the chapter on "What is the so-called Art of Living?" it is asserted that things which seem to some to be evil—for example, incontinence, injustice, avarice, intemperance—are pursued by others as goods, so that the things said to be evil do not move all men alike either (III. 190). There are a number of general arguments in support of these two conclusions; and then Sextus embarks, almost by way of an afterthought ("perhaps it may not be amiss," he opens), on an extended demonstration by means of a renewed and far more detailed recourse to comparative ethnography. By dwelling on the notions concerning things shameful and not shameful, unholy and not so, laws and customs, piety towards the gods, reverence for the departed, and the like, we shall discover, he writes, "a great variety of belief concerning what ought or ought not to be done" (III. 198).

Since the anthropological pertinence of this demonstration lies in this variety, as also in the range of peoples whose customs and ideas are opposed one to another, I shall give a complete list of the kinds of social facts considered, though omitting for the most part the ethnographic evidences. This does not make for entrancing reading, but this degree at least of replication (cf. III. 199–232) is called for if the weight of the case is to be assessed.

Sextus begins with sodomy (that bugbear of moralists): to the Greeks it is shameful or illegal, but among the Germani (perhaps a Persian tribe) it is the customary thing, and in legendary and historical Greece there are indications that it was not always castigated. He then takes up, in each instance citing contrariant practices, the following customs: having intercourse with a woman in public; prostitution and pimping; tattooing; wearing earrings; piercing the nostrils; wearing a flowered robe reaching to the feet; marrying one's mother or one's own sister (as the Persians and the Egyptians respectively were reputed to do); sexual intercourse with one's mother; a father getting children by his daughter, a mother by her son, a brother by his sister; masturbation; eating human flesh; defiling an altar with human blood; intercourse with the wives of other men; care for the father; infanticide; homicide; polygyny; piracy; theft; cowardice; effeminacy; belief in the existence of gods; sacrifice; human diet; reverence towards the departed; ideas about death.

The range of peoples whose ideas or customs are cited includes: Germani, Indians, Egyptians, Sarmatians, Syrians, Laconians, Scythians, Athenians, Romans, Thracians, Gaetulians, Cilicians, Amazons, Jews, Ethiopians, Hyrcanians, and Troglodytes. Among the persons cited as authorities or exemplars are: Meriones, Achilles, Zeno, Cleanthes, Chrysippus, Crates, Plato, Aristippus, Tydeus, Solon, Archilochus, Diagoras, Theodorus, Critias, and Herodotus.

In the course of his exposition, Sextus observes more generally that in regard to justice and injustice and the excellence of manliness there is a great variety of opinion; that around all matters of religion and theology there rages violent controversy (III. 218); and that sacrificial usages and the ritual of worship in general exhibit great diversity (III. 220). His summing up is: "Thus none of the things mentioned above is naturally of this character or of that, but all are matters of convention and relative" (III. 232).

Sextus rounds off his ethnographic argument by asserting that the same method of treatment can be applied also to each of the other customs which, for the sake of brevity, he has not described. He adds moreover that even if, in regard to some of them, we are unable to declare their "discrepancy" offhand, we ought to observe that disagreement concerning them may possibly exist among yet other peoples (III. 233). For just as, if we had been ignorant of, say, the Egyptian custom of marrying one's sister, we should have asserted wrongly that it was universally agreed that men ought not to marry their sisters, so "in regard to those practices wherein we notice no discrepancy, it is not proper for us to affirm that there is no disgreement about them, since . . . disagreement about them may exist among some of the nations which are unknown to us" (III. 234). Accordingly, "the Skeptic, seeing so great a diversity of usages, suspends judgment as to the natural existence of anything good or bad or (in general) fit or unfit to be done" (III. 235).

Sextus closes his argument with these arresting lines: "Hence we conclude that if what is productive of evil is evil and to be shunned, and the persuasion that these things are good, those evil, by nature, produces disquiet, then the assumption and persuasion that anything is, in its real nature, either bad or good is evil and to be shunned" (III. 238).

IV

This is a resounding period to an ethical inquiry founded on comparative ethnography, and it answers directly to the concerns expressed in the opening section of the present essay. What did Sextus think should follow from it?

In the first place, quietude. The Skeptic suspends judgment, and thereby abstains from the rashness of dogmatism; he remains impassive in respect of matters of opinion, while in conditions that are unavoidable his emotions are moderate (III. 235). "The man who determines nothing as to what is naturally good or bad neither shuns nor pursues anything eagerly; and, in consequence, he is unperturbed" (I. 28). It would be a mercy if this end could be attained. What are the conditions on which it might be hoped for?

We might think that it could perhaps be had by the careful contrivance of a superior art of living, perhaps one enriched and instructed by comparative ethnography. Moreover, one of the two senses of the very "criterion" of the Skeptical school is "the standard of action by conforming to which in the conduct of life we perform some actions and abstain from others" (I. 21). But the formulation of an art of living is not at all the consequence that Sextus intends. Indeed, he declares that "it is plain . . . that there can be no art of living" (III. 239). The first reason is that if such an art exists, it has to do with the consideration of things good, evil, and indifferent; and since these are nonexistent the art of living also is nonexistent. There are other arguments; for example, that different arts of living are propounded, and their discrepancy undermines the claim that there is one such art; that an art is recognized by its own special products, whereas there is no special product of the art of living; and that most philosophers propound modes of conduct which they would never dare to put into practice (III. 249).

What then is to be done? That is, if in the tenth mode we are to be better guided in our judgments by resort to comparative ethnography, how should we frame our attitude to the many forms of life among which ours is one? (I say "ours," and "one," for the time being and in order at least to start on a

level with the Athenian Skeptics.) The answer given by Sextus is that, seeing that "we cannot remain wholly inactive,"
we should "live in accordance with the normal rules of life,
undogmatically" (I. 23; cf. 226); and, again, he says that the
Skeptic "follows undogmatically the ordinary rules of life"
(III. 235). In place of an art of living, we are enjoined to a
quiescence under the coercions of one or another form of life.
The point is that if there are no decisive reasons to live in one
way rather than in another, among the more or less disparate
forms of life that are known or that can be conjectured, then
we may as well conduct ourselves as the people around us expect—whether or not they themselves have any good reason
for regarding their rules of life as right and proper.

How feasible this compliance could be is another matter,
for it depends on a prior identification of what are the "normal" or "ordinary" rules of life; and in any real community
these will be such that divergent courses of action will arise,
or discrepant interpretations of the rules will be made. Even a
monastic order or a regiment or a traditional college will not
define its normal or ordinary rules of life so strictly and consistently as to obviate a choice between one rule and another
or between alternative interpretations of a given rule. Moreover, to acquiesce in advance to any rule whatever, just on the
ground that it was normal or ordinary, would constitute an
affront to the spirit of critical intelligence which is the very
inspiration of Skepticism; to let this faculty decline into abey-
ance would be ignominious and in the end indefensible as
well.

It is all very well to be undogmatic, but there are limits. To
be undogmatic on principle, methodically, is to subscribe to a
kind of dogma, and to lay oneself open to Lichtenberg's ironical dictum: "All impartiality is artificial. . . . Even impartiality is partisan," so one might say of someone that "He be-
longed to the party of the impartial" (1968:539). (Not that
this was new, either. Lao Tzu is supposed to have said to

Confucius that "to make up one's mind to be impartial is in itself a kind of partiality."—Waley 1939:30.)

Likewise, to decline to choose between alternative forms of life, with the excuse that there is no reason to think that one of them is objectively better than the other, is to place oneself in the dilemma of Buridan's ass, and we know what happened in that case: the creature starved to death, between two equally delectable bales of hay, because it could find no reason to choose one rather than the other. The logical response, in the face of rival forms of life, is that the rational thing to do is to make a random choice; the practical response is that any choice, however irrational, is better than the consequences of making no choice at all. But Sextus opts for neither of these responses. He does not recommend a random choice among forms of life, and he does not concede that any choice whatever is better than no choice. Instead, he rather lamely concludes that we should "simply conform to life undogmatically, [so] that we may not be precluded from activity" (I. 226). Admittedly, he has his reasons; for instance, that Nature constrains us to eat and drink, and that the tradition of laws and customs inclines us to regard piety in the conduct of life as good. But these reasons themselves cannot withstand a skeptical treatment, and it is no more than appropriate that Sextus qualifies them by adding at once "we make all these statements undogmatically" (I. 24). All the same, this does not save his case; and it gives all the less reason to follow the ordinary rules of life, whatever that may mean. In any case, there is a still more fundamental objection to his precept.

The foregoing observations have taken for granted the force of Sextus's argument that since forms of life differ, therefore none of them is absolutely right; but this is logically mistaken. Numerous though forms of life may be, and however discrepant they may be one from another, it could still be the case that just one of them was absolutely right. It is not self-

contradictory to assert as much, and plainly it is a logical possibility. How we should discover the one right form of life is
a separate question, and not a purely logical matter, but Sextus has given us no proof that it is not to be found.

To the opposite effect, indeed, there is an interesting comparison to be made. Pascal asserted that "it would not be possible that men should have imagined so many false religions if
there did not exist one that was true" (1964:300, no. 817).
This is the dogmatic converse of the Skeptical position, and
likewise it too is logically mistaken. Another line of argument is that of Durkheim, who contended that there are no
false religions: "all are true in their own fashion; all answer
. . . to the given conditions of human existence" (1915:3).
This is not logically self-contradictory, though it is a logical
option, but then it is not a logical argument; it is a particular
expression of Durkheim's "essential postulate of sociology
that a human institution cannot rest upon an error and a lie"
(1915:2). The argument for this postulate itself is that "if the
institution were not founded in the nature of things, it would
have encountered in the facts a resistance over which it could
never have triumphed." But this means no more than that the
institution in question is whatever it happens to be, and that it
answers to whatever human interests continue to sustain it.
These circumstances tell us nothing in themselves about "the
nature of things" (however that grand phrase may be construed), and nothing about truth or falsity in any regard.

Finally, in this train of summary comparisons, there is yet
another response to the question posed by the Skeptics. This
is the position taken up by Wittgenstein with respect to "forms
of life," each of which propounds implicitly its own grounds
for the attribution of significance to human existence. This is
a complicated matter of exegesis (cf. Needham 1972:244–
45), but it can be epitomized by two passages: "What is needed
for [an] explanation? One might say: a culture" (1967c, sec.

164); and "Only in the stream of thought and life do words have meaning" (1967c, sec. 173; cf. Malcolm 1966:93). The burden of these expressions is carried further in Wittgenstein's observations on religious belief, in which he repeatedly abjures the notions of contradiction and opposite belief in coming to terms with what a religious believer asserts; one is "on an entirely different plane," Wittgenstein is reported to have said, and "the difference might not show up at all in any explanation of the meaning" (1966:53; cf. 58). In other words, truth and falsity are not immediately to the point; what counts is circumstantial cogency, in the present case the force of prevalent custom.

This may seem to take us back to the precept of the Skeptics, but it is very different: it is not an injunction about the conduct of life, it is a key to the interpretation of statements which reflect forms of life. But can it be taken to the limit, as a guide to conduct? Wittgenstein's philosophical stance was in great contrast to his personal practice; he was a man of ardent principles, and he did not resort to logic or to ethnography in order to justify these—any more than we do. Yet the Skeptics did adduce comparative ethnography in their quest for a right way of life, and if their logic was invalid the challenge they faced in antithetical moralities still confronts us—on condition, that is, that we take disparate forms of life as seriously as they did.

V

The topic that I have been treating here is the humane significance of the comparative study of social facts.

The question, morally speaking, is whether anthropology matters. The Skeptics thought it did, and their tenth mode was intended to prove as much. If they did not succeed in making their final case, we have to ask ourselves if we possess any advantages over them, especially by virtue of the modern academic development of social anthropology.

The first obvious difference between the Skeptics and ourselves is that we now have at our disposal a vastly increased record of usages and collective representations. But it is not so obvious that this is an advantage. Actually, we have altogether too many facts, so many that we do not know what to do with them; and whenever we fail in explanation or in understanding it is not usually for lack of a sufficiency of ethnographic data. There is an awkward exception to this generalization when we put a theoretical proposition to a comparative test; in this case the crucial evidence is often not to be had, for the simple reason that the ethnographers did not have the proposition in mind when they pursued their own inquiries. Either way, then, it is not in the accumulation of factual information that we can claim a decisive advantage over the Skeptics. And, in any event, it is not the availability of evidence that counts, but rather the intrinsic recalcitrance of the issue that the Skeptics formulated. The difficulty is at first that of working out how to come to terms with the problem.

Have we now, therefore, by virtue of our academic concentration specifically on problems in the comparative analysis of social facts, a superior method which gives us an advantage over the Skeptics? Hardly, for they already had an adequate method in their exploitation of the tenth mode. Moreover, all they needed to do, essentially, was to determine "discrepancies," and this was a straightforward task which they carried out perfectly well. Also, all they needed for their purpose was any solitary form of life which contrasted in some respect with their own, and their method of comparison was more than adequate to this end.

Lévy-Bruhl, writing in the heyday of sociology, thought it

was hardly to be doubted that if we possessed the static and dynamic laws of society we should be able to resolve most conflicts of conscience, and that we should be able to act economically and rationally on the moral reality of social life (1904:272). But, hopeful though he was, he conceded that the prescriptions of a rational art of morality would apply only to a single society and in certain conditions (277). He predicted no circumstances in which the comparative treatment of the moralities of different societies could resolve the discrepancies isolated by the Skeptics. Indeed, he expressly wished his argument not to be taken for a skepticism; yet his rejection of a skeptical conclusion rested not on argument but on a confidence in the possibility of a science, resembling physics, that would make more apprehensible the "plurality of moralities" among mankind. This confidence was not to be borne out, and today there are still fewer grounds on which it might be revived.

We have to ask, then, whether the development of a discipline in the universities has given us an advantage of theory over the Skeptics. Well, a realistic and even charitable view of the course of anthropological theory over the past century and more is that it has traced a sequence of failures, and that our advantage consists in being in a position to recognize these more readily as such. With the exception of very limited and fairly technical matters (for example, in the analysis of prescriptive systems), there is little in the way of anthropological theory that would have surprised or perhaps even interested the Skeptics.

My conclusion, therefore, is that the Skeptics faced the moral challenge of alternative forms of life as directly as we can, and that they did so both seriously and methodically. We cannot logically accept their response to that challenge, and we cannot follow their injunction simply to obey the ordinary rules of life—but then they themselves pretty surely did not do so either, or if they did it was probably not for the reasons they gave. For our part, consequently, what should we do? In the main, we carry on as though there were nothing to be done. Is this because we do not see a problem? Or because we do not take other forms of life seriously? Or is it because actually there is nothing much that we could possibly do about it anyway?

We accede readily enough, I should think, to the suggestion that we can benefit in our sympathies and in our judgments from moral examples in forms of art, and perhaps these advantages really can be secured—even if on rather contrived conditions and in a logical scheme that is tautological. But what inner changes can we bring about in the face of the multifarious testimonies of ethnography? Rationally, we can suspend judgment; analytically, we can situate an exotic morality more firmly in its peculiar setting; empathically, we can imagine ourselves acting without qualms in accordance with standards that are discrepant from our own. Yet none of this will automatically procure within us an altered commitment of the kind that we regard as moral.

There is nothing surprising in this, for we do not in the most apt of circumstances manage our attitudes of mind by deliberate recourse to reason, analysis, or empathy. These are not the means by which our moral commitments were formed in us, and we need not expect that they will any better accommodate our responses to alien conceptions of right conduct. They are instead, in the present context, tokens of the very concern that they are intended to direct; they are moral exercises, as it were, and in putting ourselves through them we are perhaps pressing as far in the desired direction as we can reasonably look for.

The attempt to come to terms with disparate forms of life is already a moral commitment, and one that is proper to our own critical tradition, just as is the conception of a "humane significance" in social facts. Not all actions need have separate consequences, as we know of propositions by the examples of performative utterances. The skeptical perturbations of comparativism are self-sufficient moral acts which in being conceived accomplish their right nature.

3

Robert Knox and the Structure of Absolutism

The king can do no wrong.

Sir William Blackstone

I

In his great ethnographical volume *An Historical Relation of the Island of Ceylon* (1681), Robert Knox lays great stress on the "tyrannical" nature of the reign of the King of Ceylon, Raja Singha. He catalogues in detail the king's oppressions and exactions, his ubiquitous spies, his arbitrary and ferocious punishments and executions, and his constant care to keep the people in a state of subservience, poverty, and fearful impotence.

The land that is under his jurisdiction is all his, together with the inhabitants, their estates, and whatsoever the country affords. His endeavor is to keep the people poor and in want; he takes their hens, hogs, and goats, giving little or nothing for them in return. The poverty of the people is so great that, despite their intense concern to appear in public adorned in clothes and ornaments suitable to their respective stations, they are unable to buy even "what is very mean and ordinary at best," and they constantly have recourse to borrowing in order to make a decent showing. Their lodgings are poor, their taxes and other dues are heavy, and the king exhausts them with forced labor on huge public works which may undermine even such security and sustenance as the people have.

Notwithstanding their common subjection to the tyrannical rule of the king, the people are yet divided rigidly among themselves into a hierarchy of what Knox calls "ranks." These are first noblemen; then goldsmiths, blacksmiths, carpenters, and painters; after these, barbers; then, in order, potters, washers, sugar-makers, agricultural workers and soldiers, weavers, basket-makers, mat-makers; below these come the slaves; and finally there are the beggars. The ranks are distinguished by their clothes and the manner of wearing them, by such privileges as sitting on a stool, by titles and more or less honorific personal pronouns, and above all by regulations prohibiting the members of one rank from eating with, marrying, or having sexual intercourse with a member of an inferior rank. These ranks are hereditary, and, according to Knox, they are unchangeable; neither wealth nor any office of honour has any effect on their rank "according to their Descent and Blood."

Whether or not it is agreed, as a moral judgment, that the king's rule is tyrannical, there is little doubt that "he ruleth Absolute, and after his own Will and Pleasure"; the land is at his disposal, and all the people from the highest to the lowest, who in body and goods are wholly at his command. It is this absolute character that should be stressed, for it is not only characteristic of the kingship but it governs the entire constitution of the society and sustains both social distinctions and mutual obligations. Knox's *Relation* convincingly describes to us an absolutist polity.

It is striking that the king, for all his absolute power, hardly exploits what could be unlimited sexual privileges. It is true that he sends out into the countryside for "handsome young Women" to serve in his kitchen, but otherwise his conduct appears remarkably constrained. His queen, having borne him a son and a daughter, has not been with him for twenty

Plate 2. Robert Knox (The National Maritime Museum, London)

years but has remained where he left her in the distant city of Cande. Most of his attendants are boys and young men, who are "well favoured," but Knox at once absolves the king of the suspicion of sodomy, a sin which indeed he has not even heard mentioned among this people. The king has in fact some concubines, though not many. He is abstemious in his use of women; "if he useth them 'tis unknown and with great secrecy." Chaste himself, he does not allow "whoredom" or adultery in his entourage, and if he hears of sexual misdemeanors among his nobles he executes them and severely punishes the women. Moreover, when nobles are admitted to the court, to enter his service, they are not even allowed to enjoy the company of their wives, any more than that of any other women; no one, except slaves or inferior servants, may have a wife in the king's city.

Against this background it is all the more arresting that Knox reports the king to have once been guilty of an act which seemed to argue him a man of the most unbridled lust: "For he had a Daughter that was with Child by himself: but in Childbed both dyed." However, our ethnographer explains, "this manner of Incest is allowable in Kings," though "in all other 'tis held abominable, and severely punished."

The reason adduced by Knox to explain this license exercised by the king is that it is permissible "if only to beget a right Royal Issue, which can only be gotten that way." But then he goes on to draw an intriguing parallel which does not answer particularly to this reason: "And here they have a common and usual Proverb, None can reproach the King nor the Beggar. The one being so high, that none dare; the other so low, that nothing can shame or reproach them." We shall take up this comparison in a moment. First, let us note another report by Knox on the topic of incest, this time as expressed in the ordinary speech of other ranks of society.

Some of their words of Reproach, or Railery are such as these. One brother will say to another, and that in the presence of their Mother,

Tomotowoy, go lye with your Mother, the other replyes go you
and lye with your Mother. And the Mother will say to the Daughter, Jopi oppota audewind, go lye with your Father; intimating she
is good for nothing.

There is great difficulty in construing the phrases as Sinhalese via the seventeenth-century English orthography. The
-*moto*- component in "tomotowoy" may be connected with
the Pali *mātā*, mother, though the usual word is *amma*. As for
the other phrase, "jopi" may be a misrendering of *topi*, you;
"oppo" is apparently *appa*, father, with the suffix -*ta*, meaning to or towards; while "audewind" would mean to go. In
neither objurgation, however, does it appear that there is a
verb standing literally for "lye" in the sense of to have sexual intercourse. Nevertheless, Knox is definite that there are
forms of abuse referring to incest between mother and son
and between father and daughter. On the other hand, he also
says that people's "usual manner of swearing in protesta-
tions"—which he thinks are merely customary rather than
truthful—is "by their Mother, or by their Children . . .
oftner than by their Gods."

If we now return to the beggars, we shall see that in most
respects they make an extreme contrast with the king. They
have indeed "by former Kings been made so low and base,
that they can be no lower or baser." In token of this, they are
obliged to give to all other people such titles and forms of
respect as are due to kings and princes. The reason traditionally given for their low estate is that they are descendants
of Veddah (hunting people) who used to bring venison for
the king's table but one day brought human flesh. The king
liked it very well and demanded more, but his barber told
him what it really was. The king was so enraged that he accounted death too good for the perpetrators, so he com-
manded that all of this rank or tribe should be expelled from
among the people and not be allowed to practice any calling.

Instead, they were only to beg, from generation to generation and from door to door, and "to be looked upon and es-
teemed by all People to be so base and odious, as not possibly
to be more."

Henceforth, beggars are so detested that they are not permitted to draw water from people's wells, but only out of
"holes" or rivers; and nobody will touch them, for fear of de-
filement. They travel in troops, begging and also dancing
and performing conjuring tricks. They are importunate in
their begging, but people cannot "without horrible shame"
raise a hand against them or push them away, so rather than
be troubled by them they give in. The beggars live in small
hovels, in distant places or by the highway; but they live as
well as others, or better, since they do no work and are free
from all sorts of services which respectable people are obliged
to render to the king. On occasion they turn their vileness
into a weapon; thus when weavers make to exercise their
right to the flesh of naturally dead cows, the beggars run at
them and threaten to pollute them. So contaminating are the
beggars that the king resorts to their power of pollution in
order to inflict punishment on great and noble men who have
fallen out of his favor. He delivers their wives and daughters
into the hands of beggars, which is a far worse punishment
than any form of death. Indeed, it is reckoned such a horrible
cruelty that even the king shows the victims some kind of
mercy; the women are taken to a riverside, there to be handed
over to the beggars, and they are given the opportunity if they
choose to throw themselves into the river and be drowned.
That this punishment is so dreadful is underlined by the fact
that "the worst railery" that can be levelled against a woman
is to allege that she "has laid with ten sorts of inferior ranks of
People"—that is, with her social inferiors, not especially with
beggars—"which they will rather dye than do."

It is precisely of the beggars that we are told that incest is
common among them: "These Men being so low that noth-

ing they can do, can make them lower, it is not unusual for
them to lay with their Daughters, or for the Son to lay with
his Mother, as if there were no Consanguinity among them."

II

There is a proverb: "No body can reproach the King and the
Beggar." This is because "the former is above the slander of
the People, and nothing can be said bad enough of the latter."

Whether they are reproached or not, the telling point for us
is that the king has had sexual intercourse with his daughter,
while the beggars are said to have sexual intercourse with
their daughters and sons. At the zenith of the social universe
and at the nadir the common feature is incest, an act held by
all others to be abominable.

The reason advanced by Knox in explanation of the king's
incest with his daughter is that this is the only way to be sure
of getting a right royal issue; that is, of having a descendant
who is equally royal through the father and through the
mother. At least, this is presumably what Knox means, for it
could be inferred that by this way also the king was more assured of the fidelity of the woman who was to bear his child.
Given the extreme strictness of the king's surveillance, this is
by far a less likely interpretation, but the possibility of it still
stresses that the report bears more than one interpretation.
Also, we do not know to what degree the explanation given
by Knox is an ethnographic report of what he was told. He
writes that this manner of incest is allowable in kings "if it be
only" to beget right royal issue, and these words too leave
room for qualification. They read like a defense of the practice, though by whom and in what circumstances does not
appear.

Two points can be made more surely, however. The first is
that for the king to beget a child by his own daughter can as-

sure him of a truly royal offspring only on condition that the daughter herself is equally royal with himself, and this is indisputable only if she too is the offspring of just such an act of congress in the preceding generation. In other words, if this particular practice is to have the effect in question, it must be a regular institution and not a sporadic indulgence for which the effect would then be a justification. This inference adds weight to the second point, which is that Knox says such incest is "allowable in kings," in the plural; that is, not only in the case of Raja Singha. It would seem therefore that we are dealing indeed with a regular institution. There is no need that it shall regularly have been put into practice, or even that it should ever be done, just so long as it is accounted allowable in kings.

Similarly, there may well be no factual content in the allegation that the beggars commonly have sexual intercourse with their children. This is the sort of thing that is often said in other parts of the world about the lower orders or about despised foreigners, and in the case of the beggars also it may be no more than a standard idiom of derogation. At any rate, it deprives them of an essential moral quality and it thrusts them thereby to the very edge of human society. This of course is where they belong as the consequence of the heinous crime of their ancestors in having brought human flesh to the king's table. We are not told for what reason the latter should ever have done that, and we are left free to think that such conduct is typical—and all the more so if gratuitous—of their intrinsic vileness. Moreover, it may be significant that they should have brought human flesh, not to nobles or to commoners of any rank, but to the king himself. A practical gloss might be that in this rigidly hierarchical and tyrannical society it is only the king who has the power to consign any sort of people to a condition of perpetual baseness and indigency, just as it is the king alone who has the power to elevate by conferring honors or by admitting to his service. Yet clearly this is only a correlative capacity in company with which the mythical act of the original beggars makes its contribution to a social and moral ideology. The essential is that the loathsome crime attributed to them is of like nature with the abomination of customary incest that is charged against their descendants. Neither type of act need have any empirical foundation, but they are mutually consistent collective representations characterizing the beggars as the lowest and most contemptible rank in the social order.

We see therefore that not only are king and beggars linked by the imputation of incest, but that they are also proverbially connected in their immunity to reproach. It is for a commentator who is struck by this assimilation to see what interpretation can be placed on such apparently incongruous facts.

III

The ordinary recourse of comparison with other societies does not at first appear to serve very well, and for two reasons.

The first is that Raja Singha has intercourse with his daughter, whereas in better known and apparently more institutionalized cases the relationship is with the sister, and it is not merely sexual either but marriage. Thus in the Egyptian royal family, brother-sister marriages are known as far back as the eleventh dynasty in about 2000 B.C. (Hopkins 1980:311); and among the Inca the emperor could commit incest with his sister, who was also his principal wife (Moore 1958:74). The second reason is that the assimilation of king to beggar is not, so far as I know, replicated in societies that are known to have permitted royal incest in any form.

Nevertheless, there is perhaps something to go on if we compare the Ceylonese king with the Inca emperor in other respects. Moore points out the striking fact that the Inca himself had the privilege to commit certain crimes, "or rather acts which were crimes if committed by a commoner." Not only incest, but also homicide and theft, which carried the capital penalty, were in certain forms permitted to the Inca. The Inca could apply the death penalty as he saw fit; that is, he could "commit a legal homicide." Also, the Inca could confiscate the property of those who were considered to have committed a crime against him, and he could in some cases, if not in all, apply the property to his own use; "the Inca could, in short, with certain limitations, commit a legal theft" (75).

Knox's relation of the powers of Raja Singha is full of instances of royal execution and of the arbitrary confiscation of the estates and goods of those who offend him or fall out of his favor, so that the Ceylonese king can readily be said to have the privilege of committing incest, homicide, and theft with impunity. The parallel with the Inca is modified, however, by the fact that the Inca nobility, though they did not enjoy all these special privileges of the emperor, had considerably more than the commoners: "any illegal act committed by a noble invariably carried a lesser penalty than the same act committed by a commoner" (75). Thus incest, which carried the death penalty for commoners, involved merely a public reprimand for the nobility (75); murder of a wife, which entailed death for a commoner, was in the case of a noble punished as the Inca saw fit, "short of death" (168). Overall, it could be said that among the Inca there was a scale of immunity from the law, according to rank, whereas in the case of Raja Singha there is an absolute contrast between the total immunity of the king and the complete subjection of the nobles and commoners. And then of course there are the beggars, with their special defense from legal blame, and they appear to have no parallel in Inca society.

The feature of absolutism insistently attracts attention: not only the absolute power of the king but also the total contrast between his privileges at the apex of society and the refusal of any to the beggars at the base. We can see this pervasive absolutism as expressed in the form of myriad prohibitions, and under this aspect there seems a chance to approach the topic of incest from a different direction. It has been argued elsewhere (Needham 1974:61–68) that "incest" is a mistaken sociological concept and not a universal: what is at issue in the study of incest prohibitions is simply the negative aspect of the regulation of access to women, and all that is common to incest prohibitions is the feature of prohibition itself (68). If we abstract the special connotations that are ordinarily attached to incest—for example, horror and abomination— there is no compelling reason to separate the king's incest with his daughter from his acts of homicide and expropriation. In committing all these acts the king is exercising, without distinction, his absolute power and privilege to flout any prohibition whatever. This, it may be said, is the absolute expression of the governing principle of an absolutist polity.

Sally Moore, writing about the Inca emperor, who was not bound by the rules which bound others, concludes that it may not be that power corrupts and that absolute power corrupts absolutely: "It may simply be that power is desirable because it gives license" (134). She sees in the privileges of the Inca emperor and nobility "the urgently pressing human wish to be free of the usual social disciplines." We can readily grant as much, even if it cannot be intended to explain the distinctive incidence of privileges in any particular case. But how, if at all, does this formulation help us to understand the explicit assimilation of king to beggar?

A pat way to represent the situation is to say that they are assimilated structurally; that is, as poles, one at the very top of the social scale (and it is, by virtue of its gradation of ranks, a scalar society) and the other at the very bottom. The king is the exemplar of all that is most admirable; the beggars stand for everything that is most despicable. If both the king and the beggars commit "incest," this act bears quite different connotations in the two cases: the king does so because he is above the law, the beggars do so because they are without the law. The act they perform, apparently in common, has no intrinsic value in common. What they do equally is to flout a prohibition that is essential to the system of prohibitions by which the society is made up; but the evaluations placed upon their respective acts of incest are just as much opposed as are the statuses of king and beggar.

If we wish to relate this opposition to the scalar constitution of the social order, we can do so by conceiving the hierarchy of ranks (or "castes") in the frame recommended by Dumézil; that is, not as a linear series but as a succession of binary oppositions (1948: 76). An inducement to do so is that the definitive statuses of king and beggar are absolute, just as are the ranks themselves by reference to the polarity of purity and pollution. On these premises it can be conceived that the absolute prohibition on incest is significantly flouted in opposite senses: by the king, for the sake of purity; and by the beggars, as a token of their irremediable pollution. And in the end we can see this entire scheme of ideas as yet another collective representation of an innate proclivity of thought and imagination, namely a natural tendency towards the employment of polar opposites in the construction and interpretation of social experience.

The present collocation of dispersed evidences in Knox's *Relation*, like the train of concomitant interpretations, has been directed by abstractions that are far from the practical concerns of Knox himself, and indeed it would not be much to our credit if our critical concepts had retained the more concrete forms of his description. Yet at the same time it is a tribute to his ethnographic acumen that his reports should respond so aptly to what have latterly proved some of the central lessons of comparativism: the stress on relations in place of substantive properties, the contrast between institution and system, the independence of value and structure, the free play between motive (lust, wish for true issue, desire for license) and mode of action, and the determination of categorical experience by subliminal vectors of cerebration (cf. Needham 1978). This may seem a refractive apparatus through which to scrutinize Knox's rough-cut gem, but the task of analysis here is, on the contrary, precisely to discriminate aspects which otherwise might remain refracted by the style and expectations of another period.

4

Locke in the Huts of Indians

It is possible that in one way it may be intellect that divides, but in another way the divider may not be intellect.   Plotinus

I

A main benefit of the systematic comparison of social forms is the discernment of certain primordial images and subliminal connections which, it can be inferred (Needham 1978), represent fundamental inclinations of the psyche. These obscure motives have been alluded to as "primary factors of experience" (Needham 1981:1, 3–4, 24–25), but usually in particular settings and not in any concerted fashion. In the present essay that enigmatic topic will be taken up once more, and in a renewed consideration of what justification can be found for proposing such problematical aspects of human nature.

It can be suggested that the primary factors correspond in some respects to what are traditionally known as "innate ideas," and it is this qualified isomorphism that we shall pursue. There is a long philosophical tradition focused on innate ideas, from the Platonic forms onward, some thinkers maintaining that they are basic constituents of thought while others argue that they are empty fictions. Without attempting to adjudicate between these opposed contentions, we can well begin, for the present purpose, by considering a classic case against the postulation of innate ideas. This is the argument presented by Locke in Book I of *An Essay concerning Human Understanding* (1690). His conclusion was that "ideas and notions are no more born with us than [are] arts and sciences." This is not the only conclusion that he arrived at in the consideration of this issue, but as it stands it will help us to decide what to look for, under the guise of "primary factors" or whatever term may appear more apt, if we first examine Locke's reasons for rejecting any kind of "innate notions."

Locke's announced purpose in the *Essay* was "to inquire into the origin, certainty, and extent of human knowledge, together with the grounds and degrees of belief, opinion, and assent"; alternatively, "to consider the discerning faculties of a man, as they are employed about the objects which they have to do with" (Bk. I, chap. 1). A crucial and recurrent term is "idea," which stands for "whatsoever is the object of the understanding when a man thinks, . . . or whatever it is which the mind can be employed about in thinking." The first task that Locke sets himself is to prove that no ideas are innate.

The description under which innate ideas are introduced is actually "innate principles," and in the course of Book I Locke calls them also by a variety of names: "characters . . . stamped upon the mind of man," "constant impressions," "truths imprinted on the soul," given by "native inscription"; they are "imprinted on the understanding," or else they are "natural characters engraven upon the mind." Whatever they may be called, the "established opinion" against which Locke argues is that these are ideas "which the soul receives in its very first being, and brings into the world with it." Against this opinion Locke maintains that the mind is at first an "empty cabinet," which becomes furnished by the senses with particular ideas; also that it is a "white paper" which "receives any characters." Men, barely by the use of their natural faculties, can, he asserts, attain all the knowledge they have, "without the help of any innate impressions," and they can arrive at certainty "without any such original notions or principles." How these ends are brought about is the subject matter of the *Essay*, but before Locke makes that argument he tries to dispose in advance of the possibility that some ideas are innate.

The first contention that he addresses is that there are certain "principles," both speculative and practical, which are universally agreed upon by all mankind; their universality stems, it is said, from certain constant impressions which the souls of men bring into the world with them. But, responds Locke, this universal consent—even if conceded—would not prove the truths innate so long as there were any other way by which men might reach universal agreement. Worse, he continues, the argument from universal consent, to prove innate principles, demonstrates that there are none such, because there are none to which all mankind give a universal assent. To show as much, in the case of speculative principles, he adduces two "propositions" which of all he thinks have best title to be considered innate: namely "Whatever is, is" and "It is impossible for the same thing to be and not to be." Yet children and idiots know nothing of these propositions and do not think of them, so that as far as they are concerned the criterion of universal assent, as "the necessary concomitant of all innate truths," must fail. For it is almost contradictory, Locke thinks, to say that there are truths imprinted on the soul but which it neither perceives nor understands. Indeed, "to imprint anything on the mind without the mind's perceiving it, seems to me hardly intelligible."

This objection, "it is usually answered," is avoided by the argument that all men know the speculative principles in question, and assent to them, when they come to the use of reason. But that can certainly never be thought innate, Locke replies, which we have need of reason to discover; unless, that is, all the certain truths that reason ever teaches us are likewise to be regarded as innate. Alternatively, if it is said that children come to assent to these maxims when they reach the age of reason, this is false, for they certainly give many instances of the use of reason long before they have any knowledge of the maxim "It is impossible for the same thing to be and not to be." All the argument really amounts to is that these maxims are never known before the age of reason, but may possibly be assented to some time after, during a man's life, though when is uncertain. This is so with all other knowable truths, yet it is not held that all such are therefore innate.

Nor can it be shown that ready assent to a proposition, upon first hearing and understanding the "terms," is a certain mark of an innate principle; for then all propositions that are thus assented to must count as innate, and the proponents of this demonstration "will find themselves plentifully stored with innate principles." Moreover, if such principles were innate, why should they need to be proposed in order to gain assent? It may be answered that the understanding has an implicit knowledge of these principles, but not an explicit; but then, answers Locke, it will be hard to understand what is meant by a principle imprinted on the understanding implicitly—unless all this means is that the mind is capable of understanding and assenting firmly to such propositions, which is hardly the same as to prove that they are innate.

There is moreover a further weakness in the argument, namely that men are thereby supposed not to learn anything absolutely new, when in fact they are taught and do learn things that they were ignorant of before. It is evident, in particular, that they learn the terms of the maxims, and their meanings, and neither maxim nor meaning was born with them. "I would gladly have any one name that proposition whose terms or ideas were either of them innate." (Locke seems rather to enjoy asking if "identity" and "impossibility" are two *innate* ideas.) Certainly innate principles must have universal assent, but then they cannot be assented to by those who do not understand the terms, nor by many who do understand them but have never heard or thought of those propositions.

Finally, in this consideration of speculative maxims, Locke comes to a point of argument that touches closely on the comparative analysis of social facts. There is, he says, yet a further argument against their being innate: namely that these characters, if they were native and original impressions, ought to appear most clearly in those persons in whom we find in fact no trace of them (Bk. I, chap. 2, sec. 27):

> For children, idiots, savages, and illiterate people, being of all others the least corrupted by custom or borrowed opinions; learning and education having not cast their native thoughts into new moulds; one might reasonably imagine that in their minds these innate notions should lie open fairly to every one's view.

But alas, he responds, what general maxims, or what universal principles of knowledge, are to be found among such individuals? Their notions are few and narrow, borrowed only from those objects they have had the most to do with, and which have made upon their senses the most frequent and strongest impressions. Hence Locke concludes, apparently rather ironically: "Such kind of general propositions are seldom mentioned in the huts of Indians."

The reason for this lack is that propositions of the kind are the language of academics in learned nations, who are accustomed to that sort of conversation, in which disputes are frequent. The maxims are suited to artificial argumentation, but they do not much conduce to the discovery of truth or the advancement of knowledge.

As for practical principles, in the form of moral rules, Locke finds that these fall far short of universal assent from all mankind. Since we can readily agree with his contention that they are not innate, we may pass over the details of his argument about them.

In sum, then, neither speculative nor practical principles—
or the ideas that enter into them—are, in Locke's view, to be
accepted as innate. The truth is, he concludes, that some ideas
are generally and easily received by the understanding among
all men, and it is by reason of this facile reception that the
ideas have been "mistaken for innate."

II

Locke's account of innate ideas is by no means the only one
that might be cited from the course of this antique debate,
and of course he did not pronounce the last word on the
topic.

Hume, in his *Enquiries* (1758), already charged that Locke's
reasonings, misled by the undefined terms of the schoolmen,
were affected by ambiguity and circumlocution. Nevertheless, Locke's statement of what must be required of innate
ideas, together with his refutation of them in those respects,
remains basic and fairly comprehensive; and it is also, on his
premises, largely cogent. Whether his premises were themselves sound is a matter that we shall take up later. The point
for the present is that Locke, in a well-known argument, entirely undermined the case for supposing that certain "notions" are innate. What then is to be made of the suggestion
that primary factors of experience correspond in certain senses
to what are traditionally known as innate ideas?

If the existence of innate ideas themselves can be cast so
radically in doubt, the obvious question is whether the postulated primary factors are in any better standing. Locke submitted that "at least it is reasonable to demand the marks and
characters whereby the genuine innate principles may be distinguished from others." With an irony more marked this
time, he continued: "When this is done, I shall be ready to
embrace such welcome and useful propositions; and till then

I may with modesty doubt; since I fear universal consent, which is the only one produced, will scarcely prove a sufficient mark to direct my choice, and assure me of any innate principles."

Since something like "universal consent," in the form of a global distribution of certain social facts, is the most general mark of the primary factors, there is all the more reason to demand to know what is the true character by which such factors can be recognised. In what follows, therefore, we shall quickly run through a number of factors, with the aim of giving the kind of account that might have answered to Locke's demand. Since the evidences have been treated elsewhere, if partially and in a number of scattered places, the stress will be laid not so much on the distinctive phenomena themselves as on testing their distinctiveness against skeptical criteria.

First, however, it is necessary to say something about the "global" distribution of primary factors. By this epithet let us mean, perhaps rather unconventionally, a worldwide incidence of similar social facts; hence in disparate cultural traditions in far-separated parts of the globe. This is not the same as "universal," that is occurring everywhere. It can indeed be claimed that some institutions, such as language or dance, are literally universal, but this is a condition which it would be impossible to satisfy in the case of primary factors. To do so would depend in the first place on a sure circumscription of social units, in each one of which a given factor would need to be found; but there is no valid definition such that a unit could not be considered as divisible into parts, in some of which the factor might then not be found. This is a formal objection attaching to any quasi-universal comparison of social facts, and it cannot be evaded by the claim that the necessary character attributed to at least some primary factors makes it certain that they must exist even where they have not been reported. What alone must count, if the description of "universal" is to be aimed at, is that a given feature must be reported from absolutely everywhere—but "everywhere" cannot be given a practicable application.

In default of this universal distribution, we have to fall back on a global incidence, and what will then count is that a feature shall occur in as many different parts of the world as will indicate that neither historical connections nor similar local determinants were responsible for the resemblances in question. Thus the image of the half-man can be traced on every continent and in practically every quarter of the globe, from Oceania right round the great Asian land mass, throughout Africa, in Europe, and in North and South America down to Tierra del Fuego (Needham 1980, chap. 1). If the image is not universal, it yet has a distribution which precludes certain conventional explanations and attracts instead the supposition that the feature possesses an archetypal character.

This particular description may not be the right one, but the global incidence answers as nearly as may be to Locke's criterion of "universal consent." Despite all the inevitable qualifications, this kind of distribution is the first mark whereby the fundamental nature of the type of social fact at issue can be recognized. Let us now therefore survey a range of features which have been claimed to qualify, on this score, as fundamental in the sense required.

III

1. Certain a priori relations count as primary, and hence as fundamental, by definition; examples are duality, symmetry, transitivity. There need not, however, be any cultural recognition of such relations; they frame social facts, and it is the structure of the frame that displays the relations. On occasion they are indeed given a local definition, and they may even become objects of a detached critical attention, but this is not

necessary to their postulation as primary factors of experience. This character accords with the hypothesis that the fabricators of institutions ordered by such relations were guided, probably subliminally, by the same mental impulsions and constraints as are isolated critically by the analyst.

If it is objected that the conception of these relations reflects our western tradition of formal logic, and that therefore they are not proper to other social forms and ideologies, it needs to be shown that different formal or logical considerations actually obtain elsewhere. So long as this cannot be done, or remains merely an open question (cf. Needham 1972:158–75), the primary character of these relations will stand.

2. Logical possibilities and constraints have a similar claim to acceptance. For instance, in assessing resemblances among concepts of "descent," the premise is that two procreative sexes are recognized (Needham 1974:44–50). Where this premise agrees with cultural tradition, the logical consequences must follow, namely the severely limited number of possible modes in which rights can be transmitted from one generation to the next according to sex.

If there were ever discovered a society in which a different number of procreative sexes was recognized, we should have to reconsider the fundamental determination of types of descent system. As matters stand, however, the premise appears universal, and so therefore are the logical constraints on the regulation of rights by descent. The constraints are purely formal, moreover, and they have no exclusive or peculiar connection with the social facts in question, so that in this regard also they can be regarded as primary factors.

3. An inductive conclusion from the comparative study of symbolic classification is that there are points of attraction to which the imaginative unconscious tends naturally to respond.

Examples are the right and left hands as paradigmatic of dyadic opposition, the triad of colors white-black-red as natural symbols, percussion as a fundamental signal (and, in the event, as regular concomitant of transition). These mediators of significance have no logical character, and they could not have been deduced; nor are they, as a class, the outcome of deliberate choice on the part of those who resort to them. Their character is indicated by their global distribution and, what is particularly decisive, by the agreement among a great many cultures in their reliance upon a common stock of such symbolic vehicles.

4. Among civilizations of the most disparate kinds there recur synthetic complexes of symbolic elements which cohere into regular and easily detected ideological images. Examples are the characteristic features of the shaman and the image of the witch. These are patent phenomena, as social facts, and to discern them calls for little in the way of abstraction or analysis. Such complexes are as quickly recognizable as are the numinous features of Greta Garbo, the Hawksmoor towers of All Souls, or the pinnacles of Monument Valley. They are so steady in their constitution and in their characteristic significance that they can be taken as spontaneous symbolic constructions; and because their forms are comparatively invariant they are recalcitrant to causal or to correlational analysis. These prominent and characteristic features lead to the inference that synthetic complexes of the kind are products of imaginative inclinations which have an archetypal character.

5. The constituents of culture, whether conceptual or imaginative, are sometimes connected up in regular ways, and one of the outstanding modes is by analogical association. A striking example, both formally and semantically, is the chain of relations right : left :: male : female :: jural : mystical :: light : dark :: active : passive. Such concatenated

ideas rest on a capacity to detect resemblances which extends to the detection of resemblances among resemblances. In this instance, also, there is evidently a positive determination which inclines men to posit resemblances where no common properties are patent.

Classifications which are the products of semantic analogy can be consistently analyzed, but not causally (Needham 1980, chap. 2). The recognition of analogical classifications does not depend on any particular explanation of their form or of their universality, but instead these aspects provide grounds to infer that such constant features of social facts reflect unconscious operations of thought and imagination.

6. Among the forms and influences which attribute order and meaning to human life, amid the incessant flow of impressions and representations, there can be isolated a class of what I have called paradigmatic scenes.

These are in the main affective and iconic, and their impact is such as to convey a sense of deep and directive significance in the interpretation of human experience (Needham 1981: 88–89). These scenes are not all alike; in their particular conformations, they differ from culture to culture and also from individual to individual. Some are collectively contrived, others are the products of individual artistry; some are communally interpreted, others are idiosyncratically construed.

Locke wrote that "there is scarcely any one so floating and superficial in his understanding, who hath not some reverenced propositions, which are to him the principles on which he bottoms his reasonings" (*Essay*, Bk. I, chap. 3, sec. 24). In like manner, there are moving depictions which are exemplary in the comprehension of life and in the guidance of conduct. These iconic representations serve imaginatively and psychically as do rational principles in an intellectual appreciation of experience. Although they are highly contingent in what they happen to depict, they show forth in each instance

a more constant and fundamental tendency to condense con-
tingencies into steady and exemplary images of a tellingly
emotive kind. They are complex symbols in the main; for example, religious depictions such as the Crucifixion or Śiva
Ardhanārīśvara, and also a range of domestic, erotic, and
natural situations such as have become standard resources for
pictorial advertisements in the commercial press.

Apart from citing examples, to which others may or may
not respond, it is difficult to stipulate by what general marks
and characters these paradigmatic scenes are to be objectively
distinguished. If it is not too flexible and accommodating to
do so, perhaps the notion is to be tested chiefly by whether
others agree in recognizing in themselves the kind of source
and the kind of effect suggested, especially with the gloss that
such scenes need not be specifically religious or metaphysical,
nor overtly didactic in any manner. It may be helpful to compare them with the idea of a "tone of thought" such as Waismann adduced to characterize the intellectual attitude of an
age; this too is hard to isolate or define, yet it is a pervasive
and powerful feature in the life of a civilization. A more particular comparison can be made with the exemplary scenes
depicted in emblem books. It is true that, unlike the affective
paradigms in question, the emblems are deliberately instructive, but they testify to the same kinds of prompting and response. The paradigmatic scenes, however, can be regarded
as more resourceful, in that while they must be characteristic
of a form of life (whether taken collectively or individually)
they can yet be adventitious.

It might be objected that moving and memorable scenes of
the kind derive their peculiar force from the mere power of
drama, but this can be met by instancing events from straight
drama. When Kurwenal rushes on to the stage, urgently calling to Tristan to save himself ("Rette dich, Tristan!"), this is
electrifying—and is to be miserable in its consequences as
Mark groans at trust betrayed—but it has not the quasi-

hermeneutic significance that can be ascribed to paradigmatic scenes. In Hitchcock's film *Psycho*, the terrifying sequence in which the identity of the killer is disclosed makes a breathtaking dramatic impact, but it has nothing of the deep exemplary import that is characteristic of scenes that serve as affective paradigms. When Lulu is murdered by Jack the Ripper, the screams of Berg's dissonant chords are blood-chilling, but their savage force serves only the interests of the drama. Yet drama alone is not enough, and conversely there can be paradigmatic scenes (for example, the Buddha in the attitude of Fear-not) which are devoid of any drama.

In the matter of distinguishing marks of such scenes, there is a further serious question. If there is a disagreement over whether or not certain phenomena constitute a paradigmatic scene, can the issue be settled? One answer is to say that it does not matter crucially if a particular representation is or is not agreed to be paradigmatic, just so long as it is agreed that scenes of the kind can be coherently posited. Of course, this stance means that a paradigmatic scene may not be a clear-cut social fact, such as a marriage rule or a form of punishment or a regular ceremony, but a degree of indefinition does not entail that the notion cannot in fact be revealingly employed. Much in the field of symbolism is vague, obscure, or even subliminal, yet we do not permit these characteristics, which after all are no more than appropriate to the phenomena, to preclude analysis or investigation. At the very least, if it is conceded that paradigmatic scenes can be isolated in one's own culture, or even in one's own inner life, the presumption is that subtle and sympathetic inquiries will be able to discern them in another.

There is also a more general reason, grounded in comparative epistemology, to entertain the notion of paradigmatic scenes. This is that they can be seen as instances of the familiar process of condensation. Under this rubric they can be assimilated to categories, types, and generalizations, all of which condense the characteristic features of large sets of various particulars into an economy of manageable concepts. In the same way, paradigmatic scenes exemplify a common inclination, and even a practical necessity, in coming to terms with experience and its fluctuating press of particulars—only in this kind of mental construct the operation of condensation is not analytical or rational or cognitive but iconic and affective.

IV

In this summary conspectus of primary factors, I have devoted only a few lines to those which I consider best established, and I have dwelt longest on the most uncertain. Although I have omitted any lengthy factual demonstrations, the marks and characters of primary factors of experience can be claimed to include the following:

1. They are of different kinds: perceptions, images, abstractions, logical constraints.
2. They are independent of the will; intrinsically they are neither created nor altered deliberately, but they originate unconsciously.
3. They are not as a class connected up into systems, but they can be variously combined.
4. They are primary but not elementary; each is analyzable into a complex of grounds or possible determinants.
5. Characteristically, though not exclusively, they are manifested in symbolic forms, not in cognitive or rational institutions.

Granted this much, it is still possible to ask what is the point in trying to isolate primary factors, if only because the aim may have something to do with their definition.

The first answer is that the venture is a continuation of an age-long concern to find out what is fundamental in human nature. The second is that the procedure may facilitate comparison, and also make this more comprehensive and effective. And a third might be that, methodologically, the point in trying to isolate primary factors is whatever proves to be the point of having isolated them; that is, that even if they may be purely hypothetical, it is reasonable to postulate them for the sake of whatever heuristic advance they may turn out to secure.

Nevertheless, given the highly variegated characters of these factors, it is not to be looked for that they will be capable of systematic combination and permutation such as might yield equivalents to the calculations of physics or chemistry. Their methodical value, rather, will reside in their relative discreteness and in their capacity for indefinitely changeable conjunctions in the composition of collective and individual representations.

V

We are now in a position to assess Locke's case, with regard to speculative principles, and in general the case for innate ideas.

We do so, however, not only from a different empirical basis but with a different direction of interest. Instead of concentrating on "ideas," we have focused on whatever might be found to be innate, and this has displayed the issue under a new aspect. Let us look, then, at the contrasts between Locke's contentions and the findings of modern comparativism.

The chief point to take is that Locke's argument applies to propositions. Sometimes he explicitly calls them "propositions," at others he writes alternatively of "principles," "maxims," or "truths." The components of these propositions are "terms" and "ideas" or "notions," though on occasion no distinction is drawn between a principle and an idea. The propositions are explicit; they must be present to the consciousness and they must be assented to. They serve functions of knowledge and reason; that is, of intellectual discernment.

By contrast, the primary factors indicated above are not intrinsically propositional, and they cannot be true or untrue. They are hence not ideas, in these respects, and they are not deliberately made up of cognitive or rational terms. Their operation is implicit; they are not, as "notions," present to consciousness, nor are they, in general, explicitly formulated or assented to. Although they provide means for coming to terms with the world and society, they are not instruments for the better attainment of knowledge; and although the logical factors guide thought, or compel the form of conclusions, they are not rational concepts.

If we consider the primary factors in an etymological perspective, there are in fact grounds to admit them as ideas, for the first sense of the word "idea" (from the Greek for "to see") is given as "archetype" (*Shorter Oxford English Dictionary*); but since Locke's day the definitive sense has been that of any product of mental apprehension or activity, existing in the mind as "an object of knowledge or thought," and under this interpretation the primary factors are not ideas. They do however testify to what I earlier called fundamental inclinations of the psyche, and an appropriate designation for them is "innate proclivities."

That such proclivities are in fact innate is shown by their global distribution, by their constancy within any tradition, and (with the exception of the semantic particulars of paradigmatic scenes) by their remarkably economical agreement from one civilization to another. They are in the main neither taught nor learned, and it is only by comparative analysis that they are brought to consciousness as objects of intellectual scrutiny.

If, then, we venture into the huts of Indians, we find that the mind at birth is not an empty cabinet or a white paper. It is a complex of proclivities which, though brought to expression by society, are, as mental forms, independent of semantic tradition and resistant to social pressure. Through many remarkable congruencies among collective representations, examined on a worldwide scale of comparison, it can thus be determined that there are indeed "natural characters engraven upon the mind."

Presumably, innate proclivities are generated by natural operations of the brain. These cannot be entirely spontaneous, but they are conditional (as is pathetically underlined by the wild boy of Aveyron) on communication with other brains in a tradition of civilization. There is at present not even any prospect of determining what particular neuro-physiological events or functions are responsible for any of the proclivities. In any case, a reduction to cerebral vectors cannot be the affair of comparativists. Our field of evidence is representations, and we have no call to posit a correspondence with any other kind of phenomena. So far as the evidence of social facts carries us, in the determination of any innate proclivity, the order detected in those facts constitutes the proclivity. The order is in fact the only immediate contact with the proclivity that we can have. That is, there is nothing of the kind subsisting behind the order itself and to which—if only it could be discovered—the order in the analysis would really correspond (Needham 1979:60).

However that may be, there are grounds to suspect that to postulate innate proclivities, ascribing to them thereby an archetypal character, could provoke resistance on the part of some social anthropologists. A likely ground of objection is that this kind of undertaking is part of a deep analysis of the psyche, and hence not appropriate to a certain conception of what social anthropology should be. My own response, in that event, would be that it was the professional definition of social anthropology that was itself inappropriate, and that any characteristic manifestations of human nature should be central to anthropological inquiry. If the present exercise in particular were called into question, the rejoinder would need to respond to the terms and concerns of the objection actually raised, but a general point can be made in advance.

There are no decisive reasons to reject in advance any form of conceptual atomism or any mode of reductionism, and it is surely an accepted theoretical ambition among anthropologists to establish basic features of human society, conduct, and representations—though what is to qualify as basic cannot be deduced and cannot usefully be stipulated before the event. If the postulated innate proclivities, considered in the form of social facts, can be shown by comparative analysis to match certain criteria of the fundamental, why not accept them as empirical discoveries? It is hard to see why we should not concede that, for once, we have actually found what we were looking for.

5

Psalmanaazaar, Confidence-man

A secret and benevolent society . . . arose to invent a country. . . . After several years of secret conclaves and premature syntheses it was understood that one generation was not sufficient to give articulate form to a country.　　　J. L. Borges

I

In all science a basic precondition of progress is confidence in the integrity of one's colleagues. They may not all be of the highest intelligence, imagination, or perceptiveness, but it is essential that we trust them absolutely, as if in this one respect they were paragons.

In the experimental sciences this confidence is safeguarded by the possibility of empirical proof and replication; in the exact sciences generally it is buttressed by the canons of formal demonstration and especially by the rigorous consistency of mathematics. In the humane disciplines these checks are not usually feasible, and beyond the ordinary requisite of logical coherence there is no means of being sure of one's colleagues other than by going back to their sources. But then ethnography is in the worst case of all, for it is quite common that the reporter is the only source of information on the society in question, or at any rate over a particular period or from a certain point of view. In that event, professional confidence in the integrity of the ethnographer may well be the decisive factor in the acceptance of what he reports. Scholarship is always a moral undertaking, and when one's sources are practically inaccessible the sense of conscience needs to be at its highest pitch; every particular assertion calls for the ethnographer's total scrupulosity with regard to criteria of fact, value, evidence, and every conceivable form of bias. In the outcome, there is probably no ethnographic statement that an outsider can confidently accept entirely as it stands, but the one thing that we should not be able to call into question is the ethnographer's trustworthiness.

Nevertheless, there are two kinds of allegation, both touching on the question of trust, that are commonly levelled against the ethnographic data on which comparativism must rely. They are probably voiced more often outside the anthropological profession than within it, but this likelihood does not affect the crucial issue. One allegation is that the ethnographer is systematically deceived by the natives, so that what he reports in good faith is still not to be relied upon. There are many good reasons to doubt that this ever happens. It is not to be denied, of course, that individuals under the pressure of an ethnographer's questions will on occasion, and for one or another of a variety of motives, give answers that are evasive or misleading or downright untrue; but this is a far cry from a total and concerted deception of such a kind that the ethnographer will record what is in effect a fictitious set of institutions. One reason that this is unlikely is the endemic factionality of any form of social aggregate, and there are other reasons also that readily propose themselves, but the chief obstacle to the supposed enterprise is the sheer difficulty of it. This is a main consideration in the way of the other allegation, namely that which asserts that the ethnographer himself may just make things up. From a professional point of view this is the more worrying imputation, not merely because it more directly attacks the professional himself but because the deception would in this case be more likely to succeed. However little we may think of the scientific progress made by social anthropology, by way of theories and tested hypotheses and abstract propositions, the ethnographer ought at least to have a far wider knowledge of social forms, their variety and their limits, and of how institutions tend to fit together, than would the most ingenious group of indigenous deceivers. Just how successful he could be would depend in part on his scholarly knowledge, his power of imaginative invention, and his rhetorical capacity; but the general presumption would seem to be that a professionally trained confidence trickster, in ethnography as in other enterprises, would stand the best chance of an effective deception. This is not to say that he would in fact succeed, but only that he would be the most likely to carry it off. Is this kind of deception, then, really likely to be put into effect?

In posing this question, I am not considering human folly or wicked ambition, nor the gullibility of those who might be (or want to be) deceived. What I have in view is the intrinsic difficulty of inventing a society. By this I mean the conception of an account so plausible as to persuade readers that it is a veracious work of ethnographic description. The essential is that it must be intended to deceive. This rules out such fictions as *Gulliver's Travels* and *Erewhon*, which, whatever their plausibility as the depiction of possible forms of social life, were never meant to deceive as to matters of social fact. Nevertheless, the avowedly fictional can give us some idea of what may be required in the interest of plausibility, and thus provide a scheme for a fiction that was intended to deceive.

Borges, in his classic tale "Tlön, Uqbar, Orbis Tertius" (1981:27–43), expands the scope of the fantastic; he imagines not only a secret society that is founded to invent a country, but also a bolder thinker (an American) who suggests the composition of a methodical encyclopaedia of an imaginary planet. The forty volumes of this, the First Encyclopaedia of Tlön, are to be the basis of a more detailed edition, written moreover not in English but in one of the languages of the fictitious planet. (We shall see below the pertinence of this ultimate detail of false authenticity.) As time passes, in the tale, the imaginary world intrudes testimonies to its reality, in the form of characteristic material objects, into the everyday world. Whether this device goes too far is a matter that will find its place as we consider further the components of an effective ethnographic deception. In any event, it is not Borges who intends to deceive; it is his inventive conspirators who are described as responsible. Furthermore, the story is a metaphysical entertainment, and if there is a deceptive aspect to it the effect is epistemological, not ethnographic.

Where Borges approaches closer to the topic of the present essay is in his later tale, "Doctor Brodie's Report" (1976). This purports to be based on a manuscript left by a Scottish missionary who had ventured into the heart of Africa. Borges declares that the story "obviously derives from Lemuel Gulliver's last voyage" (12), and he employs a literary tactic that is at least similar to Swift's. The fictional society is that of the Mlch, and the characteristics ascribed to this exotic people are repellently different from those of western Europe. Their language is harsh; they have no fixed abodes; only a few individuals have names; they live on roots and reptiles, and they imbibe the milk of cats and chiropterans; they perform all their bodily acts, except eating, in open view; they devour the raw corpses of their witch doctors and of the royal family; the king is hideously mutilated and is anointed with excrement; the people are insensitive to pain and pleasure, save for the relishment they get from raw and rancid meat and evil-smelling things, and an utter lack of imagination moves them to cruelty; they cannot manufacture the simplest object; their numeration stops at four, their memory is greatly defective or perhaps nonexistent; they conceive of hell as dry and light, and of heaven as marshy and beclouded. All in all, the Mlch are a terribly barbarous nation, yet they do have institutions of their own: they enjoy a king, they employ a language based on abstract concepts, they believe in the divine nature of poetry (even if they have free license to kill poets), they surmise that the soul survives the body (even if those who go to heaven are the merciless and bloodthirsty), and they apply a system (however unjust in our eyes) of punishments and rewards. "After their fashion, they stand for civilisation . . ." (100).

In this case also Borges has no intention to deceive, and he does not even imply any deceit on the part of his missionary ethnographer. The institutions he attributes to the Mlch may be barbarous, but they are institutions all the same; the qualities of their way of life may be repulsive, yet they compose a form of civilization. Nevertheless, despite the extreme contrasts with our own social forms, it is not self-evident that Mlch society would be recognised as fictitious if Dr. Brodie's report were presented as a sober and hard-won ethnographic description. It could be true, and the question then is by what marks we can hope to distinguish the invented from the ethnographic. Mere internal consistency is not enough, of course, and this is demonstrated moreover by professional responses to the structural interpretation of ethnographic data: if the analysis proves to be consistent, it is suspiciously neat; if inconsistencies remain, these are contradictions which invalidate the analysis. Nor is familiarity with the type of society a sure criterion, for every type is unfamiliar until it is discovered; if we do not know of any society which treats its king as horribly as the Mlch do theirs, this does not entail that there is none that does so. Indeed, the only safe guide appears to be that whatever conduct can be imagined will be put into practice, if it is feasible, by some people somewhere and for some time.

How, then, are we to distinguish fake ethnography from the genuine article? Let us examine a genuine example of the fake, and see what it can teach us.

II

George Psalmanaazaar, author of *An Historical and Geographical Description of Formosa* (1704), caused a great stir at the beginning of the eighteenth century with his account of the religion, customs, manners, and much else of the inhabitants of that island.

Formosa was then practically unknown, and Psalmanaazaar's description enjoyed the greater authority in that he had been born there; he had been lured away, at the age of nineteen, by a scheming Jesuit who had brought him to Europe; he spoke the Formosan language fluently, and he wrote it in the Formosan alphabet; in his way of life, moreover, as for example in eating herbs, uncooked roots, and raw meat, he continued to follow Formosan customs.

Not a particle of this colorful background was true. His family name was not Psalmanaazaar; he was perhaps born in the south of France; and he had never been nearer to Formosa than the Rhine. The language and its alphabet were his own inventions, and the oriental customs were mere acting. His *Description of Formosa* was a fiction, and the institutions he ascribed to the inhabitants of the island were fake ethnography.

We have no independent means of determining the course of Psalmanaazaar's life before he came to England, where his book was first published, for the one major and detailed source is his own *Memoirs* (1764), and we cannot be sure how far these are to be relied upon. Farrer says they put "a severe strain on belief" (1907:94), Lee describes them as "vague" (1921–22:439), and Hill writes: "How far his *Memoirs* are truthful is somewhat doubtful. . . . There are passages which are not free from the leaven of hypocrisy, and there are, I suspect, statements which are at least partly false" (in Boswell 1934, 3:444). His birthplace was apparently a city lying on the road from Avignon towards Rome; the editor of the *Gentleman's Magazine* concluded that it "could not be more than

100 miles from the city of Lyons in France" (Anon. 1764b: 543 n., 574 n.); but Hill, after collating the various hints provided, declared "I do not think such a place can be found" (in Boswell 1934, 3:446). He may have been born in 1680 or in 1684; Winnet reasonably thinks the earlier date the more probable (1971:7); Walckenaer puts it at 1679 (1843:453), and so, with a query, does Lee (1921–22:439); and there is a possibility that it was earlier than that. The nearest that Psalmanaazaar himself came to any precision was that in his will, dated 1752, he wrote that he was "in the 73rd year of my age" (1764:5), giving a birth date of 1680; but, if this looks certain, other relevant particulars are not (cf. 174).

Psalmanaazaar's family name is unknown, and the most he intimates is that it was rather grand. Writing of a time when he had embarked on a vagrant life and was resorting to all kinds of shifts in order to survive, he says that his pride would not let him forego his name "because it had something of quality in it" (1764:117–18). Later, however, he decided to pass himself off as a Japanese, and he called himself Salmanazar, after the Assyrian king Shalmaneser (2 Kings 17:3). When he was taken to England he altered the spelling, "by the addition of a letter or two, to make it somewhat different from the biblical name" (1764:169), and became Psalmanaazaar, a form which itself was eventually simplified to Psalmanazar. A contemporary challenger took him to be Jewish, but, as Psalmanaazaar slyly replied, his name (which of course was not his given name) was not Jewish but Assyrian, and "a Jew would as soon call a son of his Beelzebub, as Salmanazar" (1764:358–59). Later in the eighteenth century, nevertheless, Richardson bluntly described him as "the Jew Psalmanasar" (1778:247). As for the rest concerning his background, he conceded, in a rather odd wording: "Out of Europe I was not born, nor educated, nor ever travelled" (1764:70). He said he lived in the southern part of Europe until he was sixteen years of age. A clergyman called Villette, who was well acquainted with him for some twenty-four years, said that he spoke French so well that he was unquestionably a Frenchman; he even had a Gascon accent, and he was so masterly in the dialect of that province that he could be presumed to have been born in the Languedoc (1764:i–ii). Soon after his death, it was definitely concluded that he was "undoubtedly a Frenchman born" (Anon. 1764a:66), and this was what his friend Dr. Johnson also imagined him to be (Piozzi 1786:173). All the same, late in his life Psalmanaazaar wrote on this score: "I can safely say that I never met with, nor heard of any one, that ever guessed right, or any thing near it, with respect to my native country" (1764:199). Perhaps he was playing on the distinction between the country in which he had been born and that in which he was brought up as a child.

Psalmanaazaar was described in 1704 as "a middle sized well shaped man of a fair complexion" (Gwinnett 1731:58; Anon. 1765b:78), though a few years afterwards he was "known" by his features "to be of India by an ingenious Gentleman who had been many years there" (Anon. 1710:48). He was found "an ingenious man, and a good scholar"; "he is allowed by all to have good parts, both natural and acquired; he is master of six languages, has an acute apprehension, tenacious memory . . ." (Gwinnett 1731:65; Anon. 1765b:78, 79). An engraved portrait published as frontispiece to the *Memoirs* shows heavy features and large dark eyes (see plate 3).

Psalmanaazaar's life during his education and his European travels need not much occupy us; it has been well summarized in the *Dictionary of National Biography* (Lee 1921–22:439). For the present purpose we need remark only certain decisive points. He was educated in Roman Catholic institutions (Psalmanaazaar 1764:27), successively by Franciscans, Jesuits, and a Dominican, and then at a university. At the age of sixteen he made his way, in a state of destitution, to Germany in search of his father. Finding no support from him,

Plate 3. George Psalmanaazaar (Bodleian Library, Oxford)

he went on, as a mendicant student, through Germany and the Low Countries. Reduced to the utmost hardship, he thought of "a more cunning, safe, and effectual way of travelling." Recalling what the Jesuit tutors had told him about the East Indies, China, Japan, and elsewhere, he decided to assume the character of a Japanese. He invented an alphabet and writing that, like Hebrew, ran from right to left, "a considerable piece of a new language and grammar, a new division of the year into twenty months, a new religion, &c. and all out of my own head" (1764:134–36). Under the name Salmanazar (he never does tell us why he thought the name of an Assyrian king was suitable to a Japanese), he passed himself off as a heathen and exhibited outlandish customs. This recourse did not mend his fortunes, however, and he sustained himself by enlisting as a foot soldier. After many vicissitudes he joined his second regiment at Cologne; towards the end of 1702 the unit moved to the town of Sluys, where his behavior drew him to the attention of the military governor. This officer, Brigadier George Lauder, invited Isaac Amalvi, the minister of the Walloon church, and William Innes, chaplain to a Scots regiment stationed there, to examine him. This was the turning point in his career and was to lead him into an extraordinary notoriety.

The key figure was Innes. Psalmanaazaar found he had "a much smoother and less overbearing way of speaking than the other gentlemen" (1764:178); later he judged the chaplain to be ambitious and avaricious, and according to a note added to the draft of the *Memoirs* Innes was afterwards convicted of repeated untrustworthiness and ill conduct (180). Psalmanaazaar declared in his last will and testament, not long before his death, that he had been "in some measure unavoidably led into the base and shameful imposture of passing upon the world for a native of Formosa" (1764:5), and if only half of what he tells us is true it is at any rate easy to concede that he was not solely blameable. Innes quickly proved Psalmanaazaar to be a fraud. He had him translate a passage from Cicero into the invented "Formosan"; this version he took, and then he demanded another. Psalmanaazaar was unable to remember exactly what he had first written, and was exposed when Innes pointed out the "palpable difference" between the two versions, for not more than half the words in the second were in the first (184–85). Yet Innes did not give him away. Instead, he conceived a plan to gain "some preferment" from the Bishop of London by claiming the credit of converting a heathen Formosan to the Christian faith (179). Psalmanaazaar fell in with this deceit, was publicly baptized, and, possibly at the end of 1703 (Lee 1921–22:440), was taken by Innes to London. He aroused much interest and was taken up by persons of eminence including Sir Hans Sloane, secretary to the Royal Society, and the Earl of Pembroke. Innes then "prevailed upon" him to write the history of Formosa (215), and with this undertaking he was irrevocably committed to the bold imposture for which he was to become famous. Innes gave him a copy of the description of the kingdom of Japan by Varenius (1649), and Psalmanaazaar also read, in some source, that of Candidius (1704).

The fictitious account of Formosa was written in two months, under pressure from Innes and from the bookseller who was to publish it; and the translator from his Latin into English, a certain Mr. Oswald, assisted him to correct many "improbabilities" which he had not had time to discover (216–17). Compton, the bishop of London, and certain friends sent him to Oxford, where he was assigned "a convenient apartment . . . in one of the most considerable colleges" (221), in fact at Christ Church (Hearne 1885, 1:271), where Compton had been a canon (Lee, *Dictionary of National Biography*, 4:899). He stayed almost six months at Oxford, and revised his "romance of Formosa" there (226). He was a social success, especially perhaps as he was rumored to be a king's son (Gwinnett 1731:66); and he soon afterwards implied in print, with a feigned reluctance, that his "Father's Quality" was that of king, viceroy, prince, governor, or the like (1705a, 3 obj. 1 answ.). On one occasion he regaled a company of ladies and gentlemen, at their request, with an account of the "diabolical sacrifices" of young children on Formosa, and also with details of cannibalism; "I think it no sin, continued he, to eat human flesh; but I must own it is a little unmannerly" (Gwinnett 1731:61; cf. Anon. 1765b:79).

Psalmanaazaar's *Description of Formosa* was published in 1704, with a fulsome dedication to Compton; this epistle stressed the general ignorance about Formosa and the baseness of the "wicked Society" of the Jesuits. The latter imputation was prudent, given the religious politics of the day (cf. Bracey 1925:78) and Compton's reputation for persecuting Roman Catholics (Lee, *Dictionary of National Biography* 4: 899); and it was also tactically advantageous, for a Jesuit missionary to China, Father Fountenay, was then in London and had proved a menacing critic. Psalmanaazaar devoted half a dozen pages of his preface to an account of three occasions on which he had publicly confronted the "Spite and Malice" of this priest, and by his own reckoning he won hands down each time. He also prefaced the *Description* with a number of more general defenses (to which we shall revert below), for there was much skepticism abroad about the truth of his tale. Nevertheless, the book quickly sold out, and Psalmanaazaar was asked to prepare a second edition, which appeared in 1705, and this he introduced with a second preface of thirty-four pages in which he answered "those Objections which the unmerciful Criticks have rais'd against me and the Book." In the same year a French translation was published at Amsterdam; Psalmanaazaar complained that the translator had "taken but little care to stick to his Original," and that this version contained "many gross Faults" (1705a, second preface). Two other French translations followed, in 1708 and 1712, and a

German translation was brought out in 1712 and 1716 (cf. Walckenaer 1843:440).

The French edition provoked a reply by Amalvi (1706), who protested against Psalmanaazaar's report of his implication in the (fraudulent) conversion. In the next year Psalmanaazaar published a *Dialogue* between a Japanese and a Formosan (1707), but, according to Lee, the tide of incredulity rose and after 1708 he was the butt of much ridicule (1921–22:441; cf. Anon. 1711). About two years after this date a group of investigators published anonymously *An Enquiry into the Objections against George Psalmanaazaar of Formosa* (Anon. n.d.). It was dedicated to Henry Compton, bishop of London, on the ground that it was at his command that Psalmanaazaar had been brought to England. The authors had collected as many printed accounts as they could find, interrogated as many travelers as they met, put out a public notice of their inquiry, and issued in the *London Gazette* a general challenge to the "World" to send them whatever people had to say against Psalmanaazaar (cf. Psalmanaazaar 1764:202). Their conclusion, after all this, was definite and positive: "We have made Enquiry, which we hope will satisfie the World, that P———r is the Man he pretends to be, and that the History of Formosa, and of his Travels, is true" (1710: 53). To this there was conveniently appended an answer to Amalvi by their cooperative subject in which Psalmanaazaar rebutted objections attaching to his conversion and baptism and also to certain doctrinal points (Psalmanaazaar 1710).

Nevertheless, things must have been getting too hot for him, and he withdrew from public notice into a life of dissipation. Eventually he found respectable employment, first as a private tutor and then, in 1715, as clerk to a regiment in Lancashire. In this latter post he was made much of by some of the officers and was even credited by his sponsor with having been knighted by Queen Anne. In 1717 he left the regiment and turned first to fan-painting for a living and then to literary work for a London printer. A serious illness in 1728 made the occasion for him to read certain devotional works; he renounced his past life, and in the same year he embarked on the memoirs that were to be published after his death. Thereafter he maintained a laborious existence in London as a hack writer and independent scholar, especially in the study of Hebrew. He is generally credited with having been the actual author of *A General History of Printing* which was published under the name of the man who printed it (Palmer 1732). Between 1735 and 1744 he contributed eleven articles (for titles, see Psalmanaazaar 1764:321–22; Lee 1921–22: 441) to the *Universal History*. In 1747 he wrote an unsigned article on Formosa for Bowen's *Complete System of Geography*, and, referring to his own *Description of Formosa*, "as it were by a third hand" (1764:339), declared that Psalmanaazaar had "long since ingenuously owned" that the account was untrue (Bowen 1747, 2:251). Six years later, he published under a pseudonym a volume of essays on the reality of miracles and on biblical subjects (Psalmanaazaar 1753). He continued for another decade to survive by literary drudgery, until he died in Ironmonger Row, Clerkenwell, London, on 3 May 1763. In the following year his *Memoirs* (Psalmanaazaar 1764) were published by his executrix; they were issued in a second edition in 1765, at London and Dublin.

Psalmanaazaar's design in leaving his memoirs for publication was, very handsomely, "to undeceive the world with respect to that vile and romantic account I formerly gave of myself, and of the island of Formosa" (1764:11). All the same, his fake ethnography had a long run. The *Description* was reissued in a French translation in 1739, and in 1808 it was drawn upon by Boucher de la Richarderie (1808:289–91) as the authority for an entry on Formosa. Psalmanaazaar was described as "a man born in the country" (290), and with this assurance the compiler attributed to the Formosans the eating of raw meat, snakes, and human flesh. On this last count, indeed, he went further and added a gruesome story: "Palmanaazaar himself, transported to London, had retained this depraved taste to such an extent that, excited to eat the flesh of a woman who had been hanged, he did so without repugnance" (290). He gave no source for this tale, but the likelihood is that it has a connection with Swift's "Modest Proposal." Swift introduces the suggestion that the lack of venison in the country might be supplied by the bodies of young lads and maidens, who otherwise would starve for want of work. Then his supposed interlocutor explains that this expedient was put into his head by "the famous *Sallmanaazor*, a Native of the Island *Formosa*, who . . . told my friend, that in his Country when any young Person happened to be put to death, the Executioner sold the Carcass to *Persons of Quality*, as a prime Dainty, and that, in his Time, the Body of a plump Girl of fifteen, who was crucified for attempting to Poison the Emperor, was sold . . . *in Joints from the Gibbet . . .*" (Swift 1729:10). After these authoritative details, it was easy to debit the Formosans with the abominable habit of immolating multitudes of children. For the rest, however, the compiler contented himself with noting the great detail with which Psalmanaazaar describes the Formosan language, ceremonies, and so forth, and he concluded merely that in these respects the Formosans show much similarity to the Japanese. As for the connection with Swift, there is, as Napier has pointed out, a further correspondence in the matter of trampling on the crucifix. Psalmanaazaar says that Christians were prohibited to enter Japan and that they were found out by the test of trampling on an image of Christ crucified; those that refused were themselves put to death by crucifixion (1704: 316–17). In the third book of *Gulliver's Travels*, first published in 1726, there is an incident in which Gulliver begs of the Emperor of Japan that he be excused the ceremony of trampling on the crucifix (Napier 1979; cf. 1981).

Finally, as perhaps the latest example of the resonance of Psalmanaazaar's deceit, his *Dialogue* was reprinted in 1896 together with a genuine translation of the Articles of Christian instruction into Favorlang-Formosan (Campbell 1896:103–21). The editor's explanation of the decision to include Psalmanaazaar's composition, without reference to his imposture, cited the *Dialogue*'s brevity, its rarity, its total contrast (no wonder) with another dialogue, and its interest at a time when the Japanese were "encountering" the hill tribes of Formosa (xviii).

These testimonies to the lasting persuasiveness of Psalmanaazaar's forgery would surely have saddened the culprit who, in his later and reformed years, was to be named by Dr. Johnson as "the *best* man he had ever known" (Piozzi 1786:173).

III

The *Description of Formosa* was published, as we have seen, in two editions: the first in 1704, the second in 1705. Although it was reset and rearranged for the new edition, the text was not substantially altered; the account of the author's travels and conversion was placed after the ethnographic description instead of before, and a map and one additional plate ("The Idol of the Devil") were supplied. An expository change of some significance is that whereas in the first edition a chapter heading read "Of the Marriage" (XI) or "Of the Opinion concerning the State of the Souls after Death" (XIII), in the second edition it is boldly altered to "Of our Marriages" and "Of our Opinion . . . ." A typical touch also is that where in the first edition Psalmanaazaar alludes to a letter from Meryaandanoo, a fictitious personage, to the King of Formosa, in the second edition he adds a corroborative footnote: "My Father has a Copy of this Letter by Him" (1705a:11 n. *a*). The chief difference between the two editions lies in the

Second Preface, "clearly answering every thing that has been objected against the Author and the Book." We shall take this up after we have very briefly surveyed the text of the *Description*, and for this purpose we shall rely on the original edition of 1704.

Plainly it would be impracticable to summarize here the 182 pages of supposedly ethnographic description, full of details of many kinds as they are. What is represented as the history of Formosa, moreover, has little methodological interest and can be passed over. In the main, we have to deal with some thirty-two chapters that can be called ethnographic. A list of their subjects will give an idea of Psalmanaazaar's range and also some indication of the mass of the material that cannot, in the present space, be treated item by item. The chapters in question, then, cover: government, religion, fasting-days, ceremonies, priests, objects of worship, postures of adoration, ceremonies at births, marriages and deaths, after-life, vestments, manners and customs, physical appearance, clothes, habitations, commodities, weights and measures, superstitions, diseases, revenues, natural produce, foodstuffs, animals, language, shipping, money, weapons, musical instruments, education, liberal and mechanical arts, and the vice-regal retinue. This is a very wide variety of social facts to adduce, and no doubt the comprehensive nature of Psalmanaazaar's monograph contributed to its plausibility and success.

The institutions are not described in formal terms, or systematically, but instead the *Description* proceeds by the accumulation of particulars. Nevertheless, it is possible to isolate certain features that may well have exerted a special appeal in opposite senses. On the one hand, readers at the beginning of the eighteenth century in England were presented with a set of familiar and perhaps reassuring institutions: monarchy, a strict social hierarchy, a revealed religion with a sacred book, processions, even the wearing of black for mourning. On the

other hand, the majority of readers could be righteously re-
pelled by a tyrannical priesthood that invented profitable
falsehoods and kept the sacred book to itself alone, a god appearing in the shape of an ox or of some other beast, the
burning of incense, immolation of thousands of small children, and even cannibalism. Some exotic details were merely
piquant, for instance that the "Formosans" ate venison and
fowls raw (1704:263), a practice that Psalmanaazaar himself
publicly followed in London (xi). On the whole, in these respects, he seems to have struck an effective balance between
the acceptable and the detestable. Yet, all the same, there is
much evidence, from himself and from others, that his integrity was doubted and that the authenticity of his *Description*
was gravely questioned.

Psalmanaazaar's attempt to disarm criticism was first made
in advance in the opening pages of the first preface (1704:v),
where he wrote:

I pretend not to give you a perfect and complete History of my Island, because I was a meer Youth when I left it, but nineteen Years
of Age, and therefore incapable of giving an exact Account of it.
Besides, I have now been six Years from home, so many things of
moment may perhaps slip my Memory.

But his main defense was offered in a series of responses to
twenty-five objections which he set out to refute in the preface to the second edition of the *Description* (1705a, unnumbered pages; citations by objection and answer). With false
candor, he begins by admitting that to him "it does not seem
strange . . . that Men should suspect the first Accounts of
any remote Places," and he surmises that if he were to return
to Formosa his own countrymen there would not readily believe his description of England. But he does profess himself
surprised that he should be taken for a European rather than
for "what I really am, a Japannese, born in Formosa. . . ." He

confesses, too, that the first edition of his book was "imperfect," and that it omitted many curious and valuable things which long thinking, and the various questions since put to him, have at last brought fresh to his memory, a faculty which in him he acknowledges to be "treacherous" (1 obj. 4 answ.). He passes over many "little Arguments" of his "trifling Opponents," and comes to what he considers objections of the first magnitude. We in our turn shall have to pass over most of even these, astute and revealing though his responses are, and instead take up just certain points of present interest.

Perhaps the most dramatic report in the *Description* is that the Formosans are obliged to sacrifice annually 18,000 boys under the age of nine (1704:178—the true page, not the repeated p. 178). It appears that Psalmanaazaar once committed himself to this figure in a conversation and thereafter printed it (1764:218). At any rate, once the figure was published it became a topic of controversy; and not surprisingly, for the children's throats are cut and their hearts are plucked out and laid on a gridiron (187). "Mexico itself," one commentator has remarked "never offered a picture more horrible" (Farrer 1907:86). Since the God of the Formosans requires the hearts of so many young boys, and lest the population be thereby extirpated, polygamy is allowed (200). This recourse on Psalmanaazaar's part answered the practical objection that the figure was "incredible" (1705a, obj. 19), for in this case twenty men can have as many children by eighty women as these could bear in any other nation where polygamy was not allowed (answ. 2). Also, many of the children are sacrificed very young, and few of them (if they had escaped the knife of the Sacrificator) would have lived until the age of twenty-one (answ. 3). Finally, England loses so many men by emigration each year that the Formosan annual sacrifice would not cause so great a loss (answ. 4). In addition to these responses, moreover, Psalmanaazaar desires the reader to observe "that I assert the Law commands us to sacrifice so many, but I do not tell you it is a matter of fact that we do every Year Sacrifice the full number" (answ. 1).

Another kind of defense is more sophistical. Psalmanaazaar is challenged to explain how it is that he learned Greek at home, and how the Japanese or Formosans came to be such masters of Greek as to teach it in their academies (1704:290). To this he answers: "you may as well ask me how Formosa came first to be inhabited, and, because I cannot tell you, conclude there is not a Man upon the Island" (1705a, 2 obj. 1 answ.).

A wider objection elicits a shrewd response. It is contended that since Psalmanaazaar's historical description differs so much from what previous writers have said, then with so many witnesses against it his account must be false (1705a, 14 obj.). To this, Psalmanaazaar replies that "this Objection rather confirms than discredits the Account I have given," for if any European intended to pass for a Formosan or a Chinese his best way would certainly be to read Candidius and other reporters and so frame his tale "that he may not be contradicted by the Romantick Authors that have already written of these Countries" (1 answ.). As if this refutation were not enough (we shall see in a moment just how tricky it is), Psalmanaazaar adds the further response that in any case the authors in question "make no difference between Formosa and Tyowan"—which he asserts to be different islands (3 answ.). He goes even further, in fact, and actually alludes to "the forgeries of Candidius" (18 obj.). And of course he has the ultimate defense of the ethnographer, let alone of a writer who claims to be "a Native of the said Island" (*Description*, title page): that if anyone will obstinately deny what he reports, "the best advice I can give him is, to go to Formosa, and, if he can, confute me" (2 obj. 2 answ.).

But even these explicit and often ingenious defenses were not enough to quell the criticism, and in July 1705, only six weeks after the date of the second preface, Hearne noted:

"Tho' there be a II^d Edition of Psalmanezzer ye Formosan's Book, giving an Account of his Country, &c. come out, wherein he has answered most of ye material objections made against him, yet I am told he is still taken to be a Cheat in London" (Hearne 1885, 1:17).

Evidently, however, this opinion did not universally prevail, for about five years later there was published the *Enquiry into the Objections against George Psalmanaazaar of Formosa*, composed by a group of authors who did not supply their own names (Anon. n.d.). A set of addenda, prefixed to the text, reports the testimony from an unidentified source of a number of kingdoms on Formosa, the eating of raw meat and human flesh, the existence of many languages that are mutually incomprehensible, the mining of gold, and the fact that the mountainous part of the island was still unknown—"All of which make Ps——r's account highly probable in the whole, and confirm it in some material parts" (unnumbered pages). It is more than possible that the source of these details was the *Atlas Chinensis* of Arnoldus Montanus (van Bergen or van den Berg; ca. 1625–1683), a work commonly known, after the editor and translator, as "Ogilby's Chinese Atlas" (Montanus 1671). This contains a long section (9–39) on Formosa, citing inter alia Georgius Canidius (namely Candidius), a minister of the gospel who was on Formosa in 1628 and resided there several years. The account contradicts Psalmanaazaar's on certain important points; for instance, it says that the island has no king (12), and that the Formosans cannot write or read and have no books, letters, or characters (15). But it does say that the skulls of human victims are hung in the houses as trophies (14), that the natives eat venison, pig meat, and fish raw, without boiling or roasting it (23), and that there are different and mutually incomprehensible dialects (35). It also states that the island of Taywan, otherwise called Tayovan and Tayowan, lies south of Formosa (39), a point that will be seen to have its importance. These latter particulars appear to count in Psalmanaazaar's favor, though in another way they also tell against him. The weight of these points respectively will come to bear as we proceed.

The authors, who declare themselves plebeians who have not been educated beyond grammar school (51), state their intention as being "only to find out the truth" about Psalmanaazaar (1), and they adduce in the main two sources of evidence about Formosa. The first is a writer, unfortunately also unidentified, of two letters dated April and May 1705 and addressed to a "Mr. H. N." in London (12–15); the letter writer visited the island in 1672, but he does not contribute decisively to the chief points of contention. The other source of testimony, rather more substantial, is "A Short Description of the Isle Formosa" (21–25) by Johannus Albertus Lubomirski. This gentleman asserts that the chief idol of Formosa is called Moloch and that it is made of pure gold, and also that children are sacrificed to it annually. He does not comment on the remarkable correspondence of the name with Moloch (or Molech), the Canaanite god of fire to whom children were offered in sacrifice and whose worship was repeatedly condemned in the Old Testament (for example, Leviticus 18:21; Jeremiah 32:35), and possibly he was not aware that Moloch was an Assyrian god (cf. Psalmanaazaar's name, taken from that of an Assyrian king). At the feast of the new moon, according to Lubomirski, men offer themselves as sacrifices; a priest cuts open the chest and pulls out the heart (24). "These things about the Isle Formosa," Lubomirski declares, "I have heard to be very true" (24). He has no more than heard so, for he himself was evidently never on the island. What he relates is what he had from a Father Basilius of Cremona, a missionary who had been forty years in China and on the adjacent islands, including three on Formosa, and this priest affirmed that he had seen what he told Lubomirski (25).

The main part of the *Enquiry*, however, does not rest on these rather unsatisfactory sources but consists of individual answers to a paper of twenty objections which were received by a bookseller in response to the inquirers' advertisement; these are questions which had been heard leveled at Psalmanaazaar's book, but most of them relate not to ethnography but to points of Christian doctrine. There are a couple of matters among them, though, that do concern social facts. One is that the Formosan dress illustrated in the *Description* is "such as Stage Players use, and taken thence" (see plates 4 and 5). To this objection the authors reply: "Ps——r tells us he gave only general Directions to the Engraver, who added some Ornaments to the Habits . . ." (35). Another objection raised is that "there is a great deal of Greek" in the Formosan language. The authors reply that in Varenius there is a short sentence in Japanese containing six words, and that one of these "both sounds and signifies like Greek" (39), though they do not locate the sentence or isolate the actual word.

To these proofs that Psalmanaazaar "is the Man he pretends to be, and that the History of Formosa . . . is true" (53), the subject of the inquiry added the twenty-three pages of his own answers to Amalvi's protests about his conversion and baptism (1706); there is much emphasis, naturally, on doctrinal points but there is nothing of pertinence to the ethnography of Formosa.

The public trust of Psalmanaazaar's defenders may have been somewhat ingenuous, but they were not to know to just what an extent they had been cheated. The author of the *Description* had resorted to such bold and determined deceptions that they could hardly have conceived how devious he was. After all, he had candidly written in his preface (v) to the first edition of his monograph:

I assure you, I have not positively asserted any thing which is not as positively true; but if I have said what I did not know, as a certain Truth, as such I have admonish'd you of it. I have discharged my Conscience.

Plate 4. The King (Bodleian Library, Oxford)

He also gave the assurance that he had "oblig'd the Translator to make no Additions or Alterations" and that "'tis mine, and not his Fault, if you meet with any Imperfections" (xii). It was not to be known that in his *Memoirs* Psalmanaazaar would admit that actually the translator assisted him to "correct many more and greater improbabilities" which he had not had time to detect for himself (1764:216–17). In the text, moreover, there were little touches which appeared to testify similarly to a nice scrupulosity on the part of the native historian. For instance, at one place he reports a legend by which the Formosans are supposed to explain the existence of a certain fountain, and, after providing fair detail of the matter, he adds: "The History I do not deliver for a certain Truth, but neither do I account it altogether fabulous; for it seems to me very probable that there is something of truth in it . . ." (1704:239). And then he offers his detached conjectures as to the reasons that might have inclined the Formosans to fabricate the legend he had fabricated.

In the second edition, Psalmanaazaar resorted to a less polished deception concerning the translation, and to an effect which, considering what he had already asserted on this score, even his defenders could have found perturbing. At first he says that "Many improprieties, vain repetitions, and indeed mistakes of one of the Translators of the former Edition, are left out, or corrected in this" (1705a, second preface). This is ambiguous, and it permits some of the discredit to reflect possibly on the author himself, even though in the first edition he had clearly stated that the book, with the exception of certain pages on the author's conversion (94–144), "was translated out of the Latin by Mr. Oswald" (1704:xiii). But later in the second preface he does not leave open such an agreeable construction. He is countering an objection which expresses the doubt that a Japanese sword "will cut at one blow a large Tree in sunder" (22 obj.). He admits the reason-

Plate 5. The Viceroy's Lady (Bodleian Library, Oxford)

ableness of the query, but replies that the phrase did not run so in the original, where he had written merely of "arborem mediocriter magnam," a medium-sized tree. "And now how," he continues, "that Translator who is old Dog at Latin came to make this mistake, I know not." He implies that the Latin manuscript is still extant, but one wonders—just as one wonders if Oswald was still extant, and, if so, what he would have thought of all this. He would have been, if living, a dangerous man to turn into an ally of Psalmanaazaar's critics.

More fundamental, in any case, were the principles according to which Psalmanaazaar had very deliberately composed his fake ethnography, and his defenders could not have inferred these from the *Description* itself. He knew that "the place [Formosa] was upon the whole so very unknown to the Europeans" (1764:216); he found this "a great help and relief," and it meant he had a pretty free hand in what he was to invent. Thus he could assert, on the very title page, that Formosa was "an Island subject to the Emperor of Japan," whereas it was known to the Chinese from the eighth century A.D., settled by them from the twelfth century, extensively occupied by Chinese immigrants in the seventeenth century, and incorporated into the Chinese empire in 1683 (Gordon 1970:3; Hsieh 1964:146, 149). Nevertheless, there was something known about the island, notably in the account by Candidius (1704; cf. Montanus 1671), and here Psalmanaazaar brought his first and basic principle into play. He resolved to give a description of Formosa such "as should be wholly new and surprizing, and should in most particulars clash with all the accounts other writers had given of it" (217). And then, in support of this brazen tactic, he resolved on his second principle of method. This was the bold maxim never to retract what he had once asserted in conversation, so that when for instance he said on one occasion, "inadvertently" (1764: 218), that 18,000 infants were sacrificed each year, this was the figure that he afterwards adamantly maintained, though it cost him considerable trouble. These principles, held to with resolution and cunning, set Psalmanaazaar in a strong position, yet he had in his favor another factor which, in the event, also did much to mask his imposture. This was the general supposition as to the intrinsic difficulty of inventing a society.

When the *Description* was published, it occasioned a "variety of opinions concerning it, . . . some thinking it above the capacity of such a young fellow to invent, and others believing it the result of long thought and contrivance" (Psalmanaazaar 1764:134). Now, although Psalmanaazaar had begun to concoct fictitious Formosan institutions while he was on the continent of Europe, he did not write his book until he was settled in London. He arrived there towards the end of 1703, probably, and the date of the preface to the *Description* (supplied, incidentally, when it was reprinted in the second edition—but for some reason absent from the first edition itself) is February 25, 1703. If we take the year to be old style for 1704, there is left enough time for the "two months" in which Psalmanaazaar says the book was written (1764:217). If this period of composition was known, or accepted as true, it would have followed the more plainly that the *Description* was indeed above the young Psalmanaazaar's capacity to invent in the time. To judge by these circumstances, not to mention the author's impressive narratives and his command of the "Formosan" language, the fake ethnography made a colorable claim to be accepted as true; for, as Psalmanaazaar impudently wrote in the second preface (1 obj. 2 answ.):

He must be a Man of prodigious parts, who can invent the Description of a Country, contrive a Religion, frame Laws and Customs, make a Language, and Letters, &c. and these different from all other parts of the World.

IV

Later opinions about the quality of Psalmanaazaar's achievement were, like the estimations during his lifetime, of opposite kinds. D'Israeli thought it "an illusion eminently bold, and maintained with as much felicity as erudition" (1932:104); Bracey judged him "a genius of the first rank" (1925:81); and Farrer accounted his imposture "a triumphant fraud" (1907:95). But others, if well after the event, were not so impressed. Aikin said that the *Description* was "replete with improbabilities and inconsistencies" (1813:372); Walckenaer asserted that "it would have been easy to determine, by an attentive examination," that Psalmanaazaar's description "was nothing but a gross fiction" (1843:439); even Farrer concluded that "Herodotus himself could hardly have put human credulity to a more severe test than did Psalmanazar" (1907:85), and that "it seems incredible that so many of our ancestors should have been the dupes of all this" (90).

The most glaring form of inconsistency is a contradiction, but Psalmanaazaar of all people is not to be caught out in this way, and the instances in his *Description* are minor and remediable. At one place he says that "some of the Sons are Sacrific'd, but the Daughters are all preserved for Matrimony" (1704:200), whereas in a conversation reported from about the time of publication of the book we hear that if boys are scarce "they take girls, under the age of nine, whom they purify with much ceremony" (Gwinnett 1731:59; Anon. 1765b:79, letter dated June, 1704). This is not a contradiction within the book itself, though the reported conversation is too circumstantial to be easily discounted, and there is no doubt that Psalmanaazaar could have made up a suitable qualification which would have reconciled the two statements. Another instance of apparent contradiction does come from within the text. Psalmanaazaar says that the Formosans eat serpents (1704:263; Gwinnett 1731:61), and that they have "familiar Serpents, which they carry about their Body" (265); yet at another place he says also that damned souls may inhabit the bodies of "evil Beasts" such as serpents (209). As it stands, this looks like a contradiction, if perhaps a minor one since nothing else seems to hang on it, but it too could easily have been smoothed over.

An obvious field for a test of consistency is language. The "Formosan" texts supplied by Psalmanaazaar (1704:271–76) are not really extensive enough to serve as evidence, and all we have to go by are two general characterizations. One is by Psalmanaazaar, and therefore suspect. He says that the Catechism in "Formosan," written out by himself, was examined by a number of persons "who all found the language so regular and grammatical, as well as different from all others they knew, both with respect to the words and idiom, that they gave it as their opinion, that it must be a real language, and could be no counterfeit" (1764:215). The other is by Richardson, an Oxford orientalist, who much later in the same century remarked how difficult it was to detect "the forgery of books" (1778:26–27) and cited as an example Psalmanaazaar, who "invented even a language, sufficiently original, copious, and regular, to impose upon men of very extensive learning" (247 n.*f*). We do not know, in either case, who were the linguistic judges, and it is not clear how far Richardson's report reflects independent evidence and is not merely taken from Psalmanaazaar's memoirs.

On the score of language, incidentally, it has been proposed as "highly probable" that Psalmanaazaar was "influenced in the method he adopted by the work of earlier English and Continental universal and ideal-language planners," such as John Wilkins; "it may be that Psalmanaazaar had direct knowledge of one or several of these artificial language schemes" (Knowlson 1965:876). The proponent of this view adduces no particular evidence, and he does not carry out an analysis to make his case, but it may be as well to respond that the supposed influence is most improbable. It is true that, in England, Rose's *Philosophicall Essay for the Reunion of Languages* had been published in 1675, and Wilkins's *Essay towards a Real Character and a Philosophical Language* in 1668; but nothing that we know of Psalmanaazaar's life makes it at all likely, or even very possible, that he should have been acquainted with these or other such works either when he began to invent "Formosan" or when he wrote the Catechism and the *Description*.

As for the virtuosity of speaking an invented language, "he must . . .have a more than humane Memory," as Psalmanaazaar observed (1705a, second preface), "that is always ready to vindicate so many feign'd particulars, and that without ever so much as once contradicting himself." But we have been told that he himself had in fact a tenacious memory (Gwinnett 1731:65; Anon. 1765b:79), and in any case if his hearers were to stand any chance of catching him out they would have needed even superior faculties.

The printed examples of "Formosan" consist of a table of numbers (1704:247); several isolated words for officers of state, relatives, and natural features (269); the Lord's Prayer (271); the Apostles' Creed (272–73); and the Ten Commandments (273–76). The numbers are regular in their formation; "41" is a misprint for 40, and "17" for 70, but as for the principles of the scheme, Psalmanaazaar is right to say that the example suffices. Given that a comparison with genuine Formosan dialects was not feasible at the time, the individual words would have had to be taken as they stand. The examples of prose are internally regular, and consistent with one another. In what one takes to be its sound, the language has what can be regarded as a pleasing ring: for example, *Amy Pornio dan chin Ornio viey*, Our Father who in Heaven art (271); *Jerh noskion Pagot Barhanian Pornio*, I believe in God the

almighty Father (272). But there are resonances which, as we
have seen, led critics of the day to suspect a pastiche: for example, *kay*, and (cf. Gr. *kai*, and); *noskion*, believe (Lat. *scio*, I
know); *Korian*, Lord (Gr. *kyrios*, lord); *carokhen*, crucified
(Lat. *crux*, cross); *Chslac*, church (Lat. *ecclesia*, church). *Apo*,
as, can be considered as bearing only an accidental phonetic
similarity to Gr. *apo*, off, away, but it could well have aroused
suspicion all the same. *Malaboski*, evil, could be seen as com-
pounded from Lat. *malus*, bad, evil. *Mios*, my, looks too
close to It. *mio*, my (and Psalmanaazaar was a "master" of
Italian; 1764:198). There is little to be said about the grammar, for there is no intrinsic reason to contest Psalmanaazaar's reports that there are three genders, no cases, and so
on—though it is a nice touch that certain tenses are said to be
indicated merely by tone of voice (266).

The alphabet is the sort of thing that any schoolboy could
make up, with the quirk that it is written from right to left,
though of course it would have cost Psalmanaazaar much
practice to write it easily. Here is his name in his characters:

ǫɪɪн̨ɪɪυɪ ɹɾɪϦᴉ̄

In this also there is nothing inconsistent or greatly improbable.

Since Aikin does not specify what he takes for improbabilities, and Walckenaer does not identify what to him are the
signs that the *Description of Formosa* is a gross fiction, it is not
clear what would have given Psalmanaazaar away to these
critics if they had been his contemporaries. If he says that the
Formosans eat snakes, or even human flesh, there are numerous reports from other societies, and by more acceptable ethnographers, that these practices are common elsewhere in the
world. If he recounts the infliction of horrible punishments
on law-breakers, such as burning alive or beheading or bor-
ing the tongue with a hot iron (1704:164–66), the histories
of modern Europe, including France and England, can testify
to worse. If he says that the chief Sacrificator wears a sky-

blue mitre, signifying his dignity, and a red bonnet, signifying his sacrificial office (211), these are rudimentary symbol-
isms in comparison with the liturgical semantics of Christian
vestments.

It is a question, then, on what grounds Psalmanaazaar could
have been detected as an ethnographical forger by the men of
his time, in the first decade of the eighteenth century. This
leads us to the question, touching modern students of social
facts more directly, on what grounds a comparativist toward
the end of the twentieth century could hope to do much better in the detection of Psalmanaazaar's fake ethnography.

V

We shall continue, naturally, from the premise that we know
nothing of the genuine ethnography of Formosa. Factual
knowledge of the island and its inhabitants would be irrele-
vant to the fundamental issues of method and diagnosis, and
mere contradictions on such grounds would be theoretically
uninteresting.

What we need is such general knowledge of social forms,
and in particular of the systematic aspects of civilization, as
will provide skeptical criteria for the assessment of what are
presented as ethnographic reports. Psalmanaazaar's *Description of Formosa* does provide some such testing points, and in
respects that he could not entirely have known of or prepared
himself against when he composed his fiction. They are not
numerous, but this fact in itself will be seen to have some
significance.

Psalmanaazaar's figure 1 (plate 6) depicts "A Temple," and
the legend explains that "the place for Men" is on the second
floor, while that for the women is on the first (1704:173).
Since women in this society are under the subjection of men,
to the extent that a husband has "full power" to punish an
unfaithful wife as he pleases, even with death (165), it can be

Plate 6. A Temple (Bodleian Library, Oxford)

inferred from the vertical disposition of the sexes in the temple that what is above is superior to what is below. This example is confirmed by the relative positions of the three altars which each city builds on a neighboring mountain. One is the altar of the sun, another is the altar of the moon, and the third is the altar of the ten stars (192–93). The sun is at the top, the moon is in the middle, and the stars are at the bottom (fig. 3, fac. p. 194). These heavenly bodies are appointed by God as "Governors to Rule the World" (190); God has declared the sun to be "the first and most excellent Creature," the moon is placed "in the next degree below him," and the stars are "Inferior to the other two" (191). In this instance there is an explicit scale of evaluation on which what is above is superior to what is below, and that not in a simple contrast (as in the temple) but in a sequence. This disposition of spatial values may not appear very remarkable, and it is true that Psalmanaazaar could have taken it from various models including the Bible, Christian liturgy, and even monarchical ceremony in Europe. Moreover, it is so familiar as to seem obvious. But it is not necessary, and Psalmanaazaar was not obliged to adopt it, especially since he wished his account to clash with others. For the present, however, let us not worry about this question but instead pass on to a more impressive piece of spatial symbolism.

In Psalmanaazaar's figure 1 (plate 6) the central roof of the temple is surmounted by a branched arrangement of religious symbols. The top one is the head of an ox, "or a Symbol of God" (173); to the proper or heraldic right is an image of the sun; to the proper left is an image of the moon. The same arrangement is to be seen above the door to the temple. God is thus above the creatures which he appointed as governors, which agrees with the preceding examples. Furthermore, in this case lateral values also come into play: right (sun) is superior to left (moon). This disposition of symbols is repeated in figure 2, "The Tabernacle and Altar" (plate 7). .Here, above the altar, the head of an ox as symbol of God is in the center;

the sun is to its right and the moon is to its left; the stars are below, in two groups, five on one side and five on the other. The symbolism is found again on the piece of steel money called a *colan*, shown in Psalmanaazaar's fig. 16 (fac. p. 278). A compound image, referred to as "the Arms of Religion" (280), shows the upper part of an ox in an upright posture; at its right hoof (as though held in a hand) is the image of the sun, and at its left is that of the moon. The same set of symbols is borne also by the iron coin called the *riaon*. In salutations as well the symbolism of right and left is put into effect. The Formosans salute viceroys by "bending one Knee": the left to the viceroy of a foreign king, the right to one of their own kings (215). This again implies the superiority of right over left.

A further instance of spatial symbolism relates to the cardinal points. The temple has two towers: that in which God appears in the tabernacle (A) "looks towards the East" (174), while in the other tower (B) are the singers and musicians. It is not evident how the phrase "looks towards" is to be interpreted. The meaning could be that the entire temple is oriented, though in this event it is not only the sacred tower that faces east; or it could be that God's tabernacle is to the east while the profane accompanists are to the west. In either case it seems that Psalmanaazaar intends to make a positive association between God and the east.

These various instances cohere into a familiar symbolic scheme:

man	woman
above	below
superior	inferior
right	left
sun	moon
east	west
sacred	profane

Plate 7. The Tabernacle and Altar (Bodleian Library, Oxford)

This is a system of analogical classification that has a world-wide distribution (cf. Needham 1973a). It can indeed be seen as corresponding to a global inclination for men to resort to a common stock of things and qualities which they tend to interconnect by analogy (Needham 1980, chap. 2). Again, though, it is not necessary, and there was no obligation upon Psalmanaazaar to attribute this form of symbolic classification to his fictitious Formosans. Yet, we may say, he got it right. There were two distinct impulsions that could account for this outcome in what is after all a work of the imagination. One was the ceremonial tradition, ecclesiastical and so-cial, of Europe; the other, more suppositiously, was an innate proclivity of thought and imagination by which both this tra-dition and Psalmanaazaar were subliminally influenced. We have no means, in the present instance, of disentangling these factors, but the regularity of the "Formosan" symbolism leads us to an important diagnostic feature in the detection of fake ethnography. This feature is that the terms and values are articulated into a system.

Now it is quite striking that elsewhere in his *Description* Psalmanaazaar reports practically nothing under a systematic aspect. The nearest he comes to doing so in reporting institu-tions is in the hierarchical delegation of administrative power; but this is so minimal and commonplace an arrangement, by comparison with the civil service of the day, as hardly to per-mit the suspicion that it is fictitious. Where Psalmanaazaar might have given himself away, from our modern vantage point, is in the construction of a social system of any intri-cacy, such as a system of prescriptive alliance with its termi-nology and prestations and congruency of numerous social forms. In this case there would indeed be abundant grounds—comparative ethnography, technical resources, formal con-siderations—on which to make a skeptical assessment of the ethnography. But so long as Psalmanaazaar sticks to the mere accumulation of exotic cultural particulars, avoiding the postulation of systematic relationships among them, he is fairly safe.

VI

What, then, does the case of Psalmanaazaar teach us about the requisites of a convincing fake ethnography? Apart from the obvious advantages of writing about a society of which little or nothing is known—or, in the case of a fictitious subject matter, of which nothing can possibly be known or checked —there are certain circumstances and personal qualities that seem to be called for.

Perhaps the first is secrecy, and it is on this score that Psalmanaazaar was vulnerable from the start. The instigator of his imposture, according to what he tells us, was Innes, and this man seems to have been unscrupulous enough to expose Psalmanaazaar whenever it might serve his own ambition to do so. We do not know that in fact he ever did let on, but he was certainly not the right kind of man to rely on in such a surreptitious undertaking. Then there was the translator, Oswald, who actually assisted Psalmanaazaar to make his forgery more plausible. Also, Innes "got several of his and my acquaintances," Psalmanaazaar was later to write, "to back the notion" of writing a history of Formosa (1764:215), and while the phrasing is ambiguous it may be that some of these persons too were parties to the deception.

After secrecy, a necessary element is consistency: the fictitious details must agree one with another, and the impostor must take constant care that they shall not vary. Psalmanaazaar needed his "tenacious memory," and he was astute in recognizing that once he had committed himself to any statement, even if inadvertently, he had to stick to it and retract

nothing. In these regards a systematic organization of the fictitious particulars can be helpful, though it also heightens the
risk from some technical critique; so the precept appears to be
that a forger must either supply no sociological system or else
take special pains to get it right, the former course being decidedly the safer.

In his encounters with skeptics or with professional judges
the forger needs also an unusual effrontery, and there are numerous indications that Psalmanaazaar certainly possessed
this. For instance, when challenged by Dr. Burnet, bishop of
Salisbury, to prove that he was really a Formosan, he cheekily
answered "You look as like a Dutchman as any that traded to
Formosa" (Gwinnett 1731:66). We may add to this bold gift
a sheer recklessness, for Psalmanaazaar must have known
that in the end he was bound to be found out.

With luck, however, the day of reckoning might be put off
by yet another factor which, characteristically, he thought of:
namely that "it was next to impossible for the ablest heads to
have guessed what my motives were, or for what, or by
whom, I was induced thus to impose upon mankind" (1764:
204). Finally, there is the desirable element of personal presence and persuasiveness, and there are many signs that
Psalmanaazaar possessed these advantages also; Gwinnett
wrote that "there is an Air of Sincerity accompanies all he
says, as well as what he writes" (1731:65).

This is a long list of requisites for the successful prosecu-
tion of an ethnographical deception, and in combination they
must make a remarkable effect, just as they call for an individual of unusual qualities. Yet there is one fundamental consideration that must not be allowed to fade from view. A
Psalmanaazaar is not merely an actor, or some other kind of
professional simulator whose technical skill can evoke an admiration for its own sake: he is essentially a liar, as Psalmanaazaar in his regenerate years was bitterly aware, and what

he commits himself to is a life of falsehood and unworthiness of trust.

As things turned out in Psalmanaazaar's case, the deception was after all by no means an unqualified success. In 1704 he was already "thought by some to be a Counterfeit" (Gwinnett 1731:58); in 1705 he was "still taken to be a Cheat" (Hearne 1885:17); and Psalmanaazaar himself was later to write that, notwithstanding the defenses made on his behalf in the *Enquiry* (1710), he and his advocates "had the mortification to find . . . that my fabulous account was as much discredited by the greatest part of the world as ever" (1764:202–3). Overall, whereas he undertook his imposture, he says, "for the sake of a little popular admiration at the best," he had instead "more frequently met with mortification and contempt" (173).

In the final reckoning, however, it is Psalmanaazaar's character, not just his deception, that leaves the most lasting impression. He was not simply "an extraordinary literary impostor" (Aikin 1813:371), or an "extraordinary adventurer" (Walckenaer 1843:441), but an "extraordinary person" (Piozzi 1786:174) and in many ways an outstanding and admirable man. When one says "man," moreover, it is worth remembering that at the height of his success, when he had written the *Description of Formosa* in two months, was received by the Royal Society, and enjoyed the support of men of eminence, learning, and probity, he was apparently no more than twenty-five years old, and he may have been only twenty. And when he charmed and convinced contemporary acquaintances, with his rapid raillery and bold stratagems, he was defending his reputation and his livelihood in a language that he had only recently begun to learn. Given the opportunity, what a marvellous genuine ethnographer he could have been.

Morally, too, he presents in the latter part of his life an ex-

ample which testifies to the latent qualities which, perverted
though they may have been, must also have contributed to
the impact of his imposture, and "there are many worse texts
for a good sermon than the life of Psalmanazar" (Farrer 1907:
97). In his *Memoirs* he repeatedly laments and castigates his
"vanity and senseless affectation of singularity" (1764:57), his
"indolence and want of resolution" (60), and his "favorite pas-
sion, pride" (67). As Walckenaer rightly observes, "it is from
himself that we learn everything that is most shameful for his
memory; and as for what there is to be proud of in it, this has
to be sought in the testimony of his contemporaries and in
the great literary monument of which he was the principal
author" (1843:435).

Among his contemporaries, a weighty witness was Dr.
Johnson, no man to be readily won over, and from him we
have only the most measured tributes. He said "he had never
seen the close of the life of any one that he wished so much
his own to resemble, as that of him [Psalmanaazaar], for its
purity and devotion" (1787:206); his "piety, penitence, and
virtue exceeded almost what we read as wonderful in the lives
of saints" (Piozzi 1786:174). Psalmanaazaar said of himself
that he "deserved no other name than that of impostor" (175).

As for his "fabulous account" of the island of Formosa, this,
he wrote in his memoirs (1764:8), "was no other than a mere
forgery of my own devising, a scandalous imposition on the
public, and such, as I think myself bound to beg God and the
world pardon for writing, and have been long since, as I am
to this day, and shall be as long as I live, heartily sorry for,
and ashamed of."

6

Swedenborg and the Science of Correspondences: God's Secret Dictionary

As soon as someone begins to see everything in everything, his utterance usually becomes obscure; he begins to speak with the tongues of angels.

G. C. Lichtenberg

I

Man is characteristically a metaphysical animal. Everywhere, and in every form of social life, he reflects on his condition, and once he does so he concludes that things are not what they seem; he postulates unseen causes, secret connections, enigmatic signs. He is convinced, moreover, that intelligibility is not partial but that there must be a total order in the universe, and that by due attention to regularities and to revelatory singularities he will be able to make out the system of it all. In this grand undertaking he is never entirely free; he acts within the constraints of tradition and also under a spontaneous compulsion which leads him to feel, anxiously or with elation, that he "must conjecture the words, the definitions, the etymologies, the synonymies, of God's secret dictionary" (Borges 1968:104).

The figurative allusion to a cosmic dictionary introduces a hazardous aspiration that is peculiar to literate civilizations, namely to incorporate a universal metaphysical vision in a total representation. In the words of Borges: "The practice of literature sometimes fosters the ambition to construct an absolute book, a book of books that includes all the others like a Platonic archetype" (1968:66). This ultimate ideal imposes a strain sufficient to crack the best-tempered of minds, and it is scarcely to be wondered at that the history of speculative enquiry on such a scale is littered with the relics of those who failed in the attempt. In the nature of the case, conventional precepts and the rules of rationality are often suspended, and the sanity of the investigator is constantly at risk of question. This consequence is connected with the fact that metaphysics, taken systematically, is not progressive; each cartographer fabricates his own visionary world, and there are no generally accepted benchmarks of advance. A very great deal depends therefore on the personal authority of the inquirer and on the credentials of what he proffers as his sources of knowledge.

Within the Christian tradition, one of the most remarkable figures of the kind during the past three centuries was Emanuel Swedenborg (1688–1772), a distinguished scientist who inaugurated a distinct mystical doctrine. He claimed that this doctrine had been revealed to him by direct communication with spirits and angels, and he published their teachings in a sequence of weighty volumes which by their heavenly inspiration had a title to an absolute character. Inevitably, he was called mad, but it was not easy to make this charge stick against an assessor to the Royal College of Mines, a leading mathematician, a campaigning social reformer in the House of Nobles, and an ingenious engineer who by his practicality had rendered great services to the state. His life has been narrated in a number of biographies (for example, Toksvig 1949; Sigstedt 1952), and his worldly doings are not in dispute. It is his mystical faculty that has made his name famous, and it is

Plate 8. Emanuel Swedenborg (Svenska Porträttarkivet, Nationalmuseum, Stockholm)

his spiritual assertions that I want to examine in the present essay.

Swedenborg (plate 8) was brought up in an intensely theological atmosphere at Uppsala, where his father, Bishop Swedberg, was a professor at the university. He himself graduated from the University of Uppsala in 1709. In 1744 he had a great vision in which he saw the Lord, and Heaven was opened to him. He resigned his official post in 1747, and thereafter he devoted himself to expounding the true doctrines of the Word as these were revealed to him. He said he had frequent conversations with angels, at times when he suddenly found himself in a spiritual state, and many of these discourses were published as "memorable relations" in support of his theological accounts of the other world. His expositions of the spiritual constitution of the universe were published abroad at his own expense; they were very long (*Arcana Coelestia* ran to eight volumes) and they did not sell. But Swedenborg sought no secular advantage, neither popular renown nor financial reward; he devoted his life to the propagation of his spiritual findings. A number of well-attested incidents gained him a reputation as a clairvoyant, and also as one who could communicate with the spirits of the departed. He died in London in 1772 and was interred there in the Swedish Church, near the Tower; his remains were removed to Uppsala in 1909, where in the succeeding year his sarcophagus was unveiled in the cathedral by King Gustav V.

II

The publications of Swedenborg are voluminous, and, notwithstanding such aids to study as the heroic concordance compiled by Potts (1888–1902), I am not in a position to present a summary of his doctrines that would comprehend his chief tenets in anything like their proper character. What I want to do instead is to list certain prominent categories of Swedenborg's thought that happen to have struck me in a number of his works and that appear to define the principles of his metaphysical scheme. A source of particular value, despite its modest proportions, is the *Hieroglyphic Key* (1784), in which Swedenborg interprets natural and spiritual arcana by way of "representations and correspondences." He was working on this in 1741, and he resumed it in 1744, probably after his vision (Toksvig 1949:150). It is possible that the work was never completed; at any rate, Swedenborg did not take up all of the examples he had listed (Acton 1955:xxvi). Nevertheless, it is of peculiar importance for the present analysis in that it is the only one of Swedenborg's works in which he deals with the science of correspondences in a deliberate exposition (xxi). Its date in relation to that of the opening of Swedenborg's spiritual eyes is not certain, but as far as correspondences are concerned the doctrine was well thought out by him some time before, and Acton (xxiv) gives reason to think that it was formulated before the end of 1739. From my own point of view it is rather agreeable to think that the "science" was worked out, and embodied in the *Key*, both before and after the great vision, for it then appears all the more constantly to be characteristic of Swedenborg's thought.

We can take as the fundamental premise Swedenborg's assertion that

there is some correspondence and harmony between all things, that is, between natural things and spiritual, and *vice versa*; or, that in universal nature there is not a thing that is not a type, image and likeness of some one among spiritual things, all of which are exemplars (1955:183).

There are subsidiary propositions also, expressing the possibility of reciprocal interpretations between things that correspond; for example, "whatever is divine, that same is presented to view in human society" (163), and "from the world we can be instructed concerning the Divinity" (167).

A gloss, given as a "rule," explains that exemplars are in the spiritual world, images and types are in the animal kingdom, and likenesses are in nature (192). It is not the case, therefore, that there is simply a dichotomy between spiritual and natural, and that the correspondences obtain only between these parts. At the beginning of the *Key*, Swedenborg says that Nature, Human Mind, and Divine Mind or God "mutually correspond." In the first "class," as he describes it (without formal definition), are contained all those things that are purely natural; in the second, those that are rational and intellectual, "and consequently also moral"; in the third, things "theological and divine" (157–58).

An appended rule prescribes that "the principal matter must be expressed not by identical terms, but by different terms proper to each class" (159). Thus the first correspondences presented in the *Key* are: motion, action, operation. Motion is attributed to nature; action flows from the will, consequently from the human mind; operation ("though it is not a spiritual word") is predicated of divine providence (157). Accordingly, Swedenborg's index to the manuscript of the *Key* includes a number of triads in which the terms are similarly to be taken as belonging to the three classes respectively, that is to realms of existence, such as: celerity, time, eternity; objects, ideas, reasons (193–94). Other correspondences apparently include synonyms, so that four or five terms are evidently meant to be read as falling still into the three classes; for example, clear, pure, sacred + holy; contrariety, opposition, hostility + enmity + hate.

These complications make for problems of exegesis, but for the present I want to pass over such difficulties and to concentrate on the relatively simple paradigmatic scheme. This (in a phrase from the earlier *Economy of the Animal King-*

dom, first published 1740–41) is that there is "a co-established harmony of all things in a single series"; these things "mutually correspond" to one another "without any difference, save of perfection according to degrees" (1955:195). Also, in a proposition taken this time from the *Arcana Coelestia* (sec. 4044; in Bogg 1915:126 s.v. Representation): "Representations are nothing but images of spiritual things in natural things; and when the former are rightly represented in the latter, they correspond."

III

It will be a little easier to come to terms with such propositions if we set them in the wider frame of Swedenborg's spiritual cosmology. This can most conveniently be taken from his *Treatise concerning Heaven and Hell* (1778).

Universal Heaven resembles a human form, that of the Grand Man (36). Heaven is divided into two kingdoms, celestial and spiritual: the angels in the former are superior, in that they have an interior knowledge of the Lord; those in the latter kingdom are inferior, in that they have an exterior knowledge (15). There are three heavens: the highest, the middle, and the lowest; these are also known respectively as the third, second, and first heavens (19). There is a correspondence of the heavens one with another; the lowest heaven "more immediately" corresponds to and communicates with the corporeal forms of men (58). There is also a partition of heaven into four Quarters, aligned with and defining the celestial cardinal points: "In heaven that is called East where the Lord appears as a sun; opposite thereto is the West; to the right hand is the South; and to the left hand is the North"; "all the four quarters are determined by the East"; and "the angels have the East always before them, the West behind them, the South on their right, and the North on their left hand" (87). Angels in the eastern heaven are under the influence of love from the Lord, those in the southern are under the influence of Wisdom from the Lord (1781, 1:457); those who excel in wisdom are translated to the South (1781, 2:77). In the northern quarter there are purportedly wise Christians who are judged to have "no Religion at all" (1781, 1:469–70).

By contrast with this heavenly scheme, all things contrary to divine order correspond with hell (1778:67). There are hells everywhere, under mountains and hills, plains and valleys, and they are dark and dismal (400–1). The exact locations of the hells are not known even to the angels, but to the Lord alone (401). What is known, however, is that the hells are "equal in number to the angelical societies in the heavens; for there is a society of infernals answering to every society of angels, according to the nature of opposites" (403). There is a perpetual equilibrium between heaven and hell such that "under every celestial there is an infernal society answering thereto as its opposite, from which opposite correspondence results the equilibrium" (407). As for the inhabitants of the infernal kingdoms, these are in a state which Swedenborg expressly describes as "the very reverse" of that of angels; they have their backs to the Lord, and instead of a sun they see a "black body" (92). "The four quarters with the infernals are opposite to those in heaven"; their east is towards the black disk, their west is towards the celestial sun (93).

The entire cosmology is organized by a principle of equilibrium: "an equilibrium is necessary to the existence and subsistence of all things, and consists in the equality of action and reaction between opposite powers" (404). Regarding our mundane environment, accordingly, "the whole natural world exists and subsists from the spiritual, as an effect from its efficient cause, therefore there is a correspondent relation betwixt them" (53). From these premises we can conceive how it is that "when men are gifted with the knowledge of correspondences, they can think in like manner with the angels" (67).

With this elating assertion, we can turn back to the particular topic of correspondences as expounded in the *Hieroglyphic Key*. We now have some idea of the regions and components of the spiritual universe, of their interrelations, and of the principle by virtue of which this metaphysical system is sustained. Let us next look more closely at the most general form of correlation.

Swedenborg names various species of "representations or correspondences." The first is "harmonic correspondence," such as exists among light, intelligence, wisdom. The second is "allegorical correspondence"; this species is "formed by similitudes," but Swedenborg does not explain this except to say that it is in this way that we are wont to "express spiritual things naturally" and to observe that in the Scriptures this species of correspondence occurs quite frequently. The third is "typical correspondence"; this also is "formed by so many likenesses," as by Christ and the Christian church. The fourth species is "fabulous correspondence"; this was used by the ancients, who clothed the deeds of their heroes with fabulous fictions, and of the same nature also are the representations of poets and those of dreams (1955:192–93). As to this last species, Swedenborg writes elsewhere that fables "were in Fact Correspondencies, agreeable to the primaeval Method of Speaking" (1781, 2:314); examples are that nine virgins stand for sciences of every kind, horses' hooves for "experiences."

This typology is not very clear: the descriptive terms are undefined, the criteria linking correspondences of each species are barely hinted at, and the lines of discrimination between one species and another are difficult to trace. Nevertheless, it is the nearest that Swedenborg comes to setting out a typology of correspondences—and then almost directly af-

terwards the *Hieroglyphic Key* comes to an end. We are therefore left to work out for ourselves the principles (if there are
such) that interconnect the correspondences into a system.

IV

One means of isolating principles is to focus on symbolic
associations that seem to be fairly constant in the use that
Swedenborg makes of his correspondences.

For instance, "the mountain signifies the highest heaven"
(1781, 1:279); "gold according to correspondency signifies
celestial good" (1778:69). Then there are associations which
are correlated with others. For instance, the Lord appears as a
sun before the right eye, as a moon before the left eye (1778:
71); the sight of the left eye corresponds to the truths of faith,
that of the right eye to their good (1778:71); in the other
world, heavens are to the east and hells, in increasing dread-
fulness, are to the west (1778:402). This last example introduces a notable feature of Swedenborg's spiritual cartog-
raphy: in what he calls his "memorable relations" of his
encounters with spirits and his journeys in their world he
usually describes the setting and his course by reference to
cardinal points. For instance, "I was conversing on a Time
with two Angels, one from the eastern Part of Heaven, and
the other from the western" (1781, 1:67); he observes a theological debate among spirits, and tells us that "they who sat
towards the North declared their Sentiments first," then those
to the south (69). In one relation after another, Swedenborg is
careful to locate persons and objects and events in their relation to cardinal points, and these are fixed features of his visionary topography.

In addition to these absolute coordinates, Swedenborg just
as constantly resorts to the relative discriminations of right
and left. Even the positions of the planets are described in

these terms; Mercury is behind the sun and a little to the right, Venus is to the left, and so on (1875:26). If we were to ask by what means cardinal points are established away from the surface of the earth, and in even more puzzlement how it is that right and left can be employed as though they were absolute spatial designations, the answers are to be found in the sketch of Swedenborg's cosmology that was given above. The angels look perpetually towards the east, where the Lord appears as a celestial sun; to their right is the south, to their left the north. It is by references to these combined coordinates that we can conceive, for instance, a journey made by Swedenborg to another earth that is in the universe but outside our solar system. He was led by spirits and was taken at times obliquely upwards and obliquely downwards but "continually to the right"—which, he explains, "in the other life is towards the south" (1875:115).

I am not sure of the doctrine on this next point, and it may be that Swedenborgians could correct me exegetically, but it looks as though right and left may acquire their absolute values by reference also to the human-like form of the universe. "The universal heaven," writes Swedenborg, "resembles one man, who is therefore called the Grand Man, and . . . all and everything with man . . . correspond to that man or heaven" (1875:5). It may be, then, that we should picture a man-like figure in plan with its head defining the north (the left as conceived by angels) and its feet towards the south (the right as conceived by angels) but looking, as it were, towards the south—rather as in a Christian burial the head of the corpse, to the west, is conceived to look towards the immanent light of the resurrection to the east. This interpretation may or may not be thought correct by those with a faithful interest in the matter, but as we proceed it will be appreciated that in either case the definitive significance of the symbolic associations of the cardinal points will remain.

As for right and left in particular, these designations are

constantly used by Swedenborg relatively to his own position in space, but just as constantly they continue to bear distinct values. In one memorable relation he finds himself in the
lower parts of Earth, lying immediately above Hell; they
open, and Birds of Night fly forth and spread themselves at
his left hand, while beautiful birds descend from Heaven and
spread themselves at his right hand (1781, 1:83). The symbolic complex that we can discern in this narrative is much
developed in another memorable relation. Swedenborg saw
a spirit speaking in a theological debate with others, and
"whilst he was thus speaking, he saw on his right hand, as it
were, the Appearance of a Sheep, and a Lamb, and a Dove
upon the Wing, and on his left hand a Goat, a Wolf, and a
Vulture" (1781, 1:96). It later appears that the goat, wolf,
and vulture are creatures in Hell (110). At the end of a debate,
intelligent spirits depart to the right, stupid to the left (101),
which adds further attributes to the connotations of the sides.
These connotations then link up with others making a comparable contrast. Spirits are conducting a debate about God
and Nature, to the accompaniment of flashes like lightning
and perturbations of the air like thunder. These phenomena
attract Swedenborg's attention, and it is explained to him that
"the Vibration of Light like Lightning, and the Clapping of
the Air like Thunder, were Correspondencies, and conse-
quent Appearances of the Conflict and Collision of Arguments, on the one side in Favour of God, and on the other in
Favour of Nature." Satans contend that God is only Nature
and that his name is a word without meaning except that of
"Nature," and their arguments are thunderous; whereas their
opponents, who are Angels of Heaven, are responsible for
the intense vibrations of light (1781, 1:105).

Swedenborg not only employs lateral values in this constant fashion; he also contrives elaborations which at first
seem inconsistent but which prove to confirm the symbolic
contrast.

In one instance the ground opens up to the left and there emerges a devil which terrifies Swedenborg by his gruesome appearance; he says he comes from a society of the most supereminent of all societies in which all are Emperors of Emperors, Kings of Kings, and the like. Then the ground opens up again, this time towards the right; another devil emerges, of a different aspect; he is worshiped by the former devil, and he explains that this is because he is God of Gods (1781, 2:274–75). In this memorable relation, therefore, we see that devils are not invariably associated with the left, and that the latter devil occupies the right. They are both devils, nevertheless, emerging from a hell to which they return, and the significance of the sides in this case is that lateral values discriminate the contrasted functions that they claim: the one who arrogates temporal power is associated with the left, whereas he who claims divine authority is associated with the right.

In another instance a marriage is being celebrated in heaven; the bridegroom is on the left hand, the bride is on the right. Afterwards, the guests pertinently ask some angels who are explaining the ceremony, "Since He represented the Lord, and She the Church, why did she sit on his right hand?" The answer is that two things constitute a marriage of the Lord and the Church: Love and Wisdom. The Lord is love, the Church is wisdom; wisdom is at the right hand of love; "the right Hand also signifieth Power, and Love hath Power by means of Wisdom." But after the marriage "the Representation is changed, for then the Husband representeth Wisdom and the Wife the Love of his Wisdom" (1781, 2:383–84), so that the positions of man and woman are transposed, the husband to the right and the wife to the left.

This operation of symbolic transposition is seen in another memorable relation, this time concerning a debate on the nature of God. Those who are immersed in vanity, thinking the Lord to be a mere man, or pinning their faith on the opinions of others, are on the left. A light descends from heaven, at which several of the debaters move from the left to the right, where the heavenly light is reflected on to them (1781, 1:197).

In these last two examples we can see the movement as a reversal: in the former, from left to right and conversely; in the latter, from left to right. Reversal is also to be seen, more clearly, in a memorable relation implicating the symbolic values of back and front. Swedenborg sees riders on bay and black horses, sitting backwards with "their bodies inverted . . . inasmuch as they . . . do not love the Truth"; whereas their opponents, mounted on white horses, sit normally inasmuch as they understand the Word of God (1781, 1:156). And a kind of reversal can be seen also in regard to light and its symbolic significance. Swedenborg was shown certain "colleges" in which people in the spiritual world "amused" themselves with debates. He approached one such college, "but no Entrance was allowed through the Door, lest Light from Heaven should flow in, and confuse the disputants." However, suddenly a window was made on the right side, and "immediately I heard them complaining that they were in the Dark." Presently another window was opened on the left side, and that on the right was shut up, and then by degrees the darkness was dispersed and the debaters "appeared to each other in their own proper Light" (1781, 2:75). Here Swedenborg seems ironical in representing the disputants as being confused by the clear light of heaven, which they perceive as a darkness, while the effect of a window on the left is to reveal them as they are. As if this were not informative enough, he then tells us that the debaters "had all of them been given to disputing, during their abode on Earth, and had never renounced any Evil" (76). As a third example of a kind of reversal we may now adduce again the fact that "the four quarters with the infernals are opposite to those in heaven," so that in hell east is towards the black disk and west is towards the celestial sun (1778:93); that is, hell too is partitioned into quarters, as is heaven, but east and west and their contrasted values have been transposed. Heaven is the original and exemplar, and notionally it is by an operation of reversal that the quarters of hell have their perverse disposition.

Let us next turn to the principle of equilibrium that we noticed earlier in the introductory sketch of Swedenborg's cosmology. "Opposite must correspond exactly to opposite, in order that there may be equilibrium" (Potts 1890, 2:518 s.v. Equilibrium). A good example is that the hells are equal in number to the angelical societies in the heavens; there is a "perpetual equilibrium betwixt heaven and hell" (1778:403, 405). This process, indeed, is explicitly described as "according to the nature of opposites" (403). The next most fundamental principle to consider, therefore, is that of opposition. This is not a strictly formal concept, and it is by no means simple (Needham 1980:51–55); much depends on the circumstances in which it is employed.

Opposition is given a fairly clear expression in the following passage from *Heaven and Hell*:

. . . Every good has its opposite evil, and every truth its opposite false, there not being anything without its relation to a contrary, by which it is distinguished both in quality and degree; nay, this gives the difference to all perception and sensation. And thus the Lord disposes and regulates the evil of hell into societies of contradistinction and opposition to the societies in heaven, for the sake of order and equilibrium (1778:373).

Some explication of the concept of opposition is to be found in the *Hieroglyphic Key*. Swedenborg writes there (Example XVII) that light without shade would not appear to be light, as neither would the perfect without the imperfect, for then there would be nothing from which it could appear. "So neither could the positive be given," he continues, "if there were no privative, for without the privative there would be nothing from which a thing could be posited" (1955:184). This is a crucial proposition, to be mirrored in a subsequent assertion that "without the negative there would be nothing from which a thing could be affirmed" (185). Hence it is that ignorance and falsity have their uses, and so also unwisdom, insanity, and unhappiness (185–86). Without evil, too, no affection would be given, no will and desiring, and no variety of desires: "From this is apparent the use performed by stupidity and evil" (186). After considering various correspondences and "opposites," Swedenborg proceeds to the confirmation of his proposition, and here he passes from analysis to ontology. After rehearsing the contentions that no perfection can be conceived of without imperfection, and so no truth without falsity, he arrives at a crucial conclusion (1955:186):

These considerations confirm the real existence of evil or the devil, to the end, not only that the idea of good may be exalted, but also that it may actually exist in the created world.

And a little later, after repeating that an entity or a quality cannot be posited if its relative (namely, opposite) is lacking, he asserts: "From this it follows that evil, that is, the devil, actually exists" (188). Thus the structure of thought and that of existence also depend upon "opposite correspondence," and from this relation results the equilibrium that sustains universal order (1778:407).

"God is Order itself," Swedenborg declares (1781, 1:94), and "everything that appears on earth is a correspondence with the affections of God's love and the perceptions of his wisdom" (109). In God himself, moreover, we see the duality—here the conjunction of affection and wisdom—which in numerous other respects pervades Swedenborg's cosmology. Another divine instance of duality is the nature of the light of heaven. This light appears in many of the memorable relations, and it is a typical accompaniment of the "influx" of God's action. But even the light of heaven does not exist independently. "The Light of Heaven is in its Essence Divine Truth, and the Heat of Heaven in its Essence is Divine Good, both proceeding from the Lord as the Sun of Heaven" (1781, 2:236). So the divine influx into phenomena, by which all comes to pass, is not single but is effected by a dyad; even the manifestations of God are framed by duality.

V

Swedenborg's central contention is that "in all and every part of the World there is a Spiritual Sense corresponding with the Natural Sense (1781, 2:459); "all things come to pass, and exist, and also are changed, according to Correspondencies" (1781, 2:77).

The meaning of correspondence is not self-evident, and in order to come to terms with the doctrine we need to work out, as we have seen, the significance of symbolic associations, cardinal points, lateral values, transposition, reversal, equilibrium, opposition, and duality. Swedenborg's spiritual metaphysics is in these respects generally consistent, systematic, and comprehensive; but these attributes still do not in themselves provide us with an explication of the concept of correspondence. Swedenborg gives a negative hint when he says, in the *Key*, that "the resolution of singulars to their universals does not pertain to this science of correspondences, but rather to first philosophy" (1955:184); yet this tells us how not to take the concept rather than how it is formally to be understood.

It is true that "correspondence," in Swedenborg's employment of the term, need have no formal definition, just as it need have no essential meaning, and that in this case we may well have to look for the meaning of the concept in the range of uses that it subserves. This recourse, however, turns out to be an extremely difficult and baffling task. I am not saying it cannot be accomplished, but that the concept has proved to resist even assiduous and conscientious attempts at decipherment.

One such undertaking is a critical examination published in 1875 by an unnamed author. He wrote at a time when many of Swedenborg's writings had yet to appear in print, and also without the benefit of Potts's concordance and of subsequent commentaries, yet all the same his main criticisms can be taken as they stand. They relate, moreover, particularly to Swedenborg's interpretations of the Bible and not to the metaphysics as a system, but this restriction need not reduce the effect of the author's argued doubts concerning the science of correspondences in a privileged sphere of its application. He finds, then, that Swedenborg's writings on this topic are full of arbitrary assertion and absence of principle: "In vain do we search among the individual instances of correspondences for the principle of the relationship of cause and effect, or for the analogy of uses" (Anon. 1875:12, 14). He judges that Swedenborg's reasoning was ever from general principles to particular facts, and that he "ran riot in similes" (21), in constant attempts to "jump at once to conclusions" (22). "When we examine correspondence," the critic concludes, "we find no science and very little art" (26).

These are hard conclusions, but they are not prejudiced. As we have already had occasion to remark, Swedenborg's own typology of correspondences is unclear in a number of critical respects; also, the numerous statements that he makes about correspondences (filling nearly 20 columns in the concordance) are so extraordinarily heterogeneous that it is hard to conceive that they are connected by any kind of principle. Toksvig imagines Swedenborg's contemporaries shaking their heads over the significance of the idea (1949:283–84):

'Correspondence' gleamed and darkened everywhere. It seemed to be a world-principle, so ubiquitous and bewildering that it had to be confronted if one would understand Swedenborg. And that was difficult, not to say impossible, on the basis of the published books, in which he never bothered to explain its many meanings, nor said how the idea had developed for him.

This does not sound very impressive on the part of someone whom even a spirit from the nether regions addressed as "the Man who thinkest and speakest concerning Order" (1781, 1:94). In fact, Toksvig concludes, much of what Swedenborg called "correspondence" was not causal in character at all, "but either analogy or simple association of ideas" (288).

It is such laxity, at any rate, that permits Bachelard, in a discussion of Balzac's *L'Enfant maudit*, to say that central to this author's thought is "a correspondence, in the Swedenborgian sense," between the life of a natural element (in this case, the ocean in a storm) and the life of an unhappy consciousness (Bachelard 1942:232). What Balzac is writing about is "the divination of the thoughts of matter," a gift with which the subject, Etienne, has been endowed by his occult science—but this is an idea which, so far as I can discover, is not to be found in Swedenborg. Apart from the logical employment of "correspondence," in which the positing of one term entails another (cf. Lalande 1950:192 s.v. Correspondance), the notion can in fact admit an almost unlimited range of kinds of connection or association, and Swedenborg's own exploitation of the term shows as much. But the accommodating nature of the word does not thereby make it right, conversely, to describe any correspondence whatever as Swedenborgian.

Emerson, in a remarkable essay devoted to Swedenborg as mystic, estimates him as "not to be measured by whole colleges of ordinary scholars," but he none the less finds a basic flaw of construction in his metaphysics (Emerson 1850:75, 104):

Strictly speaking, Swedenborg's revelation is a confounding of planes, a capital offence in so learned a categorist. This is to carry the law of surface into the plane of substance, to carry individualism and its fopperies into the realm of essences and generals; which is distortion and chaos.

In particular, he charges, Swedenborg's theological bias fatally narrowed his interpretation, "and the dictionary of symbols is yet to be written" (89).

One of the more positive things Emerson has to say about Swedenborg's work is that "we have come into a world which is a living poem" (92). At the same time, however, he writes that "Swedenborg is systematic and respective of the world in every sentence: all the means are orderly given" (75); yet also that Swedenborg's pictures of heaven and hell, as mystical representations, are "quite arbitrary and accidental" and that "any other symbol would be as good" (98). These are very contradictory things to say about a metaphysics that is intended to be taken as a divinely inspired paradigm of universal order. No wonder, then, that Kant, after an arduous attempt to draw up a clear account of Swedenborg's reports of the spiritual world, came to the conclusion: "all this labour comes in the end to nothing" (Kant 1766:113).

More than a century after this judgment, the anonymous critic of Swedenborg's science of correspondences asked: "The question naturally arises, if there is no basis for these things, how did they arise?" (Anon. 1875:20). His own answer is that they result from "the efforts of an overwrought brain to reconcile an unshaken faith in the divinity of the Scriptures with the contradictory and apparently historical and worldly nature of those records" (20). This strikes me as altogether too narrow an explanation, but it does hint at the much wider question of Swedenborg's sanity.

At the end of *True Christian Religion*, Swedenborg himself indirectly raises the issue. He describes how certain arcana are put on paper by angels and are let down to earth, but that the learned clergy and laity mutter that the arcana are "the Offspring of Imagination and a disordered Brain" (1781, 2:462–63). Having summoned up the imputation, he responds, with particular regard to his memorable relations: "I protest in Truth that they are not Fictions, but were really seen and heard" (464); and he justifies his visions by recalling that similar things were seen by John in the Apocalypse and by Prophets in the Old Testament, and also by the Apostles after the Lord's resurrection (465). The defense shows clearly enough the kind of contemporary charges that he knew were circulating. As for his own protestation that his visions were true, we have an apt phrase uttered by a much later skeptic: "He would, wouldn't he?" Swedenborg was an admirably honest man, though, and we cannot doubt that he was convinced that he really had seen and heard (as perhaps he did) what he reported. Unfortunately, this hardly settles the question of his sanity.

One of Swedenborg's modern biographers, Signe Toksvig, devotes an entire chapter (1949:156–67) to this matter. She presents psychoanalytical diagnoses to the effect that Swedenborg suffered from one or another pathological complex (162–63), and she pays special attention to the evidence of Swedenborg's handwriting when he was under the influence of spirits to such an extent that he put down in automatic writing what they told him (205f.). Her inference is that there are graphological indications of "trance or semitrance" (214) when Swedenborg wrote about his visits to other planets, and other mystical experiences, or when the spirits were supposed to be writing through him.

Now if Swedenborg's metaphysical scheme and particularly his memorable relations were the imaginative products of a disordered brain, there would be nothing surprising in the distortion and chaos that Emerson complained of, or in the failure of a critic to isolate a principle behind the correspondences. But in my opinion this is not what we are faced with; indeed, from the point of view of comparativism it need not matter whether Swedenborg was mad or not, in trance or not. The more firmly we assume that his writings are the figments of an exalted and riotous imagination, the more fascinating they become in the eyes of the analyst. Let us recall that Emerson also thought that Swedenborg was systematic: "all the means are orderly given." Well, I think he was quite impressively systematic, and it is to this general quality of his metaphysics that I now want to direct attention.

VI

In working out the symbolic structure of Swedenborg's metaphysics we have dealt individually with the steady components by which his scheme is constituted. Among these, the basic features are: duality, opposition, equilibrium; cardinal points, lateral values; reversal.

These features, although they are coherent one with another, are of different kinds. Duality is a purely formal partition; opposition is a relation within dyads; equilibrium is a state figuratively attributed to dyads conceived as forces; the cardinal points are absolute spatial coordinators; the lateral values (right/left) are by definition relative; reversal is an operation. The other features that we have isolated, namely symbolic associations and transposition, are, structurally considered, not basic. The symbolic associations are, as it were, the semantic resources which discriminate and evaluate the terms (persons, objects, directions, etc.) among which the connections are made. Transposition can be viewed as an operation that is subsidiary to reversal, in that it affects only one term of a dyad.

Despite their diversity, however, the components of Swedenborg's reports of divine order prove to constitute a distinct and readily recognizable kind of system. It is a system in at least four standard respects. First, it is articulated by a set of relations, beginning with that of opposition. Second, it is self-consistent. Third, in its empirical expressions it is regular, in that its identifications and values remain constant from one setting to another in numerous instances. Fourth, consequently, it permits a limited circumstantial predictability, in that on the basis of one symbolic identification (in a memorable relation especially) a sound inference can be drawn as to concomitant terms and values.

A conventional way of representing such a system is by means of two columns, as in table 1. The dyads (pairs of opposed terms) are listed merely in the order in which they happen to have been adduced in my brief descriptions of the several contexts and examples in which they occur. These contexts are not isolated; as examples, they are typical of the values and relations that they implicate. Taken together, what the dyads compose is a scheme of analogical classification.

This is a form of conceptual order on which a fair amount of comparative work has been done, and a compendium on dual symbolic classification, under the title *Right & Left* (Needham 1973a), brings together a number of cultural examples of the kind. Apart from the taxonomic resemblance, there are several terms in Swedenborg's metaphysics which agree remarkably with symbolic dyads which as collective representations have a global distribution. Examples are: east/west, right/left, sun/moon, divine authority/temporal power, good/evil. These have so common an occurrence in numerous societies as to prompt the inference that "there seems . . . to be a global inclination for men to resort to a common stock of

Table 1. *Scheme of Analogical Classification Underlying*
Swedenborg's Mystical System

spiritual	natural
divinity	world
celestial kingdom	spiritual kingdom
east	west
south	north
right	left
heaven	hell
above	below
angelic societies	infernal societies
celestial sun	black disk
sun	moon
right eye	left eye
goods of faith	truths of faith
beautiful birds	birds of night
sheep	goat
lamb	wolf
dove	vulture
lightning	thunder
divine authority	temporal power
wisdom	love
white horses	black horses
forwards	backwards
good	evil
truth	falsity
light of heaven	heat of heaven

things and qualities in order to convey whatever it is that they are taken to symbolize" (Needham 1980:60). Naturally, there are idiosyncratic terms also in our Swedenborgian table, such as beautiful birds/birds of night, wisdom/love, white horses/black horses. Such is the case with every classification of this kind, and, as in other examples, the idiosyncrasies are nevertheless perfectly accommodated by the principles of the classification.

These principles are: opposition, by which the dyads are constituted; proportional analogy (*a* : *b* :: *c* : *d*), by which the dyads are concatenated; and homology, by which terms that are analogically alike (such as *a* and *c* or *b* and *d*) are more sporadically related one to another. It is these principles that constitute the system, assure its constancy, and permit prediction.

In these regards Swedenborg's metaphysics can be seen as an entirely standard instance of analogical classification. There are, however, a few observations to be made about matters that appear not to fit so well.

One such matter is that there is no place in the dual scheme for the triadic aspect of the heavenly world. It will be remembered that there are three heavens, and that these are arranged in an absolute hierarchy of highest, middle, and lowest (1778: 19). But there is no contradiction here. That the metaphysics is based on a dual classification does not imply that there is nothing else (cf. Needham 1973a:xx–xxi), for there are no grounds to presume that a society—even a heavenly one—need employ only a single mode of classification (Needham 1963:xviii–xix). In the present case, moreover, the triadic hierarchy of heavens may in part be understood by reference to Swedenborg's emphasis elsewhere on the importance of degrees (cf. Bogg 1915:27–28), and to the idea that angels ascend to more blessed states according to the "degree" of perfection they attain. More generally, also, we can say in this connection that a triadic organization is appropriate to a movement or process, in contrast with a dyadic scheme of categories which simply classifies that which acts or is acted upon.

The second critical observation relates to an instance of actual contradiction to the analogical principle of the system. The four quarters of the infernals are "opposite," as Swedenborg says, to those in heaven. Accordingly, their east is towards the black disk, their west is towards the celestial sun (1778:93); everything is determined by reference to the west.

But we are told also that south for the infernals is to their "right," and that their north is to their "left." This is indeed a flat contradiction, for these are coordinates proper to the angels, facing as they do towards the east, and I can only note the fact without being able to explain it. There is no mistake in the translation, for the original Latin has: ". . . meridies illis ad dextrum, & septentrio ad sinistrum" (1758:61). No doubt it is a simple mistake in what Swedenborg wrote down, no matter from what source he had the information. Nevertheless, there are two positive points to be made: first, that this is the only such contradiction that I have discovered; second, that it is a contradiction only by reference to the principles of the system of classification that I have posited.

The third and last of these qualificatory remarks has to do with the dyad divine authority/temporal power. The devil claiming to be God of Gods emerges on the right, while the devil representing Emperors of Emperors and the like emerges on the left (1781, 2:274–75). This is a clear reflection of a complementary opposition between spiritual authority and temporal power such as is found all over the world and throughout an extensive range of institutions (Needham 1980, chap. 3; cf. chap. 8 below). But Swedenborg's vision reflects this partition of sovereignty in another way also, for the sides occupied by the two sources of sovereignty are the reverse of the normal. What we usually find in comparative ethnography is that temporal or jural power is associated with the right, whereas spiritual or mystical authority is associated with the left (Needham 1980:89, 91). That Swedenborg's god/emperor pair of devils are the other way round does not make a contradiction to the principles of the classification, but their lateral assignations are still inconsonant with what we know from elsewhere of the symbolism of jural/mystical diarchy. We can only conjecture the reason for this discrepancy, but if we are to speculate usefully on the matter we need to consider what may have been the nonrevelatory grounds of the components in Swedenborg's system.

There is little problem about some of the components. The preeminence of the right in Swedenborg is in agreement with the honor and privilege accorded to the right throughout the Bible. The orientation of the quarters in heaven, the angels facing east, and the lateral values ascribed to north and south are doubtless connected with Hebraic concepts: the Hebrews expressed east, west, north, and south by words signifying respectively before, behind, left, and right—according to the position of an observer with his face turned towards the east. (Swedenborg was given a Hebrew grammar at the age of seven; see Toksvig 1949:34.) The furniture of heaven can also in many instances be connected with biblical descriptions of chariots, marble, jewels, precious metals, and the rest; in general, Swedenborg's descriptive language has much in common with that of the Bible and especially with the profusion of elaborate material particulars in *Revelation*. There is nothing to be surprised at in all this. The biblical resonances are in Swedenborg's inspired writings either because he was, as we know, steeped in the Bible from his earliest childhood or because both the Bible and Swedenborg's visions report the same things from the mystical realm. But, granted that Swedenborg did not simply imagine certain of the components in his accounts of heaven and hell, there is still some question about the events that he says he witnessed when he was in the spirit.

The imputation that obviously can be leveled against his memorable relations is that they were really dreams. Kant, in his witty discourse on Swedenborg and philosophical metaphysicians, wrote under the title of "dreams" (*Träume*) of a spirit-seer. Swedenborg himself, on the other hand, asserted that he really saw and heard what he narrates, and he repeatedly states that when he had his visions he was wide awake, while others reported seeing him converse with empty space in broad daylight. Of course, a man need not be asleep in order to experience dream-like visions, but we do not have to weigh this issue very exactly, for the memorable relations are not actually much like dreams in any case.

Some of the most striking and immediate characteristics of dreams are "metamorphoses, transpositions, fluctuations in form and qualities, abrupt transitions, immoderate powers (including that of flight), illogicalities, and in general all manner of inconstancy and recalcitrance to constraint" (Needham 1978:64). Now, whatever may be said about the reality or the apparent veracity of Swedenborg's memorable relations, these unsteady attributes have no part in them. Apart from the opulence of heaven and the horrors of hell, which are entirely conventional properties, Swedenborg's tales are remarkably sober and consequential, much like everyday life of his day but on a different plane—which in fact is what he explicitly said the afterlife was really like.

From an aesthetic point of view, indeed, judging the narratives as though they were fictions of the imagination, the rather dejecting thing about the memorable relations is that they are pretty dull. This is not just because the inhabitants of the other world are perpetually holding debates on abstruse theological subjects (which for some is by no means dull), but because Swedenborg's narratives lack precisely the charm and irreality and fantasy that we do find in dreams. "We wander forlorn," Emerson complained, "in a lack-lustre landscape" (1850:107). If "recalcitrance to constraint" and a "disorderly" function of consciousness are indeed typical of dreams (Needham 1978:65), then Swedenborg's visions, as he relates them, were surely not dreams.

If we were to look further into the contemporary conditions of Swedenborg's works, and seek therein the mundane grounds of their style and materials, we should need to go far into the history of ideas and into his own intellectual biography. Much might then be accounted for, but not, I think, the structure of his metaphysics. Emerson opines that "genius is ever haunted by similar dreams, when the hells and the heavens are opened to it" (1850:98); and a common imaginative impulsion could well have had something to do with the more or less familiar images of Swedenborg's visions. But, all the same, where did the *system* come from?

VII

We have already remarked that Swedenborg's metaphysics is articulated by a set of relations constituting an analogical classification. This form of symbolic order is very widely attested to in world ethnography. The congruence, however, is not self-explanatory, and there are two initial obstacles in the way of making a direct comparison of Swedenborg's scheme with that which is familiar to comparativists.

The first is that Swedenborg's construction is that of an individual mind (so far as we can know), whereas the ethnographic cases are collective representations. It is true that the line between individual and collective is not easy to draw, and we have in fact already adverted to the probable impress upon him of the symbolism of the Bible, but his writings are none the less replete with idiosyncratic tropes and images and values which are as much individual to him as if they were fictions of his imagination. The second obstacle is that Swedenborg's writings are explicitly the products of a mystical participation, whereas the ethnographic classifications are the outcome of long cumulative traditions on to which have accreted all kinds of other considerations on the part of uncounted generations in the history of civilization.

For these two reasons, therefore, it is not a straightforward matter to base explanations of Swedenborg's metaphysics directly on a comparison with isomorphic schemes that are to be found in world ethnography. The articulating principles at work may well be the same, but if we are to identify their source we need to resort to a means that transcends the contrasts between individual and collective, visionary and traditional.

A hypothesis which offers some promise of such an explanation is that which posits certain innate predispositions of the human brain as the effective grounds of constant features of thought and imagination (Needham 1981:25–26). There are many uncertainties in this approach, especially to the extent that we concentrate our attention directly on the brain itself (Needham 1978:47–49); but some such difficulties are obviated or reduced if we recognize that the task of the comparativist is to concentrate on the characteristic properties of representations, and that the inferences drawn from these as to properties of the cerebral cortex do no more than indicate a material and dynamic ground to the representations. The order that we discern in representations, so far as comparative evidence goes, *is* the postulated predisposition, or the "cerebrational vector"; and the principles of a symbolic classification, for example, are the only immediate contact with the proclivity that the comparativist can have. We are not therefore doing fake neurophysiology when we attribute certain principles of representation to the brain and to its vectors of operation.

From this premise we can reconsider Swedenborg's metaphysics under a revelatory aspect. Instead of seeing his writings as the imaginative products of an overwrought or disordered brain, we can recognize them as yet further manifestations of certain general proclivities in the working of the normal brain.

We can sum up the case in the following terms. A structural analysis establishes a system of analogical classification; this system includes standard components such as are commonly found in collective representations; and the principles that articulate it reflect natural operations of thought and imagination. We can ignore the contrasts between individual and collective, visionary and traditional, and we can appreciate Swedenborg's works, in the above respects, as still another system of representations belonging to a familiar, fundamental, and even normal kind. If Swedenborg was mad, then these evidences show that in his case at any rate even a mad brain can think in a regular and comprehensible manner.

In prosecuting this analysis we have not been working out a semasiological interpretation of Swedenborg's more idiosyncratic concepts, but we have instead discerned a structure among them. In trying to come to terms with his conception of a "science of correspondences," we have discovered correspondences among his concepts and images themselves as these are ordered in a system of analogical classification. The profusion of his elaborate visions is reduced by comparative analysis to a simple economy of the orderly operation of the human brain. Framing the extravagance of his images there are common constraints, and organizing the fantastic complexities of his mystical cosmology there is a restricted set of relations. In place of the "arbitrary and accidental" that Emerson deprecated, what we find is that Swedenborg is indeed systematic, as Emerson also wrote, and that all the means are in fact orderly given. Only the system was not Swedenborg's: he did not invent it, he was not responsible for it, and he may not have been aware of it.

There remains one possibility that we have not yet examined. What if angels really were responsible, and Swedenborg merely wrote down (as he says he did) what they told him or sympathetically revealed to him by the exercise of their own thoughts? Well, how should we expect angels to speak? Lichtenberg had his own idea: "If an angel were ever to tell us about his philosophy, I believe that many of his statements would have to sound like: 2 times 2 is 13" (Lichtenberg 1968:109). Perhaps, though, we expect too much of angels. Swedenborg promised that "when men are gifted with the knowledge of correspondences, they can think in like manner with the angels" (1778:67). But Emerson observes quite justly: "These angels that Swedenborg paints give us no very high idea of their discipline and culture. They are all country-parsons" (1850:105). Angels, then, by this account, are much like us, and they think as we do. If a mystic does begin to speak with the tongues of angels, he may obscurely be seeing everything in everything, but we need anticipate no perplexity in comprehending his symbolic syntax.

7

Remarks on Wittgenstein and Ritual

The Master said, Ritual, Ritual! Does it mean no more than presents of jade and silk?

Confucius

I

The influence of Ludwig Wittgenstein on the comparative analysis of social facts has been late, little, and slow. When it has not been flippantly dismissed, as though not even calling for counterargument (for example, Augé 1979:93 n.), it has had scarcely any effect on the practice of the great majority of social anthropologists.

Nevertheless, deliberate attempts have been made to demonstrate the radical importance of Wittgenstein's thought for the working concepts of comparativism. It has been argued, for instance, that the stock terms in the study of systems of descent and affinity are so defective as to be incapable of framing reliable scientific results (Needham 1974, chap. 1); that the psychological term "belief" does not have the value, as the index to a natural resemblance among mankind, that could justify its continued use as a concept of universal application (Needham 1972); and that the discrimination of inner states is crucially affected by inappropriate taxonomic premises (Needham 1981, chap. 3). These critiques are based on Wittgenstein's exploitation of the idea of "family resemblances," and their main intended effect is to extend into comparativism a recognition of the principle of polythetic classification (Needham 1975; 1983, chap. 3). Thus it is contended that terms such as "descent," "incest," "belief," or "anger" are vitiated because they are taken to denote monothetic classes of social facts, whereas actually they are highly polythetic and cannot therefore have the uses that are normally ascribed to them. A consequence of accepting this kind of critique is that the comparison of social facts must at first become far more difficult, if it is at all feasible in such terms; but the immense potential benefit that can follow is the attainment of a more "perspicuous representation" (Wittgenstein 1967a, sec. 122) of what is really at issue when we try to understand human nature and social action.

In the cases just mentioned, Wittgenstein's influence has been exerted through the criticism of individual concepts, and for the most part this is the way he did his own work in linguistic philosophy. While he certainly urged that "forms of life" should be taken into account in the analysis of expressions in German and in English, he did not make it his concern to set his findings against the ethnographic descriptions of more alien social forms. Even in his allusions to the value of an acquaintance with many languages, he does not resort to the abundant materials on natural languages (Needham 1972:132–34). When he wants an example outside German or English, he makes up an imaginary language; and when he needs a different social setting, he asks us to imagine a primitive tribe that behaves in a way we should find strange. In these respects Wittgenstein himself behaves in the way that philosophers as a tribe usually do; and naturally enough this method does not answer directly to the concerns of those whose scientific objective is instead to study concrete similarities and differences throughout a global range of civilizations. If "the common behaviour of mankind is the system of reference by means of which we interpret an unknown language" (Wittgenstein 1967a, sec. 206), it is the task of the comparativist to determine empirically what the common features actually are. If we are to establish no more than a "natural history of mankind" (sec. 415), then we cannot just "invent natural history" (p. 230); we have to come to terms with factual accounts of what mankind really does.

We cannot reproach Wittgenstein for not making this his constant practice in relation to his philosophical interests (cf. Needham 1972:186), but his normal method attracts all the more interest when he does apply himself to social facts. This he did in his "Bemerkungen über Frazers *Golden Bough*." These remarks fall into two sets: the first were notes that he made over a period of a few weeks in 1931; the second set of remarks dates from not earlier than 1936 and probably from after 1948 (Rush Rhees, in Wittgenstein 1979:v, vi). They were published, in German as they stood, in *Synthese* (Wittgenstein 1967b), and then in an English translation, omitting several concluding passages (1967b:251–53), in *The Human World* (Wittgenstein 1971), with a long introductory note by Rhees. Eventually the German text, with corrections, and the translation, with revisions, were brought together in a single volume (1979). In the interim the remarks had also appeared in a French translation (1977b).

It cannot be said that Wittgenstein's remarks on *The Golden Bough* made any great impression on anthropologists. Apart from citations in certain predecessors to the present essay (Needham 1972, 1973b, 1976, 1980, 1981, 1983), they attracted in fact almost no professional attention. Rudich and Stassen published a critical paper on "Wittgenstein's implied anthropology" (1977), and Rhees has commented at some length on Wittgenstein's treatment of language and ritual (Rhees 1982). But anthropologists appear in general to have ignored what Wittgenstein found to say about a classical work in anthropology and about topics such as religion, magic, ritual, and symbolism which are central to their discipline. It is possible to conjecture probable reasons for this neglect, but a more useful course is to examine what is to be gained from a consideration of Wittgenstein's genius when, for once, it is applied to the explication of social facts.

To this end we shall rely on the bilingual edition of the "Remarks/Bemerkungen" (1979) and also on the passages in *Synthese* that were not included in that volume. At certain points, it should be observed, there are omissions and more or less consequential misrenderings in the translation from the German; these will be noticed explicitly only if they affect the present argument. (Page references followed by "e" cite the published translation; without this letter the passages quoted are direct translations from the German, and they differ from the English version.) Also, there are many connections to be made between the "Remarks" and one or another of Wittgenstein's other publications (cf. Bouveresse 1977); to take these up would result in a very extended and more philosophical commentary, so the investigation that follows will concentrate almost exclusively on the "Remarks" themselves and on their implications for the study of ritual.

Wittgenstein's "Remarks" are not only in two parts, written at an interval of perhaps as much as seventeen years, but neither part is composed as a sequential argument. There are connections, expectably enough, between some adjacent passages, but there is no overall development of a case. It is necessary therefore to jump from one place to another in the text and to collocate scattered remarks in order to bring out their effect in combination. This procedure may or may not result in a pattern of exposition that Wittgenstein would have been prepared to recognize; but the present commentary is not in any event intended as a reordered exposition of what we already have from Wittgenstein himself and, in the original, in the characteristic idiom that makes his writings so exciting. The object of the examination is instead one that he would surely have approved, namely to make what we can of his ideas in order to effect some advance in our own thoughts.

II

Wittgenstein's premise is that it is possible to distinguish, by observation, ritual actions from "animal activities" such as taking food. Certain actions bear a "peculiar character" and could be called ritual (1979:7; the translation has "ritualistic," which is inexact).

We are not told what it is that gives this peculiar character to certain actions and sets them apart from animal activities, but only that it can be seen when "we watch the life and behaviour of men all over the earth." What exactly can we "see" that would make this differentiation? Formality is perhaps the attribute that will come most readily to mind. But all types of social action, if they are to be recognizable as social and as the type that any of them is, must to some degree be formalized. The prescribed forms of good manners, such as standing at the entrance of a woman or a superior, certainly and deliberately have this character, and so do other and more corporate actions such as soldiers executing parade-ground drill or the fellows of a college conducting a meeting of the governing body. We cannot distinguish the ritual from the merely formal by the degree of punctilio demanded, for in that event the minutiae of everyday etiquette would have to be placed at the ritual end of the scale. And even an innovation in collective behavior can be formalized in a coercive manner; for example, British soccer players kissing and cuddling and mounting one another after they have scored a goal. On the other hand, religious ceremonies which ought to be performed in set and careful observances may in the event be lacking in due formality (cf. Needham 1981:83). And then there are activities, such as the transportation of the bier at a Balinese funeral, the formality of which consists in an appearance of boisterous informality.

Another conventional criterion of ritual is to be looked for in the inner state of the participants; for instance, reverence,

awe, inspiration, grief, and so forth, according to what the
ritual is about. It is often feasible to elicit a description of the
inner state that is thought appropriate to a given case; but
there is no certain way of being sure that a performer or
assistant in a form of action is in that state (cf. Needham
1972:98–101; 1981, chap. 3). Even when the prescribed inner
state does obtain, and is certainly in consonance with the
declared aim of the action being carried out, there is still
the possibility that the subject will also be occupied by another emotion that is inconsistent with what is prescribed;
Descartes gives the example of a man weeping over his dead
wife when he would be put out if she were to be resuscitated
(1649, art. 147). There is no doubt, however, that certain inner states are enjoined upon those who take part in what are
customarily called rituals, and if such states cannot be seen
perhaps it will serve as criterion that they should be displayed
or simulated. But then there are two difficulties: first, that it
is hard to exhibit even a genuine inner state, such as reverence, and harder still to interpret by simple observation what
state it is; second, that a prescribed expression or posture is
part of the action itself, and not a clue to an inner state that
defines the action as a ritual.

There are of course other criteria that might contribute to
the definition of ritual; for instance, it might be contended
that rituals were significantly associated with boundaries and
points of transition, so that the criterion would be, let us say,
structural. But a social or symbolic structure cannot be seen,
and we could not therefore directly identify ritual, in this
sense, by considering the "life and behaviour of men." Various further criteria attract additional objections, and in the
end there seems no secure defense of the presumption that
there is a peculiar (*eigentümlich*) aspect of social action that
provides an observable index to the ritual. Wittgenstein, at
any rate, does not say what it is. He does, however, say that

ritual can be seen apart from "animal activities," and perhaps these can help us to draw a line around ritual. The only example he cites is that of taking food, but this activity surely will not serve. The Eucharist involves the taking of food, as bread and wine, yet in the Christian tradition it is supremely a ritual; moreover, it rests on an ancient symbolic ideology, in Judaic tradition, in which dietary rules play a dominant role in the definition of status and action and in the relationship of men to God (Feeley-Harnik 1981). It is an anthropological commonplace, too, that all over the world food is far more than a merely animal concern; it is a fundamental vehicle for symbolizing incorporation, boundaries, sympathies, enmities, and much else in human relations. As for other animal activities, such as copulation or excretion or hunting, these also are never simply animal in human society; always they are governed by rules and symbolic usages which again make it not feasible to distinguish them, on the basis of their animal character alone, from what would then stand apart as ritual. If "we must begin with the mistake and transform it into what is true" (1e), the unargued premise that ritual has a peculiar character that can be observed is a prime candidate for transformation.

There is in fact another recourse in coming to terms with ritual. Instead of continuing to try to isolate the peculiar or special character of the activity, we can adopt another approach that Wittgenstein also mentions. Writing about the fire festivals of Europe, he says that what strikes him most apart from the similarities of all these rites is the dissimilarity among them. He compares them to a wide variety of faces with common features that repeatedly appear in one place and another. "And one would like to draw lines joining the parts that various faces have in common" (13e); more literally, lines that connect the common components. Now this is precisely the method for determining "family resemblances," and specifically that of Francis Galton, who in 1879 made composite portraits in order to bring out the typical characteristics of sets of individuals (cf. Needham 1972:110–13). In other words, what Wittgenstein is doing in the comparison of fire festivals is to suggest a polythetic delineation of ritual.

In accordance with this procedure, we can say then that "ritual" is an odd-job word; that is, it serves a variety of more or less disparate uses, yet we are tempted to describe its use as though it were a word with regular functions (cf. Wittgenstein 1958:43–44). It cannot be relied upon for any precise task of identification, interpretation, or comparison—as it could be if it were the monothetic concept that it is usually taken for—but this does not mean that it can have no serious use. What follows, rather, is that it has a range of uses, not one strict application corresponding to some peculiar character in the phenomena that it denotes. As a polythetic concept, "ritual" variously combines certain characteristic features, and the task of the comparativist is to identify these features and to register the patterns into which they combine.

This task is made more manageable by subsuming ritual under the more general heading of symbolic action, for we have a fair command of the vehicles, modes, and relations of symbolism. These components of symbolic classification and its social expression are marked by parsimony, regular concatenation, and a global distribution (Needham 1979; 1981:85–88). Wittgenstein suggests that in ritual practices we can see something that is similar to the association of ideas and related to it: "we could speak of an association of practices" (13e). This impression, it can now be responded, is created by the recurrence of features from among a steady repertory of such components. What we isolate as "ritual," in one or another form or context, is no more than the expression in social action of symbolic features which are by no means peculiar to it—whatever it may be.

III

To approach ritual as a polythetic concept and as a variety of symbolic action makes a useful beginning, but the identification of characteristic features does not in itself constitute interpretation or explanation.

In trying to understand ritual, a standing inclination among anthropologists is, reasonably enough, to look for the reasons behind it; either the reasons that led to its inception or those that sustain its continued performance. Wittgenstein repeatedly contends that this is a mistake. "What makes the character of ritual action," he asserts, "is not any view or opinion, either right or wrong" (7). More generally yet, he holds that "the characteristic feature of primitive man . . . is that he does not act from *opinions* he holds about things (as Frazer thinks)" (12). If this is correct, the explanation of ritual cannot consist in discovering the reasons for which the participants, at any point in its development or in the course of its practice, carry it out.

The topic of rationality has received much sociological attention, and various approaches to it have most usefully been brought together by Wilson in a collaborative volume under that title (Wilson 1970), but the basic issues have nevertheless proved very recalcitrant. On the one hand, the topic is clearly philosophical, yet on the other hand certain philosophical treatments have proved rather divagatious from the analysis of social facts. Since the problems arise typically in attempts to understand exotic forms of behavior, it seems better in this case to begin, not with the scrutiny of our own conceptual predispositions, but directly, so far as this may be done, with reports of the phenomena in question. These are voluminous, and different ethnographers have stressed different aspects and from different points of view, but certain common findings can be discerned. The most general, it seems, is that those who take part in ritual can give no reasons for it; they say that it is their custom (*adat*, as is said in Indonesia, or some such word) or that it is what they are enjoined to do by their ancestors; or else they react in such a way as to show that for them there is no comprehensible question in the ethnographer's query (cf. Needham, 1983, chap. 4). In other instances an acknowledged local authority, such as a priest or some other celebrant of the ritual, gives a traditional reason, and other participants acquiesce; in that case, the reason is to be regarded as being itself part of the ritual, not as an independent excogitation providing a rational explanation for the performance of the ritual. In yet other instances, different participants may give conflicting reasons; in such a case there can sometimes be acceptable evidence of cogitation, but there is no means of deciding which explanation is the correct one, and there are certainly no grounds to presume that the most rational explanation (if that can be isolated) will provide the real reason for the behavior. Also, Sir Thomas Browne asserted quite long ago, about the ancient Gentiles, that "in severall rites, customs, actions and expressions, they contradicted their own opinions" (Browne 1658, chap. 4); and, while it is difficult to decide, without begging the question, what is to count as a contradiction between rite and opinion, in some sense or another this is a real contingency with which in the ordinary way we are quite familiar.

All of these possibilities can be demonstrated by reference to a rite that we know especially well, and on which there is a superabundance of historical and theological evidence, namely the Eucharist. This paradigmatic rite of the Christian faith has been excellently analyzed, from a point of view made feasible only by comparativism, by Feeley-Harnik (1981). She has uncovered numerous factors that enable us to comprehend better the inception of the rite, but it is out of the question that any significant number of communicants today could know anything of these determinants. If communicants are asked their present reasons for partaking in the rite, it is sure that these will be various, even in the most strictly disciplined of churches. Ultimately, moreover, the inquirer will come up against the sophisticated response that what is in question is a mystery and hence ineffable. This does not prevent different exponents of the Christian faith from offering divergent accounts of the real significance of the rite and hence different reasons for its celebration.

The objection might be raised that Christianity is an exceptionally complex and disputatious religion, and that therefore the Eucharist is too idiosyncratic an example to rely on. But Christianity is also exceptional in the extent to which it has elaborated reasons for its tenets and their symbolic expression, and in this regard the Eucharist makes in fact an exceptionally instructive test case. Taken as such, it can readily be adduced as testimony against any theory that would explain the enactment or the form of a rite by reference to the opinions of those who participate in it. Indeed, Feeley-Harnik's analysis tends to show in another way that concomitant opinions cannot provide an explanation; for to the extent that she isolates factors which enable us to comprehend the rite more clearly, these are characteristics of symbolic ideation which are far too general, in their incidence among other traditions and rites as well, to account for the particularities of this individual rite.

If it should be thought that these characteristic features of ritual, such as the symbolism of sacrifice, contain in their turn more fundamental explanations of the rite, then the response must be that such features are not rational constructs and that they bear only contingent relations to the opinions of those who subscribe to this form of ritual. Whereas the Christian liturgy is indeed a privileged case for fundamental analysis, an enterprise in which Yarnold's study of its rites of initiation (1971) would occupy an advanced place, the conclusions to be derived are likely only to confirm what Waley

wrote in connection with Confucian practices: "The truth . . .
is that there is no 'real reason' for ritual acts" (1938:57).

IV

Wittgenstein contends that the very idea of trying to explain a
practice, say the killing of the priest-king, is a mistake (2e).
The particular case that he takes up makes the search for an
explanation seem a particular kind of mistake.

Frazer, he asserts, merely makes the practice plausible to
people who think as he does (1e), and what Frazer thinks is
that the enactors of the practice are acting out an error, a mistaken theory. But, Wittgenstein responds, it is very remarkable that all these practices should be represented in the end as
stupidities, for it never does become plausible that people be-
have so out of sheer stupidity (1). They may well have views
about what they do (and these opinions may appear mistaken), but "where that practice and these views go together,
the practice does not spring from the view, but both of them
are just there" (2). Also, as he wrote in another manuscript
(of 1945): "Why should we not say, These customs and laws
are not *based* on the belief; they show *to what extent* (in what
sense) such a belief exists" (in Rhees 1982:97).

This is cogent as far as it goes, but then Wittgenstein proceeds to a more comprehensive statement about the explanation of ritual: "I think one reason that the attempt at an
explanation is wrong is that we have only to put together in
the right way what we *know*, without adding anything, and
the satisfaction we are trying to get from the explanation
comes of itself" (2); "We can only *describe* here and say: that is
what human life is like" (3). These remarks can be subsumed
under the notion, which was of fundamental importance to
Wittgenstein (cf. 1967a, sec. 122), of a "perspicuous representation" (1979:9). The tenor of this phrase has indeed been

demonstrated repeatedly by Wittgenstein in connection with verbal concepts, but its application is not so clear when we are confronted with social facts such as the practices of ritual.

There are, in the event, considerable difficulties in construing Wittgenstein's statement about explanation. When he declares that we have only to put together in the right way what we know, his words seem to imply that "we" (*man*, one, in the German) is a constant, or at least a subject whose identity and capacities are tacitly given. But this is far from being the case, and in any case the criteria for "what we *know*" must be highly unsure (cf. 6). The first necessity in drawing on an ethnographic report, for instance, is not to presume that it represents objective knowledge but to try to assess it objectively as a representation. Ethnographic reports about alien concepts can hardly ever be accepted as they stand (cf. Needham 1972:198), but they call instead for a deliberate interpretation which is intrinsically more complex than the apprehension of what is reported. Far from not adding anything, as Wittgenstein enjoins, we need to add all manner of circumstantial particulars if we are to make a reliable cognitive assessment of what the ethnographer relates.

Concomitantly, we cannot fall in directly with Wittgenstein's assertion that "we can only *describe*. . . ." Clear description (cf. a "perspicuous representation") is a supreme art in the practice of ethnography, and the resultant account has to be assessed, moreover, in the light of the methodological principles and general concepts by which the ethnographer is guided. The observation of a symbolic act may need to be framed by notions, such as lateral values or complementarity or reversal, which are not given by observation but have to be adduced in a careful exercise of interpretation. Furthermore, such notions are ultimately scientific abstractions, and they are hence disputable. A critical apprehension of lateral values entails a resort to the relation of opposition, which is not a logical constant, and to that of analogy, which is puzzlingly obscure (Needham 1980, chap. 2); the concept of complementarity has no intrinsic logical form, but may possess a more or less adventitious use as a term of expository rhetoric; the idea of reversal is neither simple nor self-evident, but it can be decomposed into a number of more or less disparate modes (Needham 1983, chap. 5). All of these considerations, to cite no more, make it a hard matter to describe ritual, let alone to put together what we know in a definite arrangement that could be seen as the right way.

V

Another reason to think that Frazer's explanations are misleading, Wittgenstein writes, is that "we could very well imagine primitive practices for ourselves, and it would be an accident if they were not actually found somewhere" (5). This means, he continues, that the principle according to which these practices are ordered is much more general than Frazer takes it to be; it is present in our own minds, so that "we could think out all the possibilities for ourselves" (5),

For certain fields of social life this can indeed be done. Thus the great variety of descent systems, together with the recurrent resemblances among them, can be accounted for as realizations of elementary modes of descent; there are only six modes, and two of them are impracticable as operational rules of social organization (Needham 1974:47). A similar isolation of principles can be made in the case of prescriptive systems, by reference to criteria of symmetry, transitivity, and other relations; it is then readily understandable that remarkably similar systems should be found in far-separated parts of the world, and also that the discovery of additional instances of prescriptive alliance should offer no surprises as to their principles of order. It may be thought not all that perplexing that we should be able to "think out all the possibilities" when we are dealing with systematic aspects of social forms, for in addition to logical or schematic constraints there are also practical exigencies that conduce to a relatively simple economy of systems. But it is more arresting when we find that very general principles can be discerned among the imaginative variegations of symbolic forms. Admittedly, it is hardly feasible in these cases to think out the possibilities from scratch, but a number of common or basic features can still be isolated, and these can then be employed as premises in understanding the elaborations. Thus if it is accepted that men attribute symbolic significance to space, it is an obvious task to go on to work out the contrasts of values that may define the individual dimensions such as right/left, above/below, and so on (cf. Needham 1973a). Inductively, also, a number of relational constants and transformations in systems of symbolic classification can be established (Needham 1979, chaps. 4 and 5), and these in their turn lend weight to the precept, expressed in phrases taken from Wittgenstein in another connection, that in comparativism "our investigation . . . is directed not towards phenomena, but, as one might say, towards the 'possibilities' of phenomena" (cf. Wittgenstein 1967a, sec. 90; Needham 1974:71).

Wittgenstein's examples of thinking out possibilities of ritual conduct are not so comprehensive as this formulation, but they are telling enough. We can readily imagine, he says, that in a given tribe no one is allowed to see the king, but we can also imagine that everybody in the tribe is obliged to see him; and in the latter event it will certainly not be left more or less to chance, but he will be *displayed* to the people. Perhaps no one will be allowed to touch the king—but perhaps they will be *compelled* to do so (5). These examples make Wittgenstein's point, but then they are entirely overshadowed by another example that is one of the most enlightening paradigms in all that has been written about ritual and its purposes. This concerns the treatment of Schubert's manuscript scores.

After Schubert's death, Wittgenstein relates, his brother cut some of the scores into small pieces, of a few bars each, and gave them to the composer's favorite pupils. "This action, as a sign of piety, is *just* as comprehensible to us as would be that of keeping the scores undisturbed and accessible to no one. And if Schubert's brother had burnt the scores, this also would be comprehensible as a sign of piety" (5).

To this splendid paradigm Wittgenstein appends a gloss: "the ceremonial . . . as opposed to the haphazard, . . . characterises piety." In other words, it would seem, the inner attitude is given expression through a formal outward observance. Here, then, we have a fine demonstration that even a given sentiment of piety, together with a deliberate purpose to fulfill the duty of commemoration, can be expressed equally comprehensibly through very contrasting forms of conduct. The premise, of course, is that the particular formality that happens to be enacted will be recognized as inspired by that sentiment, or as intended to symbolise it, and as directed by the concomitant intention. The ritual, as we may call it, thus has a patent meaning that may not be characteristic of traditional and collective formalities of the kind. Nevertheless, the arbitrary connection between meaning and form remains strikingly demonstrated. Moreover, the paradigm has an important converse; namely that we cannot infer from the form of a symbolic action what its meaning may be (or may previously have been), and hence cannot conclude that rituals with a common form will have any common meaning or purpose.

This outcome reinforces Wittgenstein's contention that "what makes the character of ritual action is not any view or opinion, either right or wrong, although an opinion—a belief—can itself also be ritual, can belong to the rite" (7).

VI

Nevertheless, it remains deeply perplexing that certain actions of a formal or symbolic kind, whether or not we should be justified in labeling them as ritual, seem to express something that we feel called upon to comprehend in a special way. We still need to explain them, in the literal sense; that is, to unfold them, smooth out their anfractuosities, and expose some plainer significance that will allay our curious sense of puzzlement. With the concept of "ritual," one is reminded of what Wittgenstein says about thought: it is like silver paper, and once crumpled it cannot ever be quite smoothed out again (1977a:39).

If concomitant sentiments or opinions or purposes do not provide the key to what is enacted as ritual, perhaps the answer lies in a distant past, possibly in a period which saw the origin of the practice. Wittgenstein has a number of corrective observations to offer on this score. A historical explanation, as a hypothesis of development, is, he says, "only *one* kind of summary of the data—of their synopsis"; it is equally possible to see the data in their relations one to another and to fit them together into a general picture without putting this into the form of a hypothesis about chronological development (8). Certainly it is possible to conceive of facts of ritual as governed by some law, and to set out this law by means of a developmental (or evolutionary) hypothesis; but the idea can also be expressed just by arranging the factual materials in a perspicuous representation, and this makes possible the comprehension which consists simply in "seeing the connections" (8–9). Hence, Wittgenstein adds, the importance of finding intermediate links. But for him, he explains, a hypothetical link "is not meant to do anything except draw attention to the similarity, the connection, of the *facts*" (9). Then he makes the illuminating comparison: "As one might illustrate an internal relation of a circle to an ellipse by gradually transforming an ellipse into a circle; *but not in order to assert that a given ellipse in fact, historically, developed from a circle . . .* but only to sharpen our eye for a formal connection." So also the hypothesis of development can be seen as nothing but one way of expressing a formal connection (9).

These considerations do not mean that rites have no beginnings, or undergo no historical changes, or that their development cannot ever be traced or reconstructed; the Eucharist alone would suffice to refute such inferences. But the remarks do imply that we should not assume the significance of a rite to reside in its origin alone, or that the original significance has survived only as an ineffectual relic of custom, or that the present performance of the rite provides an insufficient justification of its existence.

The historical example that Wittgenstein reflects upon is the Beltane custom as reported from western Perthshire toward the end of the eighteenth century and as recounted by Frazer. A feature of this practice was that special cakes were baked for the occasion and that these had small lumps in the form of nipples raised all over the surface. In the reported practice of the custom, whoever got a particular piece of the cake was seized by the other participants, who made a show of putting him into the fire, and for a time thereafter this person was spoken of as dead. Frazer offers the "conjecture" that this looks like the relics of a casting of lots. "And through this aspect," remarks Wittgenstein, "it suddenly gains depth" (15e). If we were to learn that the cake with knobs on had originally been baked in honor of a button-maker on his birthday, and that the practice had persisted in the district, it would in fact lose all "depth." (Unless, he adds, the depth should lie in the present form of the practice itself.) Suppose further, Wittgenstein continues, that nowadays the Beltane custom is performed only by children, who hold contests in baking cakes and decorating them with knobs. "Then the depth lies consequently only in the thought of that ancestry" (15). It is as though it were the historical hypothesis that first gives the affair depth—"its *connection* with the burning of a man" (14). The question, to Wittgenstein, is consequently: "does the sinister character of the Beltane Fire inhere in the usage itself, or only if the hypothesis of its origin is confirmed?" (14).

Wittgenstein's remarks about the "depth" of a ritual are clearly important to him; as he proceeds the topic is more frequently mentioned. It is as though he were working toward the contention that what distinguishes ritual, its "peculiar character," lies in something deep in it. This depth is not simply that of historical antiquity; the celebration of a button-maker's birthday might be just as old as the ceremonial survival of human sacrifice. Why then does the Beltane custom lose all depth, in his eyes, if it commemorates a button-maker? Is it because making buttons is a priori less important than killing a man? Or because the button-maker himself, or in his social standing, was less important and memorable than a victim of ritual burning? These contrasts in evaluation are not self-evident, and in the nature of the case they do not repose on historical evidence. So either they are arbitrary premises or else they reflect moral and other estimations which, apposite though they may be today, need not have prevailed at the time of the inception of the practice. The conviction of depth therefore calls for some other justification. Certainly a historical reconstruction will not serve: Wittgenstein later suggests that "what is sinister, deep, does not lie in the fact that this is how the history of this practice went, for perhaps it did not go that way; nor in the fact that perhaps or probably it was like that, but in what it is that gives me grounds to assume so" (16). For that matter, he asks, what makes human sacrifice something deep and sinister anyway? Is it only the suffering of the victim that impresses us in this way? But all kinds of illnesses cause just as much suffering, yet do not make this impression. "This deep and sinister character does not become obvious when we just learn the history of the external action, but *we* derive it from an experience in our inner selves" (16).

It is possible to feel that we can sympathize with Wittgenstein in the way he seems to respond to the "deep" nature of a practice originating in human sacrifice, but from a more detached standpoint there are numerous obscurities in his account. The example he considers is gruesome, we might well say, but then so, in physical terms, was the Crucifixion, and this is not supposed to create an impression of a "sinister" depth. Evidently, too, the depth does not depend exclusively on a terrible character in what is commemorated. Suppose a symbolic action represents something sublime, such as the Ascension or the Enlightenment of the Buddha, then presumably this too will have "depth." So the particular evaluation placed on the prototypical event is not what confers depth, and neither does a particular emotional response derived from our inner experience. Nevertheless, Wittgenstein insists on the "terrible," and again in a way with which we can sympathize ("we" in this instance having had, let us assume, much the same moral and religious education as he had) but which analytically is hard to sustain. He says that in the casting of lots (to determine who shall be the victim) the fact that a cake is chosen has something particularly terrible about it, "almost like betrayal through a kiss"—clearly in reference to Judas identifying Jesus in the Garden by kissing him before the multitude who had come to lay hands on him. This fact, he asserts, "is of central importance for the investigation of such practices"; the impression he gains is "very deep and extremely serious" (16). Well, no doubt the Beltane cake can be seen as a terribly deceptive or mocking means of sending a man to his death, but compared with the ghastly outcome the form of the lottery is surely quite trivial in importance. Suppose an unlucky dip were held instead. Concealed in a container are various objects, such as a nut, a cork, and other things, and the victim is the man who gets a flint or a steel (for making fire). Here the lot is of the same kind as the fate of the victim thus selected, but this symbolic appositeness does not self-evidently make the proceedings any less terrible.

It is a general finding in the study of symbolism, moreover, that anything can be made to stand for anything else; whatever it may be, a thing can bear practically any meaning in the eyes of those who use it for a given purpose. But then how do we know what meaning the Beltane cake had in addition to its function in determining the victim? There is no prior reason to think that for those who took part in the practice there was anything terrible about it. To judge that possibility we should have to know a great deal about foodstuffs, dietary laws, alimentary symbolism, types of cake, and much else among the hypothetical originators of the practice. And even then it would need to be discovered that those people actually regarded burning a man alive as being in itself terrible. But, alas, there is abundant historical evidence from elsewhere that they might well not have done so—and there is no intrinsic necessity, in any case, that they should have found terrible what they regularly practiced.

So neither the method of the lottery nor the fate of the victim has inherently any character or meaning other than what is ascribed to the festival by the practitioners. If there is anything deep or sinister going on, it is they who must tell us so. Only what they will tell us is not in general going to stand in any determinate connection with the way the particular symbolic action came into being; and there is even less chance that their ideas and emotions will correspond to those of an alien inquirer. On the one hand, therefore, Wittgenstein has good reason to abjure an explanation by historical reconstruction; but on the other hand he has not supplied the grounds to accept that the character of a rite is to be elicited from our own experience. In particular, the character of "depth" has not been shown to belong in a vocabulary for the comparative analysis of ritual.

Wittgenstein says that what gives depth to the consideration of characteristic features of ritual is that which connects these with "our own feelings and thoughts" (13). In the concluding lines to the first publication of the "Bemerkungen" (1967b:253), he alludes to the embarrassment that we feel by reason of our physical or aesthetic inferiority; "we" (*wir*) is what he writes, but he revealingly qualifies this pronoun by adding at once, "or at any rate many people (I) [*ich*]."

VII

At the end of his "Remarks," Wittgenstein turns to an alternative interpretation of the Beltane festival: the people cast lots in order to have the fun of threatening to throw someone in the fire. This would be disagreeable, like a practical joke, and might procure the same kind of satisfaction. But such an explanation would take away all "mystery" from the festival, were it not that it is different in action and in mood from familiar games (18). There is still something about the rite that the explanation does not touch.

In the same way, he continues, the fact that on certain days children burn a straw man could make us uneasy, even if no explanation were given for it. Strange that they should celebrate by burning a *man*! And then Wittgenstein makes a remark that attaches in general to the search for such explanations as Frazer proposed. The German goes, "Ich will sagen: die Lösung ist nicht beunruhigender als das Rätsel" (18; cf. 1967b:251). The English translation has, quite correctly, "What I want to say is: the solution is not any more disquieting than the riddle" (18e). But this really does not fit as a conclusion to Wittgenstein's preceding remarks. It may be that he intended to write "nicht minder beunruhigend" but left out *minder*, less, though this slip would still leave the comparative adjective *beunruhigender* unaccounted for. Whatever may have happened, the expectable sense of the passage would read: "The solution is no less disquieting than the riddle." This is not only a contextual improvement, from a logical point of view, but it is worth special stress because of its far wider implications. The methodological point to be taken is that an explanation should explain. If we are disquieted by a problem, and an attempt to explain it leaves us no *less* disquieted, then the explanation has failed.

In the case of the Beltane festival, the ground of Wittgenstein's disquiet is apparently moral, not analytical; the explanation that originally a man was burnt alive, and that this is what is celebrated, is "sinister." Nevertheless, it could still be a correct explanation. But the methodological point obtains in more pertinent regards. To say that the reported practice, which mimicked the burning of a man, commemorated an earlier practice in which a man was really burnt, is no explanation at all. Even if it could be proved that this was what was originally done, and that the ceremony later became reduced to a mere simulation, still the custom would not be explained. What we want to know is why a man should have been burnt alive anyway. To say that this was an instance of "human sacrifice" would be no answer, and would fail in three distinct ways. First, it merely replaces a description by a label. Second, the label does not denote a class of events for which there already exists a proved explanation. Third, the particular motivation of the originators of the Beltane festival is inaccessible and cannot be adequately surmised; so just to be assured that they did sacrifice a man would still leave us knowing no more than that they burned him. We are left wondering, therefore, what would qualify as an explanation, not only in this case but in a very extensive range of cases of which the present one is typical.

Wittgenstein says that what we strive for through an explanation is "satisfaction" (*Befriedigung*); and he thinks this can be attained, even if the attempt to find an explanation is wrong (2e). Perhaps there is a clue here to his understanding of ritual. He later alludes to satisfaction in another connection (4):

> Burning in effigy. Kissing the picture of a person one loves. This is *obviously not* based on a belief that it will have a definite effect on the object represented by the picture. It aims at a satisfaction and it also achieves it. Or rather: it does not *aim* at anything; we act in this way and then feel satisfied [*befriedigt*].—One could also kiss the name of the beloved, and here the substitution by means of the name would be clear.

Kissing a picture (for example, a photograph) is a recognizable and perhaps even normal thing to do among ourselves; that is, among people who are brought up to kiss as a sign of affection and who are familiar with the pictorial representation of individuals. But the point of the practice—to the uncertain extent that it may in fact be a practice rather than a sentimental convention—is a matter of empirical psychology which cannot be presumed, only discovered. Perhaps in the minds of some it really does have an effect on the person represented, rather as blessing or prayer is taken to confer grace or protection at a distance. In the minds of others it may not be inspired by such a pragmatic confidence, but may express a longing, a wish, a hope, or else unease or desperation or whatever other state of mind may accompany the action. The likelihood, at any rate, must be that only the vaguest of affectionate commitments will inhere in the practice, and that an extensive variety of inner states and more or less clear-cut intentions can be accommodated by it.

The action of kissing a picture may or may not be aimed at some effect; this also is a matter of fact, not inference. But then the consequences for the actor will be just as uncertain. Wittgenstein states that "we feel satisfied," but as a matter of fact this is highly disputable. It can easily be conceived that the actor might instead feel frustrated, for example, or resentful or despondent after kissing the picture. And even if someone did say that he himself felt satisfied after doing so, it would not be at all clear what state he was reporting. We should at least have to elicit from him what his motive was, and what expectations he had in view, for only in the light of these factors could we begin to assess wherein he was satisfied. This alone, however, would still not be enough, for the actor's own explication could not always be accepted at face value; and even if what he said were accepted as being entirely candid, there might nevertheless subsist other factors of a subconscious nature which, if uncovered, could tell a different story. Moreover, in even the best of cases we should thus be provided with no more than the grounds for interpreting the actor's report that in the end he did feel satisfied; we should not know, just from that epithet, what was the peculiar quality of the inner state in question. The verb "to satisfy" means, with reference to feelings or needs, "to meet or fulfill the wish or desire or expectation of"; to be satisfied is "to be content (with)," to find something "sufficient" (*Shorter Oxford English Dictionary*). Surely none of these conditions obtains, typically, when someone kisses a picture. Only if kissing the picture were all he wanted to do could he be satisfied by doing only that.

Wittgenstein arrives at this example via that of burning in effigy, in connection with the Beltane custom. Although kissing a picture is less dramatic than mimicking the burning of a man—indeed, while conventional it is essentially private—it poses the same questions and gets the same answers as does any instance of what is ordinarily typed as ritual. When we designate ritual as symbolic action, the implication is that the analysis of it will be as intricate as is that of any other insti-

tutionalized form of action; the main difference is that the
"symbolic" aspect makes it all the more obscure and problematical. The intricacy and the obscurity together extend to
purposes, means, effects, inner states, and reasons. What is
enacted is not really carried out, but we are confronted with
representations and substitutions; the explanations that we
are offered do not explain; and the plausibility of metaphors
that seem at first to answer to the case also dissipates under
the intensity of analysis. For all the salutary changes of aspect
under which Wittgenstein exposes new facets of ritual, or
presents the familiar in inventive formulations, the topic is
still recalcitrant to a theoretical explanation.

VIII

If we take stock of the problem of ritual, in positive terms,
we find in Wittgenstein's remarks two propositions that are
particularly worth dwelling upon.

The first is that we have to do with the "ceremonial" in
contrast with the haphazard (5, 16). This reinforces the property of formality that we began by ascribing to ritual. Admittedly, the formality is not a specific feature, since, as we have
seen, it is shared by many other forms of conduct that we
should not wish to call ritual. Nevertheless, it is a characteristic feature (cf. Needham 1972:120–21), and it suggests a shift
of method. In other fields of investigation a useful precept, it
has been found, is to concentrate not on types but on properties; once these are isolated, the task is to see what they are
properties of (Needham 1978:57, 60), and only then may it
be helpful to circumscribe a type of social fact such as "ritual." In the present instance, the significant property is formality, and it is this property itself that might repay comparative examination. That would take us very far beyond ritual,
however, and for our present purpose we need not try to

foresee what the outcome of such a comparison might be. It is enough to remark the formality that is a characteristic feature of ritual, and to affirm that this property is well founded by empirical generalization. The generalization finds expression in Wittgenstein's remark that we might almost say that man is a "ceremonial animal" (7).

The other proposition to be retained from Wittgenstein's remarks, as a clue to what may be a significant property of ritual, responds to the question: What makes us unwilling to assume that the Beltane festival has always been celebrated in its present (or very recent) form? Wittgenstein replies, "We feel like saying: it is too meaningless to have been invented in this form" (17e). He compares the case with seeing a ruin and saying that it must have been a house once, for nobody would have set up hewn and irregular stones in such a pile as this. "And even where people really do build ruins, they give them the forms of tumbled-down houses" (17). Here the presumption is that the festival (rite) must once have had an intrinsic significance which, if it could be reconstructed, would constitute an explanation of the practice. But it is none the less a presumption, and the analogy with a ruined house is in fact crucially misleading. It may help us to see on what grounds people do tend to assume that there must once have been an intact and identifiable meaning to a rite, and that what we now observe are "ruins," relics, survivals that have lost their original form and significance. It does not, however, justify such an interpretation on the part of an analyst, who ought indeed to be skeptically on his guard against the temptations of precisely this kind of analogy. The comparison of a "meaningless" rite with a ruined house expresses a theory—and the theory is not proved by merely assuming the aptness of the analogy.

So a main question remains: Why should a supposedly original form of a rite have had any more clear and intrinsic a meaning than does the present form? After all, if a rite can be performed today by participants who ascribe disparate and even conflicting meanings to it, or if it can be properly performed even while appearing to be meaningless, why should its performance ever have been inspired by a clearer ascription of significance? What calls for examination is the very assumption that the rite must have had a clear meaning once.

In certain cases it may seem that an original meaning can be determined, and it may therefore appear that such rites exemplify a general rule which could explain other rites for which no such historical demonstration was possible. The Eucharist, again, is apparently such a case. But when Christ enjoined his disciples, "This do in remembrance of me," he was already drawing on a multifarious complex of meanings centered on the Passover and on Judaic dietary laws and commensual practices; and in these respects he was not inventing an integral significance that would constitute the unique explanation of the subsequent enactment of the rite. It could still be, of course, that some other rite would actually meet this condition, but in the normal run of things we have no means whatever of determining any earlier meanings, let alone a single original significance for any particular rite. This general fact takes us back, therefore, to the medley of interpretations by which participants in rites currently offer to explain what they are doing, and we have already seen that these provide no analytical explanation. If this situation can in some way be seen as comparable with a ruin, in that it lacks form or coherence or the fulfillment of a unifying intention, there are still no grounds on which to infer that it must at some former time have been any different.

The foregoing considerations stem from Wittgenstein's remark about our unwillingness to accept that a rite may be meaningless. The unwillingness may well be a fact, but that a rite must possess a meaning that is the explanation for its performance is not a fact. The question then is: Why can a rite *not* be meaningless? After all, if we cannot determine an original meaning, and if there is no unitary significance agreed to by its current participants, then we have already acceded to the very fact that in these regards there is no meaning. In that case, then, a rite can indeed be intrinsically meaningless.

Naturally, we could also say conversely that in the circumstances of the matter there can be a superabundance of meaning, in that a variety of opinions may be held about a rite and its origins and occasions, but this contention would not settle the point at issue. What we have been looking for is a meaning that will explain the rite, and in this respect it can well be that there is no such meaning to be established. More fundamentally, also, a rite could be meaningless in that even in the minds of the participants it was not regarded as having any significance beyond itself. It would be, in Waley's words, "customary" or "the thing to do" (1938:58)—and this is precisely the kind of statement that ethnographers so frequently meet with. It is not at all a queer state of affairs, in other words, for it is something that is encountererd all the time by professional investigators of formal symbolic behavior.

In that case, though, why do we not just accept what we already know? For it is a fact that ritual can indeed be meaningless in the sense required. It may well be that the purpose and meaning and effect of a rite will consist in no more than the performance of the rite itself. Ritual can be self-sufficient, self-sustaining, and self-justifying. Considered in its most characteristic features, it is a kind of activity—like speech or dancing—that man as a "ceremonial animal" happens naturally to perform.

8

Dumézil and the Scope of Comparativism

Ne considérer ni la hardiesse ni la prudence comme "la" vertu par excellence mais jouer de l'une et de l'autre, vérifiant sans cesse la légitimité de chaque démarche et l'harmonie de l'ensemble.

Georges Dumézil

I

When a polymathic scholar undertakes to reinterpret the ideological foundations of an entire field of civilization, as Dumézil has done for the Indo-European linguistic tradition, he is bound to meet opposition and criticism from specialists.

Some of the objections raised against Dumézil's arguments are textual and have to do with points of grammar and disputed readings. These issues are more or less straightforward, and they call for particular resolution; they do not affect Dumézil's method, and on this count in any case I can offer no contest to his critics. More important are those objections, whether in print or in common allusion, that attack the theory of the three functions. These criticisms are of two main kinds, and they are mutually contradictory.

On the one hand it is said that the theory is unsatisfactory because it is not universal, so that even if it is correct it is not a sociological proposition but a limited historical finding. Dumézil has never claimed, however, that the ideology of the three functions had a general theoretical application; he maintains that the ideology is characteristic of the Indo-European tradition—and if this is a limited finding, the limits are those of a great and ancient civilization.

On the other hand, it is objected that the three-function ideology can be found in non-IE civilizations—for example, in the Bible—and that it rests on so simple a division of labor as to be traceable anywhere. But Dumézil has made it quite plain that what he is concerned with is a classification that is intrinsic to a particular civilization; in that context, he has written, "le système est vraiment dans les faits," and those who employed the ideology in their myths, rites, and formulas were conscious of this system.

More specifically, criticism has been leveled at the Mitra-Varuṇa model of the sovereign function. Textual questions aside, a chief gravamen has been that the opposed personages are not clearly separated from each other but share attributes and tasks to such an extent that the complementarity asserted by Dumézil is not to be found in the ideology itself. Dumézil's own defense, offered already in the preface to the first edition (1940) of *Mitra-Varuṇa*, was that classifications are always less clear in practice than in theory, and that many ambiguities and compromises are only to be expected.

Clearly, this defense is forceful, not evasive. Any social ideal, however explicitly subscribed to by those who intend it to direct their lives, is liable to local adjustments, tendentious manipulations, various contradictions, and some degree of confusion. So if it is demonstrated that a partition of the sovereign function, in particular cases, is not fully carried into effect, this is not in itself a decisive refutation of the proposed complementary opposition. For that matter, if it can be shown that even ideally the ideology does not exhibit a clear partition, this too can be attributed to a normal erosion of categories; it does not necessarily mean that the theoretical construct is artificial or mistaken.

Much depends, of course, on the extent of the alleged disparities, but even in the event of a preponderance of ambiguities or contradictions there is still a methodological defense to be made. This is that a theoretical pioneer always has to go too far, to postulate more than he can be sure of, to exploit an idea beyond its due credit. When an advance cannot be well sustained, or a position cannot be held, it is easy enough to draw back within more defensible limits. It is the initial impetus that is really difficult, and this should not be reduced by theoretical inertia when what is at stake is the prospect of an advance.

There is, however, a contrasted precept of method which I suspect lies behind much of the resistance to Dumézil's ideas. This is that one should propose only what one is absolutely sure of, and venture no further beyond this point until it is safe to do so.

Which of these methodological alternatives is adopted depends on at least two factors which are not to be decided by considerations of method alone. The first consists of criteria of certainty which themselves are, as Wittgenstein has shown (1969), infinitely disputable. The second factor is that of individual predispositions, and these are even less calculable. The criteria of certainty can at least be argued, but they too may reflect unargued inclinations of a personal nature that cannot strictly be argued with.

At first sight, therefore, the contrast of approach between the bold and the prudent does not seem susceptible to a purely methodological resolution. If the Mitra-Varuṇa partition of sovereignty is called into question, in the respects so far adduced by certain of Dumézil's critics, the outcome is likely to be determined by influences that are not written into either theory or criticism. But there is a further test of Dumézil's ideas that I should like to propose, namely to resort to comparison by structural analysis outside IE civilization. Ultimately, this test also is likely to lead back to the irresolutions that have just been mentioned, but at very least it offers a vantage point from which the issue may be seen under a new aspect.

II

Three examples will serve to make the case; two of them have latterly been recapitulated in my *Reconnaissances* (1980), where also the ethnographic authorities are listed, so I can be brief. One example comes from Africa, another from eastern Indonesia; the third refers to a type of organisation that is found in a number of areas and linguistic traditions.

The Meru of Kenya were organized traditionally into a segmentary system of clans. There was no centralized government, and no supreme head such as a king. Instead, all kinds of juridical, political, and economic decisions were in the hands of the clan elders. In addition there was in each sub-tribe a personage called the Mugwe; his function was essentially to bless, and this activity was indispensable to such major events as the constitution of age-sets, marriage, war, and the sentencing of offenders. The jural power of the elders and the mystical authority of the Mugwe stood in a relation of complementary opposition; that is, sovereignty was partitioned between them, each party having a distinct role, and neither was sufficient for the governance of Meru society without the other. In my original analysis of this system, first published in 1960, I made a special point of the striking similarity of the Meru institutions to the Mitra-Varuṇa model of sovereignty as represented by Dumézil. This similarity is especially noteworthy, furthermore, in the symbolism of the partition: elders ($\equiv$ Mitra, jurist) are associated with this world, the day, masculine, senior, and the right; the Mugwe ($\equiv$ Varuṇa, magician) is associated with the other world, night, feminine, junior, and the left.

The Atoni of Timor, eastern Indonesia, had a centralized polity in addition to the segmentary order of political territories and clans (Schulte Nordholt 1971, chap. 6). The prince resided at the centre of the domain; his designation, *atupas*, comes from the verb *tup*, to sleep, so that the prince was the sleeper. He was not permitted to be active, but had to remain in his palace, "inside." He was the guardian of the sacra of the domain, and was the principal officiant in charge of the state rituals of fertility and warfare. The prince was described explicitly as "feminine" (*feto*), and was thus contrasted with the "masculine" (*mone*) lords, *usif,* of the four quarters, ordered by the cardinal points, that surrounded the center. These lords were war-leaders and "executive authorities," hence politically active. There were also in the quarters, and thus also in the masculine outside, persons known as "great fathers"; they were the major custodians of land, and the adjudication of disputes was also their responsibility. They were wife-givers to the prince, and they were economically superior to him in that they fed the ruler by bringing him harvest gifts. In these regards there was a certain "balance of power" between the ruler in the interior and the lords and great fathers on the exterior. The partition of sovereignty in this case was not absolute, for the prince had the political power to issue orders, and those on the outside had ritual functions, but there subsisted nevertheless a characteristic symbolic opposition of the Mitra-Varuṇa type: outside/inside, active/passive, masculine/feminine, jural/mystical.

My third example is that of systems of asymmetric prescriptive alliance. Societies of this type are marked by their own peculiar complications, and the analysis of them can run into technical difficulties, but structurally they are exceedingly simple. A society of this kind is ordered by an absolute classification in which descent lines and categories are articulated by a constant relation; women, goods, and services are conveyed in only one direction (whence the designation "asymmetric"), proper to each class of valuable, and never in the reverse sense. Affines stand to one another in enduring relations as wife-givers and wife-takers, and this opposition is crucial to the constitution of the society. It is characteristic of asymmetric systems that sovereignty is partitioned between the line of reference (for example, one's own agnates) and one or other of the two categories of affines. Jural power rests with lineal kin, and mystical influence is ascribed to one party of affines, but systems vary as to whether the latter will be wife-givers or wife-takers. Among the Karo of Sumatra, Indonesia, it is the wife-givers who are the sources of mystical benefits; they are "visible gods." Among the Purum of Manipur, on the Indo-Burma border, it is on the contrary the wife-takers who are in charge of all rituals in which their wife-givers are the principals (cf. Needham 1979, chap. 6). These occasions include name-giving, marriage, entry into a new house, funerals; and in none of them can a Purum act without the mystical aid of his wife-takers. In these societies, then, there is a partition of governance between the jural power of agnates and the mystical authority of a category of affines. The variation in the side (wife-giving or wife-taking) that is ascribed mystical influence emphasizes the importance of the partition in itself; what counts is not which party does what, but that there is a constant relationship of complementary governance in agreement with the Mitra-Varuṇa scheme.

There are numerous other societies or institutions in world ethnography from which the Mitra-Varuṇa principle of diarchy can be illustrated, but the present examples should serve to make the comparativist's point. Common features of the partition are: (1) structural, namely bipartition, opposition, complementarity; (2) iconic, namely darkness, passivity, femininity, the left. The symbolic attributes can vary, and in asymmetric systems (in which wife-givers are normally associated with the masculine, whatever their ritual status) there is not such a regular concordance as in other social forms. Nevertheless, the Mitra-Varuṇa mode of opposition recurs with striking frequency on a global scale, and very often with characteristic symbolic attributes as well. In its definitive form it can indeed be said that the system is in the facts. Whether those who live by it are in every case

conscious of the system is an open question; what is sure is
that they need not be deliberately aware of the structural
aspect, or even the ideological order, of the dual form of
sovereignty.

III

A recourse to wider comparison, on a scale that subsumes instances from far beyond the area of IE civilization, tends
therefore to confirm the validity of Dumézil's analyses of the
sovereign function.

The admitted uncertainties in Dumézil's readings of the
texts on the Mitra-Varuna relationship can be thought to lose
some of their weight once it is seen that this opposition is
only one expression of a principle that has an extremely wide
distribution. More fundamentally, the case can even be made
(as I have tried to expound in *Reconnaissances*, chap. 3) that
the principle stands for a natural proclivity of thought and
imagination, and that it may be the unconscious product of a
"cerebrational vector" in the representation of those sovereign powers to which men conceive themselves as subject.

Whatever may be thought of these constructions put on the
ethnographic evidences, the facts themselves compose a remarkable complex. Binary classifications are of course thor-
oughly commonplace (more than eighty years ago Tarde
already made light of "ce charme facile et décevant de collec-
tionner des antithèses"), and the notion of opposition is one
of the most antique in all epistemology; so it can be no great
surprise that sovereignty—in its most general sense—should
be conceived in such a form. But what could hardly have
been expected is that in this particular instance the opposed
terms should carry distinct but complementary values and
that these should be symbolized by a characteristic imagery.
It is this complex of structure, values, and images that tends

to support Dumézil in his analyses of the sovereign function. The principle of diarchy is not peculiar to IE civilization and was not invented by it: it is a principle with a world-wide distribution, and it has no exclusive association with kingship or the state or the characters of gods.

Nevertheless, there is a main objection foreseeable from among Dumézil's critics. This is that the evidences adduced above are alien data, having no historical connection with IE civilization; that is, that they do not belong to the same tradition, and therefore cannot have the same meaning. One response to this objection is to ask whether Mithra-Ahura and Mitra-Varuṇa, which are closely related within the same tradition, have the same meaning. In their particulars, and in their social settings, clearly they do not; yet a student of IE civilization would not therefore reject the structural similarity between the couples, since they are confidently taken to be historically connected. But is derivation from a common source, within the same linguistic tradition, the only criterion of common significance? If Zoroastrian and Vedic ideas are mediated by translation into English or French, the common features are well represented in a medium that is distinct from each realm of sovereignty, and in terms that are not dependent on common IE linguistic forms; the assimilation could as well be effected in Indonesian, Nahuatl, or Chinese, yet the structure and content expressed originally in Avestan and Sanskrit would subsist. Suppose it were then revealed that one of the languages translated was not Avestan after all but Atoni: the historical connection would be gone, but the principle of diarchy (the "Mitra-Varuṇa" partition of sovereignty) would remain just as evident.

It has to be conceded, however, that this argument is implicitly a resort to structural analysis—that is, to a reliance on relational abstractions—and it is precisely this method of comparison that is in question. The purist could still maintain that the significance of a concept of sovereignty was to be had only in the vernacular and in its proper social setting. But this is not a position that the majority of Dumézil's critics, I think, would be likely to take up. It is not comparison that they object to, but comparison beyond a certain limit. Well, how is this limit to be decided on? I am contending that Dumézil's interpretation of the sovereign function is confirmed by non-IE evidences; and this contention rests on the practical premise that the comparativist in world ethnography recognizes *no* limit. For him, the criteria of significant resemblance are not linguistic and historical but are provided by: (1) relations, for example, opposition, transitivity; (2) forms, such as iconic, spatial, institutional; (3) values, such as superiority, passivity, fertility. Demonstrations of the effective employment of these criteria are to be found in investigations into the binary structure of systems of symbolic classification, the preeminence of the right hand, the structural and symbolic correspondences of systems of prescriptive alliance, the standard components of the imagery of witchcraft, or the operations of the imagination as collectively manifested in myth (Needham 1973a; 1978). Naturally, the force of these demonstrations rests too on the premise that there need be no limits to comparison, so that logically they cannot overcome an obdurate resistance that is premised on the semantic constraints of linguistic tradition. But it can at least be hoped that a structural comparison of representations of sovereignty will have indicated that the limits of historical connection do not necessarily set concomitant limits on comparativism.

The fact that civilizations classify things differently, by contrasting values and for various purposes, does not impede a global comparison of forms of classification. The disparate things that men say in different languages, and the variable significances that they attach to their utterances, do not reduce the possibility of comparing grammatical forms and modes of reasoning. More particularly, the comparative study of the symbolism of the sides (see *Right & Left*, 1973) shows that a conceptual scheme, expressing constant semantic values and accompanied by characteristic imagery, can be securely established on a global scale; also that the significant structure thus determined can be a reliable instrument in the interpretation of further ethnographical cases.

In the light of these considerations, therefore, I propose that Dumézil's Mitra-Varuṇa analysis of the sovereign function should be approached from the reverse direction to that of the specialist, namely in the perspective of world ethnography. Instead of beginning with one well-known cultural conception of sovereignty and then seeking ideological resemblances more widely within the IE tradition, it is advantageous to adopt the principle of diarchy as established by global comparison and then to analyse the IE cases by reference to the most general features that the principle is known to assume. Seen from this point of view, the IE conceptions of sovereignty will then be recognized the more readily as variants of the same semantic structure as are the ideologies of the Meru, Atoni, Karo, Purum, and uncounted other non-IE societies. On this scale of comparison, the textual uncertainties and other particular difficulties in Dumézil's analyses of the IE sovereign function should recede in importance by contrast with the revelatory potential of the principle of diarchy.

Fundamentally, nevertheless, it still has to be conceded that what is found acceptable as the scope of comparativism is still in the end a matter of individual inclinations towards boldness or towards prudence. Here also, as so often in the austere craft of scholarship, the determining factor is a matter of temperament.

9

An Ally for Castaneda

"An 'ally,'" he said, "is a power a man can bring into his life to help him, advise him, and give him the strength necessary to perform acts, whether big or small, right or wrong."

Carlos Castaneda

I

One of the most general attitudes among mankind is a fascination with the exotic. This more or less excited attention to what is culturally strange receives various social expressions: sometimes it is suspiciously abjured, as by Islam; sometimes it is chauvinistically repressed, as in Tokugawa Japan; often it is regarded with a wariness that is itself a recognition of the powerful allure of the alien.

Among anthropologists—including perhaps some of the best of them—a main impulsion in their avocation is, typically, a romantic interest in what is strange, colorful, and distant. This form of curiosity about foreign parts and far-off peoples is testified to as far back as we have historical indications, though it was not until the Enlightenment that it was disciplined into a distinct form of scientific inquiry. Even thereafter, it was not until the latter part of the nineteenth century that respectable schemes of explication were collaboratively conceived, and the practice of ethnographic investigation by the theorists themselves had to wait until the twentieth century. With this development, however, there emerged a change of attitude among comparativists that could hardly have been foreseen: the enticing colors of the exotic faded almost entirely, and professional ethnographic reports became distinguished instead by a sober factuality that increasingly frustrated a growing taste for the exotic. The professional attitude, indeed, hardened against any such provision, and ethnographic reports that stressed or even acknowledged the exotic, in an adventurous sense, stood out by virtue of their rarity. Malinowski's *Sexual Life of Savages* (1929) was one; von Fürer-Haimendorf's *The Naked Nagas* (1939) was another; and in recent years there has been, significantly as we shall see, Barbara Myerhoff's *Peyote Hunt* (1974). In the event, then, the very people who were most firmly committed to the interpretation of the exotic found their reasons, some of these doubtless excellent, for declining to meet the general desire for narratives conveying the piquancy of the outlandish. But the desire is not to be denied, and if professional ethnographers as a class do not satisfy it then others will.

A prior question, though, is just what it is that people are looking for in the exotic. Probably there are as many reasons as those that inspire any imaginative delight in the fictional, beginning with the abrogation of constraint that is effected by evasive fantasies of many kinds, including myth, drama, novels, and dreams. This felicitous immunity from the irksomeness of material or conceptual limitations corresponds to a normal proclivity of the imagination, and it appears to meet longings that are characteristic of the unconscious (Needham 1978, chap. 3). These properties of the psyche, being intrinsic characters, are irrepressible and insatiable, and they find their most convenient exercise in a free purchase on the alien and alternative among social forms. Society is an immediate source of constraint, but distant societies may appear to have it in their gift to confer a liberation. An account of an exotic form of life can therefore respond to such inclinations and wishes, and with the added assurance that what is so deeply desired is not merely imaginable but is real and attainable.

A most remarkable example of orectic ethnography, and indeed the most highly successful venture of the kind, is Carlos Castaneda's *The Teachings of Don Juan*, first published in 1968. This extraordinary story was followed by a series of other books about Don Juan and his mystical lessons, beginning with *A Separate Reality* and extending so far to *The Eagle's Gift*. The present analysis will be confined almost entirely to the first and second titles, though it was the *Teachings* that scored the really impressive success. Opinions about the merits of this work have been various; some have found the writing, for instance, to be outstanding, whereas others have found it clumsy and unconvincing. But we do not have to rely on such essentially contestable literary criteria, for the extent of Castaneda's appeal has been abundantly attested in other respects: a general furor about the Don Juan saga, both within and without the anthropological profession; the great number of publications devoted to Castaneda and his works (de Mille 1980:489–510, References); and reported sales of the Don Juan books running into millions. What does this singular success tell us about what people want from exotic ethnography?

In some respects it tells us no more than the Don Juan public have clearly enough told us for themselves in their other manifestations of fashionable commitment. Thus it is well recognized that the *Teachings* responded to dominant concerns of the drug culture in the late 1960s; it contributed to a rejection of the establishment and to a search for alternative realities; it promised a direct route to an "understanding" of life, bypassing formal instruction and rational argumentation; and in general it catered to an escapism from everyday constraints into a realm of magical powers. *A Separate Reality* corresponded, in its explicit "lessons," to a move in the youth culture, after the excesses of hallucinogens, toward a more sober and reflective approach to the quandaries of life. Most recently, it may not be simply coincidental that, in a period of forceful feminism, *The Eagle's Gift* includes a number of feminine characters in the cast of seekers and that the leading part, after that of Castaneda as narrator, is played by a woman. In such respects, it could be suggested, it is as though the potential readers first voiced their concerns and the ethnographer then responded to them.

There is nothing inherently objectionable in this supposed dialogue, for it is only to be expected that an ethnography, if it were fundamental enough, should be capable of answering to interests of disparate kinds. Nor is there anything improbable in the idea that the teachings of one man should attach severally to drug-induced alterations in consciousness, to moral didactics, and to feminism. What is more deeply significant, in the present perspective, is that these various expressions of inspiration should have their source in an Indian from the deserts of northern Mexico. It is this solitary figure—exotic, certainly, to Los Angeles and Oxford—whose mystical dedication has exerted, through the self-depreciating medium of Carlos Castaneda, such a remarkable effect on the distant parts to which the Don Juan saga has been propagated. From any point of view, this is a most intriguing phenomenon, and to a comparativist it calls for at least as serious a scrutiny as do such standard topics as eight-section systems or the *kula* ring or the prominence of the mother's brother.

Not the least striking aspect of this phenomenon is that serious doubt has repeatedly been cast on the essential authenticity of the Don Juan saga. To judge by the many considerations so far adduced, there is a perturbing possibility that Don Juan does not exist; or to be more precise—since Castaneda reports that Don Juan has "disappeared from the face of the earth" (1982:9)—there are serious reasons to conclude that he never did exist, and that the entire sequence of narratives about him is an ingenious fiction. The most powerful battery of critical charges to this effect is to be found in *Castaneda's Journey* (1978), by Richard de Mille, and in the subsequent

Don Juan Papers (1980), compiled by de Mille. The outcome of these skeptical inquiries is, with no concession to any kind of qualification, that the story is a "hoax." Let us take this finding as the premise to the analysis that follows. There is no call to hazard an independent assertion to this effect, but only to entertain as a working hypothesis the conclusion to which de Mille's persuasive arguments appear so cogently to lead. The Don Juan saga, then, will be treated as though it were a construction of Castaneda's imagination. But the imagination has to have something to work on, and, if we are to understand something of the enormous impact procured by this adventure in the exotic, we need to identify the sources that have contributed to that effect.

De Mille has listed numerous publications which he identifies as the originals of one or another idiom or event or theme in the Don Juan corpus (de Mille 1980:390–436, "Alleglossary"), and in doing so he raises the question of how many of Castaneda's sources remain buried in library stacks. His answer is: "Many, . . . for it seems to me that *every* element of don Juan's teachings could be traced . . . to some earlier publication" (1980:392). The intention of the present essay is to identify a possible source which has not so far been mentioned but which appears to have made a more important contribution to the *Teachings* and to *A Separate Reality* than any other.

II

An element that runs throughout the series of Castaneda's books is the theme of power. "Knowledge" is also constantly lauded, and it is commended as the object of the apprentice's efforts, but this knowledge is itself defined by reference to power. What is the power for? One aim is to protect the man of knowledge from the inimical power of others; this is a pragmatic tautology. Another major aim is to subjugate others to his arbitrary will, even to the extent of killing them; this is a self-centered and amoral exercise. There is no need, however, to assess the value of either of these aims in order to consider another question: How is the power to be acquired? The answer is: by submission to a master, in prolonged obedience and by arduous training.

This relationship is one element that is truly constant in the Don Juan series. The master is unremittingly in control, while the apprentice is supplicatory, confused, self-doubting. The master varies his attitude toward his pupil in an apparently capricious manner; he evokes respect, affection, fear, anger, bewilderment, despair. Nothing the master does can be contested or resisted, even if he resorts to violent denunciation or destructive mockery. He does not need to prove anything, either by argument oғ by demonstration; everything he asserts or commands is to be acceded to, taken on trust, without demur. This asymmetrical relationship between Don Juan and Castaneda is definitive, even in the events ascribed to the time after the master's disappearance. Without it, the mystical pedagogy would lose much of its force and its exemplary character. If the "Yaqui way of knowledge" were described merely as a system of institutionalized ideas and practices, lacking the central inspiration of the personage named as Don Juan, a very great deal of the arresting drama and the sense of contact with mystical authority, not to mention the effect of reportorial cogency (cf. Needham 1978:76), would surely be lost. If Castaneda adopted this relationship, as a unifying focus and theme of his saga, from some published source (as de Mille affirms in general), where did it come from?

There are very many possible exemplars, and from probably as many settings as there are esoteric doctrines to be transmitted. But one that seems to fit particularly well, in many of the respects just listed, is the relationship between a Zen master and his pupil. Zen is only glancingly mentioned by de Mille, and it is not in the index to either of his books, though there are a few allusions by other authors that point in that direction. Boyd, in considering the teachings of Don Juan from a Buddhist point of view, cites the Buddhist precept that a seeker must "come and see" for himself what the Truth is; and he makes a parallel between this and the case of Don Juan's man of knowledge learning how to "see" (Boyd 1976:220, 221; cf. 228). Oates, in a brief published letter, concludes by observing: "I must confess a temperamental preference for the 'seeing' of—let's say—a Dr. Suzuki" (Oates 1976:69); and the suggestions for further reading at the back of the compendium in which the letter is reprinted include the selected writings on Zen Buddhism by D. T. Suzuki. Forisha (1978) has noted a strong resemblance between Don Juan's teachings and Suzuki's *What Is Zen?* but she does not attribute the resemblance to Castaneda having read Suzuki (cited in de Mille 1980:303). The parallel passages, listed in de Mille's "Alleglossary" (1980:429 s.v. Self-b), may be thought to suggest metaphysical agreement, as de Mille proposes, but it is less easy to think them distinct enough to argue for literary influence. The model could not in any case have been this particular work by Suzuki, either for the *Teachings* or for *A Separate Reality*, since it was not published until 1971; a more likely source would be Suzuki's easily available paperback *Zen Buddhism*, which was first published in 1956. Sukenick, finally, remarks that "Don Juan's teachings have so many similarities with Zen" (1976:113). The secondary literature on Castaneda and his teacher is extensive, so it is not easy to be confident on the score, but it appears that a connection with Zen is not a line of investigation that has been intently followed.

Yet consider, to begin with, the following dialogue:

"What must I do, then?" I asked thoughtfully.

"You must learn to wait properly."

"And how does one do that?"

"By letting go of yourself, leaving yourself and everything yours behind you so decisively that nothing more is left of you but a purposeless tension."

"So I must become purposeless—on purpose?" I heard myself say.

"No pupil has ever asked me that, so I don't know the right answer."

"And when do we begin these new exercises?"

"Wait until it is time."

To a reader of *The Teachings of Don Juan* this exchange will have a familiar ring, from the self-observant adverb in the opening question to the tantalizing obscurity of the concluding answer. It comes from *Zen in the Art of Archery*, by Eugen Herrigel (1953:47–48; hereafter to be cited as *A*), and the main contention of this part of the argument is that there are such correspondences between Herrigel's monograph and the first two Castaneda titles as to make it appear that the former may have been a prime source of certain characteristic features of the latter. In addition, there is another work under Herrigel's name, *The Method of Zen* (1960; henceforth cited as *M*), which was compiled from among the papers left at his death. It is highly probable that an interested reader of one of these two attractive little books on Zen would take up the other as well, and an ancillary contention of the present argument is that the *Method* also could have been a formative influence on Castaneda's description of Don Juan and his teachings.

Some points of background information are worth noting. Both of Herrigel's books were published, in English translation, quite a number of years before *The Teachings of Don Juan* was published in 1968. *Zen in the Art of Archery* was reprinted four times (in 1956, 1959, 1964, and 1968) by that date; since then it has been reprinted, as a paperback, five times to the present date (1982). *The Method of Zen* has been reprinted three times (in 1969, 1976, and 1979). On the fair assumption that Castaneda did not read German, we need pay no attention to the German originals. Herrigel died in 1955.

Eugen Herrigel was a German philosopher who went to Japan in 1924 and stayed there, teaching at Tohoku University, in Sendai, for six years (G. Herrigel 1958:1). During that period he underwent instruction from a Japanese master in the art of archery as a "religious ritual" and as an ability the origin of which is to be sought in "spiritual exercises" (*A*:14). He was taught that archery, although no longer a practical part of war, was still a matter of life and death, to the extent that it was "a contest of the archer with himself" (15). His teacher was one of the greatest masters of this art in Japan (23), named Kenzo Awa (28–29). The master did not seek out Herrigel as a pupil, but on the contrary he at first refused Herrigel's request for instruction (29). In reporting the course of his teaching, which lasted the full six years (23), Herrigel writes: "I have no alternative but to recollect in detail all the inhibitions I had to fight down, before I succeeded in penetrating into the spirit of the Great Doctrine" (24). For mastery of the bow and arrow, far from consisting in a merely technical facility, is a mystical enterprise; the ultimate aim of the prolonged and wearing discipline is to attain the point at which "archery, considered as the unmoved movement, the undanced dance, passes over into Zen" (89). At the end of his protracted course of instruction, Herrigel had become "a different person"; touched by the spirit of the art of archery, he was to find on his return to his own country that "things . . . no longer harmonize as before" (90). This profound transformation, involving the acquisition of a doctrine (or body of knowledge) and a new apprehension of the self, was the product of utter submission to a master who had himself undergone the same strenuous apprenticeship.

Herrigel described his individual training in *Zen in the Art of Archery*, and the principles behind it in *The Method of Zen*. These two accounts can appositely be compared with *The Teachings of Don Juan* (hereafter cited, following de Mille, as *J*), in which Castaneda describes his apprenticeship, and *A Separate Reality* (henceforth *R*), in which he relates the method of mystical perception. A convenient way to make the comparison is to proceed through a dozen particular topics, from one point of correspondence to another, until the extent of overall conformity between the two sets of writings can be gauged. The case is not to be made by the force of any one instance but by accumulation. In each instance we shall first take Herrigel, as the hypothetical exemplar, and then Castaneda.

III

1. *Dramatic idiom.* Early in the treatise on the method of Zen, Herrigel describes the capabilities of the great masters: their psychological experience is "astounding," and they can do the most "amazing" things, sometimes bordering on the "incredible" (*M*:13). For practical ends, they concede the justification for the split into subject and object, though at a certain point this threatens "danger and disaster" (39). At a particular stage of higher meditation the subject feels "shattered, exhausted" (82).

Many commentators (for example, Douglas 1975:193) have remarked on the high-pitched style of Castaneda's narratives, the overwrought language in which he describes Don Juan's behavior or his own reactions. After an experience with peyote, on awakening to "serious, sober consciousness," he realizes that he had forgotten he was a man; "the sadness of such an irreconcilable situation was so intense that I wept" (*J*:44). Faced with the prospect of acquiring certain kinds of knowledge, he is "overwhelmed" by his fears (55). His very time scale has a dramatic extension; when he grinds a cupped handful (118) of seeds in a mortar, the task takes "four hours" (107); when he has to stir a mixture of dry gruel and a handful of lard into a smooth consistency, he whips the materials for "nearly three hours" (124). Holding a lizard, he has a peculiar sensation of "physical despair" (109); at a rustle in the underbrush, he wants to "scream or weep" and he falls to the ground, "whining"; in a panic, he remains in a state of "profound distress" for "several hours" (185). In his states of drug-induced dissociation, naturally enough, Castaneda's experiences call for greater intensities of expression, but even commonplace activities are reported in a tone that is decidedly histrionic. On the third day of his instruction, while merely sitting on the floor, he is told by Don Juan that he is very tired and he realizes that he is "quite exhausted" (30).

2. *The setting.* Herrigel states that he will "consciously refrain from describing the setting in which the instruction took place, . . . and above all from sketching a picture of the Master" (*A*:24). His reason for doing so is that everything must hinge on the art of archery itself.

Castaneda declares that it is not his intention to determine Don Juan's "precise cultural *milieu*" (*J*:18), and his accounts of physical settings are usually lacking in distinctive detail. It would not be possible, on the basis of Castaneda's descriptions, to identify Don Juan or his house or any other part of the setting of the instruction. The allusions to features of the Sonoran desert environment are exceedingly general, and Sebald finds that in numerous telling details of flora, fauna, and climate the desert Castaneda writes about is "quite unlike" the Sonoran desert (Sebald 1980:34); the natural setting, he concludes, is "imaginary" (38). Castaneda does not explain his deliberate vagueness or the numerous incongruities.

3. *Silence.* Herrigel reports the silence of a Zen priest in the presence of a supplicant; this is not felt by the other person as indifference, but "it is as if this silence had more meaning than countless words could ever have" (*M*:102).

When Castaneda was introduced to Don Juan, in the now famous Greyhound bus station, they shook hands and then remained silent for some time. "It was not a strained silence, but a quietness, natural and relaxed" (*J*:13).

4. *The teacher's attitude toward his pupil.* In Zen, the teachers "suppress their pupils, hold them in contempt" (*M*:12). A master is "uncompromising, strict, brusque" (21); he behaves with "pitiless severity" (22), and may dismiss a pupil with "evident disapproval" (28). Herrigel's teacher "mocked" him for his rigidity (*A*:44).

Don Juan laughs "scornfully" at Castaneda (*J*:23); he delivers a stern warning that if his apprentice does not solve a problem he may as well leave, for he will have nothing to say to him (31); he looks at Castaneda with "contempt," and addresses him in a "belligerent" tone (45); in response to a question, he replies "cuttingly" (128). After the report of what seems an ordinary encounter on a highway, he says to Castaneda that "only a fool like you" would think it unimportant (*R*:38). Repeatedly, he accuses Castaneda of "not listening" (*J*:31; *R*:40).

5. *Blows.* In Zen monasteries, a pupil performing breathing exercises may be given "a smart blow" on the back (*M*:24). When he is in a state of spiritual tension "a painful blow" may induce enlightenment (29). During archery lessons, Herrigel's master repeatedly presses one of his leg muscles in a "particularly sensitive" spot (*A*:36).

At the culmination of *A Separate Reality*, when Castaneda is overtaken by "an indescribable anguish" at the encumbering weight of his reason, Don Juan gives him "a quick blow" with the knuckles on the top of his head (*R*:268). In *The Eagle's Gift*, the female apprentice La Gorda recounts that Don Juan would give her "a sound blow" over or around her right shoulder blade; "the result was her entrance into an extraordinary state of clarity" (Castaneda 1982:148). Some "weeks" after this, Castaneda happens to remember that the same had been the case with himself; "at any given time don Juan might give me a blow on my back," high on the spine between the shoulder blades, and "an extraordinary clarity would follow" (148).

6. *Turning the back.* At a certain point in his training, Herrigel unintentionally provoked the extreme displeasure of his teacher. "The Master . . . sat down on a cushion, his back towards me. I knew what that meant, and withdrew" (*A*:71).

While searching for peyote with Don Juan, Castaneda inappositely pointed some out to his teacher and impulsively ran toward them. "He ignored me and deliberately kept his back turned as he walked away. I knew I had done the wrong thing . . ." (*J*:92).

7. *Categories.* "The Zen priest's attitude to everything has always been characterized by a renunciation of all categories of judgment" (*M*:90).

"Reflecting upon the phenomena I had experienced, I realized that my attempt at classification had produced nothing more than an inventory of categories. . . . That was not what I wanted" (*J*:19).

8. *Understanding experience.* In the transformation of a Zen pupil by enlightenment (*satori*), he seeks solitude and tranquility; "he wants only to clarify what has happened to him" (*M*:50).

Castaneda reports that during the months following his

withdrawal from the apprenticeship "I needed to understand what I had experienced" (J:19).

9. *Solutions.* The Zen *kōan*, an obscure and testing proposition that has been referred to as a conundrum, calls for the "solution" to be seen; rather than being invented, the solution has to be found (*M*:37); the pupil repeatedly fails to see the answer (26–30).

Don Juan tells Castaneda that he has to find a spot on the floor where he can sit without fatigue: he adds that he has "posed a riddle" that Castaneda has to "solve" (J:30–31, cf. 34). Castaneda repeatedly fails to find the solution before he sees the correct spot (32–35).

10. *Lotus position.* In order to perform Zen breathing exercises it is required that the meditant sit in the cross-legged lotus position, and "so much depends on the position being comfortable" (*M*:23, 24).

During a nighttime vigil, in the course of a peyote hunt, Castaneda is lying on a rock floor and keeps changing his position every few minutes. Finally he sits up and crosses his legs; "to my amazement this position was supremely comfortable" (J:94).

11. *The plucked string.* Early in Herrigel's instruction in archery, the Master grasps a bow and lets the bowstring fly back several times; "this produces a sharp crack mingled with a deep thrumming, which one never afterwards forgets when one has heard it only a few times: so strange is it, so thrillingly does it grip the heart" (*A*:30–31). Herrigel adds that from ancient times this sound has been credited with "the secret power of banishing evil spirits . . ." (cf. Blacker 1975:106; Morris 1971:292 n. 115, 342 n. 392; 1979:144–5, 178; Nijō 1983:45).

Don Juan took Castaneda out into the desert, then extrac-

ted a cord from his pouch; he looped it round his own neck
and stretched it with his left hand until it was taut. "He
plucked the tight string with his right hand. It made a dull,
vibratory sound" (*R*:167); then he kept plucking the string
while increasing the tension, and this, combined with his
voice, produced "a weird, unearthly vibration" (168). Later,
Don Juan explained that the string is a "spirit-catcher" (169).
It is a fiber with which allies or certain spirits can be called;
these spirits are helpers, but they are "hard to handle and sort
of dangerous"; "one needs an impeccable will to hold them at
bay" (233).

12. "*Seeing.*" In Zen, the specifically spiritual training starts
with "purification of the power of vision" (*M*:22); *satori* (enlightenment) is "a new way of seeing" (46).

A Separate Reality is divided into two parts: "The Prelimi-
naries of 'Seeing'" and "The Task of 'Seeing.'" Don Juan asserts that "only by *seeing* can a man of knowledge know"
(*R*:16); he stresses the word "see," incidentally, with a peculiar inflection (31).

(a) In a Zen painting, objects stand fully revealed in their
actuality; hence the impression of "continual evanescence"
(*M*:54).

Don Juan says we live in a "fleeting world"; the apprentice
has to be taught to "see," and only smoking a certain hallucinogenic mixture can give the necessary speed to catch a
"glimpse" of that world (*R*:13–14, cf. 117).

(b) Herrigel quotes Suzuki on the characteristics of *satori*:
"it is an illuminating insight into the very nature of things"
(*M*:31). In painting, it is a "vision of pure essence" (23). The
Zen priest has "the capacity to discover, in a purely receptive
vision, the essential character of an event or object" (90).

Castaneda writes that "seeing" entails a process by which a
man of knowledge allegedly "perceives the 'essence' of the
things of the world" (*R*:13–14).

(c) When a Zen priest has attained *satori*, "the things he sees

are no different from before, he just sees them differently"
(*M*:30). The center of being is beyond all opposites such as
identity and difference (61, 62).

Don Juan says: "Things don't change. You change your way
of looking, that's all" (*R*:43). Asked by Castaneda whether a
given tree remains the same every time you "see" it, he replies: "No. It changes and yet it's the same" (43).

(d) Herrigel opines that the first characteristic of "the new
way of seeing" (*satori*) is that "all things are of equal importance in its sight"; they are "all of equal rank" (*M*:32).

Don Juan says that a man of knowledge "knows, because
he *sees*, that nothing is more important than anything else"
(*R*:90); he illustrates this by saying that when we merely
look at things we catch the funny edge of the world, but that
"when our eyes *see*, everything is so equal that nothing is
funny" (*R*:88).

(e) Herrigel emphasizes that "there is not the slightest trace
of reflection in this way of seeing" (*M*:32), that is, in *satori*;
"this new vision . . . is, strictly speaking, indescribable" (30);
"everything depends on . . . 'seeing'" (34, cf. 45), and then
there is "no further need of the controlling or reflecting intelligence" (*A*:57).

Don Juan explains to Castaneda that "in the case of *seeing*, . . . thinking is not the issue at all, so I cannot tell you
what it is like to *see*" (*R*:91); "only by *seeing*" can one
know (16).

(f) Discussing a certain truth, Herrigel asserts that "you *see*
it in a seeing that is not-seeing" (*M*:92); "there is nothing like
an ego or self any more" (94). In Zen archery, "everything
depends on the archer's . . . effacing himself" (*A*:57).

Don Juan says that "upon learning to *see* a man becomes
everything by becoming nothing" (*R*:160).

(g) In Zen, "there is no direct way from the ordinary
way of seeing . . . to this new vision conditioned by *satori*"
(*M*:30); "you instantly 'see' . . ." (33).

Don Juan tells Castaneda about "seeing" that "there is

really no way to talk about it"; "*seeing* . . . is learned by *seeing*" (*R*:177).

IV

The parallels that have just been listed are not the only points of significant agreement between Herrigel's works and the first two titles in Castaneda's saga of Don Juan, but they are the most striking.

On the other hand, it is not contended that Herrigel's books alone can be considered the sources of the listed elements in Castaneda's narratives. It is noteworthy, to begin with, that, whereas the "seeing" parallels run throughout *A Separate Reality*, the parallels between Herrigel and Castaneda run out, as it were, early in the fourth chapter of *The Teachings of Don Juan*. Moreover, there are works by other authors that can be identified as possible sources of certain elements. De Mille has traced, for instance, the "spirit-catcher" to some remarkably similar passages in works by Furst and by Myerhoff on the Huichol, who tap on a bowstring to make a music that calls to spirits (de Mille 1980:430–31, s.v. Spirit-catcher). Heelas has suggested that the element of "seeing" corresponds to a passage in Aldous Huxley's *Doors of Perception* in which Huxley writes of the necessity to "look at the world directly" and not through the distorting medium of concepts (quoted in de Mille 1980:428, s.v. Seeing). Mary Douglas says that "impeccable," Don Juan's ideal epithet for a warrior, is only slightly different from the Christian "Be ye perfect" (Douglas 1975:196; cf. Matt. 5:48)—though it now seems more likely to reflect the Zen idea that "the true swordsman must also be 'a perfect man' in the Taoist sense" (Suzuki 1959:159; cf. index, s.vv. Man, perfect). Don Juan's allusion to the "fleeting" nature of the world may be connected with the ideal of Zen masters to grasp "this fleeting life" (Suzuki

1956:130), and so on. But these are fairly particular or slight coincidences, it may be thought, whatever their genetic role may conceivably have been, by comparison with the cumulative impact of the concerted parallels with the writings of Herrigel.

When there are so many precise correspondences between the publications of two authors, both writing on the theme of mystical training and insight, there is clearly a call for some kind of explanation.

Mary Douglas, reviewing the first three Castaneda titles, contends that "in itself the philosophy of ascetic mysticism, so gradually pieced together, is enough evidence of truth in the tale" (1975:193). With particular reference to the dialogue with Don Juan, she writes that: "The translation reeks with clichés of spiritual writing in all the traditions which have flowed into our language. . . . No wonder the books have sometimes been dismissed as imaginative fiction" (196). Notwithstanding this plausible imputation, she still finds it necessary to accept the three books as "a serious challenge," on the ground that "the naiveties of expression can be taken as evidence of authenticity" (197). While she concedes that the clichés may make it difficult to judge "the spirituality of the religion" revealed in the sequence of titles, she nevertheless asserts that "it would be more difficult to defend formally the view that their echoing of contemporary philosophical concerns is proof of their bogus character" (cf. de Mille 1980:436, s. v. Wittgenstein). Her reason for taking this view is that the three works are "consistently" knitted into an attitude toward life and death and human rationality whose very "coherence" is alien to our own contemporary thought (199). After a glancing allusion, not readily intelligible, to "secular modern Zen," Douglas concludes: "The young apprentice [namely Castaneda] may have imposed more than he realized of our own culture upon the non-doing of 'seeing'" (200).

The review itself is not wholly consistent, and its argument is rather hard to make out, except that the general tenor is in favor of the authenticity of Castaneda's works. None of its main contentions, however, is at all convincing. Naiveties of expression cannot be evidence of authenticity unless one also has other evidences of authenticity which incidentally explain the style of expression. Coherence is in itself no evidence either for or against authenticity; a clever writer of bogus ethnography will easily make his inventions coherent, and a cleverer one perhaps will contrive to make them just as inconsistent as may be plausible. Clichés of spiritual writing can be autonomous precepts of a genuine mysticism, especially when they are read in a translation (and Castaneda's mother tongue, after all, is not English), or they may be hackneyed formulas that have been lifted from comparative religion. If a cosmological attitude is alien to our own contemporary thought, this quality itself is no touchstone of the true; a fabricator might well devise a doctrine that was deliberately alien, and in any event we should need to know whether or not it agreed with some other tradition that was not only alien but was also known to scholarship. As for Castaneda having imposed on Don Juan more of our own culture than he realized, this is an issue touching on his good faith, and that is not to be determined by a charitable supposition.

All of these matters, however, are subsidiary to an unstated premise that appears to underlie Douglas's reception of the Don Juan narratives. This is the assumption that Don Juan's mysticism resembles other systems of transcendental ideas because he shares with them a common vision of ultimate reality. According to this view, there is a perennial philosophy that is globally subscribed to by mankind, or to which men are naturally inclined, and it is by virtue of this pattern of thought that we detect so many resemblances among the mystical doctrines of otherwise different civilizations. There is nothing intrinsically unacceptable in this idea. Eliade has plotted numerous similarities of doctrine and symbolism in shamanism as practiced around the world (Eliade 1964); Matilal has focused analysis on the extremely widespread declaration that mystical experience is ineffable (1975); and there are other arguments that certain cultural constituents and symbolic complexes are primordial characters of thought and imagination (Needham 1978). It could well be, therefore, that some general features of mysticism were aspects of a worldwide perennial philosophy of existence; and in that case it would be readily acceptable, and even (with precautions) persuasive, that the ideas attributed to Don Juan should in such respects agree with the tenets of mystical traditions elsewhere in the world.

This is all very fine, but a generic congruence of the kind cannot account for the particular parallels that have been detected between Herrigel and Castaneda. These points of agreement are so individual and so numerous as to lead to the inference that, given the chronology of their respective publications, Castaneda would appear to have adopted the common features from Herrigel's writings. Formally speaking, of course, there is also the possibility that both writers borrowed the same set of elements from some other and yet prior source, but the practical likelihood of this is fairly negligible. It is hard, then, to resist the conclusion that a crucial inspiration of the first two Castaneda titles, and especially of *A Separate Reality*, is to be traced back to Herrigel's two monographs on Zen.

This is not to deny, nevertheless, the trenchant contrasts between Castaneda's narratives and Herrigel's disquisitions. The Don Juan saga is Dionysiac in spirit: illumination is induced by hallucinogenic drugs; Castaneda pukes thirty times after taking peyote (*J*:46), and he pisses all over a dog and also gets pissed on (48); his mystical visions tend to be gruesome, terrifying, and deranged. The Zen method of instruction, on the other hand, is Apollonian: enlightenment is attained by an exacting discipline, such as years of training in archery; it is intended to inculcate a "mastery of form" (*A* : 58); its outcome is a mystical vision that confers clarity and tranquility. But these are obvious and characteristic differences, easily admitted, whereas the argument for derivation is made by the resemblances, and the impact of these is independent of the contrasts.

On the premises stated earlier, therefore, the verdict of the present analysis would appear to stand: namely that certain features of the two Don Juan titles presently in question have their source in the two works by Eugen Herrigel.

V

Granted the seeming cogency of the argument, inferential though it has had to be, we need to consider next what consequences follow from it.

What is most to be desired, of course, is that Castaneda should say whether or not the inference is correct; but he has not so far made any direct published response to his critics, even to de Mille, and there are obvious reasons to surmise that he is unlikely to do so. Moreover, he has in fact given a printed indication of what his reaction to the present hypothesis would be likely to be. In the prologue to *The Eagle's Gift*, he declares: "I must first of all reiterate that this is not a fiction" (Castaneda 1982:8). It is not clear if this assertion is meant to apply to that particular book alone, or whether it is meant to cover the previous titles as well. Castaneda also writes, however, as if in defense of the authenticity of his narrative: "What I am describing is alien to us; therefore, it seems unreal" (8). What he describes in all of his previous books is similarly alien, so it could be that he intends to state that they are not fiction either. Yet it is not because the Don Juan corpus makes an alien impression that critics have doubted its veracity, and it is not solely on the ground of an apparent unreality that the narratives have been thought fictional. The present analysis, for instance, postulates a literary source in publications about Zen, which is certainly an alien form of life to most westerners; also, the ideas and idioms are real enough in Zen, only they are not very likely to be precisely replicated in the discourse of a putative Yaqui Indian. If the Don Juan tales are taken to be fictional, this will be for reasons other than those intimated by Castaneda. Perhaps, too, there is another uncertainty in the matter. Just as it is not clear what Castaneda denotes by the word "this" (in "this is not a fiction"), so it may be that he has some more or less private connotation in mind when he uses the word "fiction."

Doubts on these scores are not allayed by a further declaration that Castaneda goes on to make. He says he finds himself in a difficult position, and: "all I can do under the circumstances is present what happened to me *as it happened*" (1982:8, original emphasis). He cannot give "any other assurance" of his "good faith," he continues, except to reassert that he does not lead a "dual life" and that he has committed himself to follow Don Juan's system in his everyday existence. Points of interpretation left aside (such as the significance of "dual," whether or not that is what is in question), this form of assurance cannot, in the circumstances, procure a complete conviction in Castaneda's favor. Psalmanaazaar averred as much, and more definitely, in the preface to his *Description of Formosa* (1704): "I assure you," he declared, "I have not positively asserted any thing which is not as positively true" —and yet his ethnography was entirely fictitious. On the barest supposition, therefore, that the Don Juan corpus may also be fictitious, it would not do much good if Castaneda were to affirm publicly and unambiguously that he did not adopt anything from Herrigel's books into his own, or for that matter if he were to state that he had never even read them. If he were in fact a hoaxer or a trickster, in de Mille's words, that is just what he would say.

Without prejudging that contingency, and without assenting to the suppositious premise, we can easily appreciate the appalling consequences when an ethnographer's integrity is called into question. These may not seem to matter beyond the limits of the dubious ethnography, even if it can be proved counterfeit; if the fraud is recognized as such, it may be thought, no harm is done once it has been expunged from the records of trustworthy ethnography. But unfortunately the consequences do not stop there. When suspicion has once set in, it continues to spread its taint, and into places that perhaps it should never have been allowed to touch. This contamination can, in the present case, affect the very works that have been identified as possible sources for the Castaneda titles, and the correspondences with the Don Juan tales reflect on them also.

VI

The uneasiness attaches in the first place to *Zen in the Art of Archery*. Read in parallel with the Castaneda successors, this otherwise attractive and illuminating monograph provokes some worrying little doubts. One is struck by the ring of the dialogue, by the shadowy character of the Master, by the deliberate vagueness about the setting.

Any implicit imputations, however, find immediate defenses. The work carries, after all, a foreword by Daisetz T. Suzuki, a renowned scholar and exponent of Zen, who calls it a "wonderful little book" (*A*:9). The archery master is identified: he is "the celebrated Master Kenzo Awa" (28–29). Herrigel's introduction to his future teacher was effected by a colleague, who is also identified: he is Professor Sozo Komachiya (28). This all looks convincing enough, but the defenses are themselves countered in part by the very comparison that evoked them. *The Teachings of Don Juan* also carries a professional foreword, by Walter Goldschmidt, a professor of anthropology at the University of California, Los Angeles. In this book as well the teacher is identified: he is "Juan Matus." The person who introduced Castaneda to Don Juan is named too, if only as "Bill" (*R*:7–8). Then it turns out that Suzuki's encomium was later rather qualified; discussing a Zen poem about archery, he appends a note in which he writes merely, in a slightly depreciating way, that this is what Herrigel "tried" to learn from his master (Suzuki 1959:120 n.). So inevitably one begins to wonder, and to worry anew. There are in fact a number of occasions for grave consideration.

The first is the long time that elapsed between the experience in Japan and the eventual publication. Not that this matters in itself, but it affects one's response to what is reported as discourse. Herrigel went to Japan in 1924 and returned from there in 1929; the book on archery was not published until nearly twenty years later. Yet much of the impact of *Zen in the Art of Archery* is produced by the immediacy of the very numerous details concerning the progress of the instruction, including in particular the quotation of many conversations between master and pupil. Herrigel says he relies upon "unforgettable memories and notes which I made at the time" (1953:12). The materials for this book could thus have been brought together two decades before it was printed; but suppose that the details were recollected so many years after the events, or were perhaps to some extent reconstructed, and the reader's confidence must wane. This source of worry attaches especially to the conversations and to the doctrinal explications of the master. The worry is hardly reduced by the assurance in Herrigel's preface (1953:12; cf. 1948:6—not in later printings of the German edition) that "there is no word in this exposition which the Master would not have spoken, no image or comparison which he would not have used."

Herrigel writes that Komachiya "participated as interpreter" in the long course of instruction (A:29). The course lasted for almost six years. We are not told how often Herrigel received instruction, but the impression given is that it was frequent and without significant break. Did a professional colleague at Tohoku University really accompany the German philosopher to each lesson and interpret for him for six years? We must not underestimate Japanese loyalty and steadfastness, but it does not seem very probable. Komachiya had already been taking lessons in archery for twenty years (28), moreover, so it is certainly improbable that he participated in elementary lessons imparted to a beginner. Perhaps, then, Herrigel at once started to learn Japanese, and as soon as he was proficient enough released his colleague from his friendly commitment. In that case, though, one is struck afresh by the intrinsic complexity of much of the discourse. Here is the master talking about how the bowstring should be held as a little child holds a proffered finger: "Completely un-selfconsciously, without purpose, it turns from one to the other, and we would say that it was playing with the things, were it not equally true that the things are playing with the child" (45). This was uttered relatively early in the course of instruction, at the stage next after learning simply to draw the bow. One wonders how the pupil managed to comprehend such expressions, unless his colleague was still interpreting. At any event, matters later became deeper, for, as we know, archery is a spiritual exercise and it exemplifies the "Great Doctrine" (57).

The incidence of quoted conversations drops off as the report progresses, but the subtlety of the instruction tends to increase. After Herrigel has for the first time made a correct shot, the master says: "You are entirely innocent of this shot. You remained this time absolutely self-oblivious and without purpose in the highest tension . . ." (74). Later, Herrigel asks how it is that hits on the target should be "only outward confirmations of inner events" (a difficult enough expression, incidentally), and the master replies with a long discourse beginning: "You are under an illusion . . . if you imagine that even a rough understanding of these dark connections would help you" (80). The entire book takes the reader through so many dark connections, and obscurities that appear without connections, that it seems indeed a marvel that Herrigel should have been able to record them accurately, let alone achieve an understanding of them that he could later purvey to his readers. No doubt paraphrase is responsible for much that we read in his narrative, but a great part of the book is actually presented as the master's verbatim utterances, and it is this aspect, in the circumstances, that must give a reader pause. If in some respects an artful form has been given to them, in the interest of apparent immediacy or conviction or didactic development, we can only speculate about the respects in which *Zen in the Art of Archery* is to be taken as a strictly factual report.

Another occasion to reconsider the descriptive status of the book is an extremely dramatic feat of archery reported to have been achieved by the master. Herrigel is trying to understand how the archer is supposed to be able to hit the target without having aimed the arrow (*A*:80). He suggests to the master that after all his years of practice he acts involuntarily with the certainty of a sleepwalker, though he does not consciously take aim. The master concedes that there may be something in this, but that his seeing the target in this way is not enough, "for I see the goal as though I did not see it" (81). Herrigel blurts out that in that case the master ought to be able to hit the target blindfold. The master (after a perturbing glance) tells him to return the same evening, and they meet in the brightly lit practice hall. The master tells Herrigel to put a taper [actually a kind of joss stick], long and thin as a knitting needle, in front of the target, but not to switch on the light in the target [stand]. "It was so dark that I could not even see its outlines, and if the tiny flame [minute glow] of the taper had not been there, I might perhaps have guessed the position of the target, though I could not have made it out with any precision" (82).

The master shoots, and his first arrow flies "out of dazzling brightness into deep night." The sound tells that it has hit the target; and so does the second. "When I switched on the light in the target-stand, I discovered to my amazement that the first arrow was lodged full in the middle of the black, while the second arrow had splintered the butt of the first and ploughed through the shaft before embedding itself beside it." The master says that Herrigel will think that the first shot was no great feat, because after so many years he is so familiar with the target-stand that he must know even in pitch darkness where the target is. But what about the second arrow striking the first? "I at any rate know that it is not 'I' who must be given credit for this shot" (83). Herrigel is virtually hit by both of his master's arrows, and he is "as though transformed" overnight.

Well, this is indeed an amazing tale. No doubt such things can happen, though even with a target rifle, and in the best conditions of lighting and steady support, it would be at least exceedingly difficult to replicate the feat. But it is not the sheer technical difficulty that prompts worry, nor the statistical probability of the trick coming off just in this particular instance. What gives pause is more the fact that this kind of tale is so common in Zen literature. Over and over again one finds a sort of parable in which a pupil or seeker or challenger has a crucial encounter with a master and is suddenly led to *satori* by a shock of some nature; this may be a gnomic utterance, a physical assault, or a demonstration of supreme mastery. Instantly the subject is transformed by *satori*; the abrupt lesson puts him into a state of enlightenment. In one such narrative the great Zen Master Shōjū Rōnin is asked by an experienced swordsman to teach him the mystery (*myō*) of the art; Rōnin strikes him with his fists and kicks him; he then has a *satori* and the experience opens up a new vista on swordsmanship (Suzuki 1959:203–4). In another encounter, some visiting swordsmen cast doubt on Shōjū Rōnin's real ability, and they challenge him; he bids them strike, but instead of wielding a sword he holds only a fan; they fail to strike him, but his fan is everywhere, and they acknowledge their defeat (204). The superb demonstration of supremacy, based on spiritual attainment, destroys the expectations of the pupil and leaves him with the realization of enlightenment. Against this standard recourse in the rhetoric of Zen, it is telling that Herrigel should write that "the Master had evidently hit me, too, with both arrows," and that afterwards he was as though "transformed."

A third occasion for reflection on Herrigel's narrative has to do with the Master's illustration of one of the incomprehensible "dark connections" that have been mentioned. The master says that it should not be forgotten that even in Nature there are correspondences which cannot be understood but which yet are real and are accepted as though they could not be otherwise. He gives Herrigel an example that he says he has long puzzled over: "The spider dances her web without knowing that there are flies who will get caught in it" (*A*:80). He uses the verb "dances," instead of "spins," probably because he has just been explaining that shooting with the bow and arrow, which is a "ceremony," must be performed rather as a good dancer dances (77). The instructional pertinence of the example is that in a similar way the archer hits the target without aiming.

The image of the spider and the flies is certainly striking, and memorable as well. A reader of Herrigel's relation may, however, also remember these lines: ". . . The spider spins her web in order to catch flies. She does this before she knows that there are flies in the world." They were written about 1784 by Lichtenberg (1971:181), known chiefly as an aphor-

ist and admired by Goethe, Schopenhauer, Nietzsche, and
Wittgenstein. As a stylist he is famous in German literature,
and his philosophical perspicacity has frequently been recognized, as for instance by Waismann (1968:6, 196, 198, 200,
202–3). A German philosopher, like an Austrian one, would
almost certainly have known of Lichtenberg and would have
been quite likely to be familiar with his writings, which were
repeatedly anthologized and reprinted from 1800 onward (see
list in Promies 1964:165).

Nevertheless, Herrigel ascribes the anecdote to his Zen
master, who is quoted verbatim, and we can only speculate
on the close correspondence with Lichtenberg's observation
in the eighteenth century. Perhaps the image is so natural as to
strike the reflective observer in any century or culture; but, if
it is, there arises the question why it is not far more common
than it appears to be, and then why it should occur just to a
German physicist and a Japanese archer.

The final occasion for a reassessment of Herrigel's writings
is presented by an enigmatic proposition in *The Method of
Zen*. He is discussing the spiritual exercises by which a Zen
priest is trained into detachment. The essential thing is for
him to become ego-less, so that his self turns into an unknown quantity; the ego-self must vanish (*M*:73). Herrigel
explains that this does not mean that the individuality of the
priest is merely submerged into the spirit of a group. Instead,
"'I' should rather be replaced by 'It'" (74, cf. 76).

This too is a striking proposition, and one can see how
aptly it registers the pitch of selflessness that the Zen postu-
lant aims at. It encapsulates, also, an epistemological objection to the Cartesian premise of the necessity of the thinking
subject. But again there is a distracting echo. In 1797 or 1798,
Lichtenberg commented in one of his notebooks: "One should
not say 'I think,' but 'it thinks,' as one says, 'it is lightning' [*es
blitzt*]" (1971:501). At another place, he elaborates the point
by adding that to say "cogito" is already too much, once this

is translated as "ich denke," I think. To suppose or postulate the "I" is a practical requirement (412); that is, not an existential verity. All we really know is the existence of our experiences, ideas, and thoughts—not the existence of the "I." The aphorism about "I" and "it" has acquired a considerable currency in western philosophy, especially, it seems, after it was advertized by Waismann (1968:196, 198), and it could easily have been more readily accessible to a German philosopher who was at all familiar with Lichtenberg's writings.

Nevertheless, Herrigel reports the spiritual precept of Zen as though it were an independent proposition that is proper to Japanese tradition. It may be such, but the possibility does not remove all question from the mind of Herrigel's reader. If both Lichtenberg and Zen arrive at the same conceptual point, despite the grammatical dissimilarity of German and Japanese, that is most interesting. On the other hand, if Herrigel is repeating Lichtenberg, for the sake perhaps of a suitable paraphrase (or even possibly without realizing that he does so), then the correspondence acquires another kind of interest.

VII

The present investigation began with a question about what people look for in the exotic. The writings of both Castaneda and Herrigel give much the same answers, namely: understanding, in the form of esoteric knowledge; authority, in the relationship of respectful submission to a master; achievement, by way of hazardous or strenuous training.

This is not to say that those to whom these writings so much appeal would themselves be prepared to do what the authors describe. This is not the point; what matters in the first place is to identify what the readers appear to seek. Why it is that westerners should look to Mexico or Japan for the vicarious satisfaction of their desires is a question that comparison cannot answer, any more than it can account for the notions that distant places are more colorful and that their inhabitants are less oppressed by the constraints of social life and the frustration of inner yearnings. Nor is the form of the civilization of evident importance; there is little resemblance between a shack in the Sonoran desert and a practice hall, as a stage for antique ceremony, in Japan. As for the persons of the mystical mentors, here too there is a great contrast: on the one hand, a practically indigent Indian, on the other a renowned Master of a publicly revered national art. What each inspiringly stands for, nevertheless, is the practical feasibility of attaining a mastery over the self and a comprehension of the ultimate sense of human existence.

These are great and admirable ambitions, but when reflected in exotic forms of life they are distorted unless two greater conditions obtain: an unimpugnable integrity on the part of the reporters, and a rigorous exactitude in what they relate. These conditions themselves are not to be met except by discipline and insight, and their attainment calls for a prior commitment that makes its own arduous and unremitting demands.

Castaneda has published, in phrases of impressive resonance, what for him has been the cost of such an enterprise. "In order for me to proceed with my scrutiny," he declares (1982:8), "I have to make an extraordinary daily payment, my life as a man in this world."

General Bibliography

Acton, Alfred
    1955 Preface to Swedenborg (1955): ix–xxxi.

Anon.
    1875 *A Critical Examination of the "Science of Correspondences" or System of Biblical Interpretation promulgated by Swedenborg.* London: Trubner.
    1965 "After Homer." Review of Davenport (1964). *The Times Literary Supplement*, February 4:86.

Archilochus
    1958 *Archiloque: Fragments.* Texte établi par François Lasserre; traduit et commenté par André Bonnard. Paris: Société d'Edition "Les Belles Lettres."
    1964 *Carmina Archilochi: The Fragments of Archilochos.* Trans. Guy Davenport. Foreword by Hugh Kenner. Berkeley and Los Angeles: University of California Press.

Augé, Marc
    1979 *Symbole, fonction, histoire.* Paris: Hachette.

Bachelard, Gaston
    1942 *L'Eau et les rêves.* Paris: José Corti.
    1949 *La Psychanalyse du feu.* Paris: Gallimard.

Banerjea, Jitendra Nath
    1956 *The Development of Hindu Iconography.* Second ed., rev. and enl. Calcutta: Calcutta University Press.

Beckett, Samuel
    1970 *Le Dépeupleur.* Paris: Editions de Minuit.

Beidelman, T. O.
    1964 "Pig (*Guluwe*): An Essay on Ngulu Sexual Symbolism and Ceremony." *Southwestern Journal of Anthropology* 20:359–92.

Blacker, Carmen
    1975 *The Catalpa Bow: A Study of Shamanistic Practices in Japan.* London: George Allen & Unwin.

Bogg, John Stuart
   1915 *A Glossary on the Meaning of Specific Terms and Phrases used by Swedenborg in his Theological Writings, given in his own Words.* London: Swedenborg Society.

Borges, Jorge Luis
   1968 *Other Inquisitions, 1937–1952.* Trans. Ruth L. C. Simms. New York: Simon and Schuster.
   1976 *Doctor Brodie's Report.* Trans. Norman Thomas di Giovanni, in collaboration with the author. Harmondsworth: Penguin Books.
   1981 *Labyrinths: Selected Stories and other Writings.* Ed. Donald A. Yates and James E. Irby. Preface by André Maurois. Harmondsworth: Penguin Books.

Bosch, F. D. K.
   1960 *The Golden Germ: An Introduction to Indian Symbolism.* The Hague: Mouton.

Bouveresse, Jacques
   1977 "L'Animal cérémoniel: Wittgenstein et l'anthropologie." *Actes de la Recherche en Sciences Sociales* 16 : 43–54.

Boyd, James W.
   1976 "The Teachings of Don Juan from a Buddhist Perspective." In Noel (1976) : 219–28.

Brochard, Victor
   1887 *Les Sceptiques grecs.* Paris: Imprimerie Nationale.

Browne, Thomas
   1658 *Hydriotaphia: Urne-Buriall.* London.

Bury, R. G.
   1933 Introduction to Sextus Empiricus, *Outlines of Pyrrhonism*: vii–xlv.

Castaneda, Carlos
   1970 *The Teachings of Don Juan: A Yaqui Way of Knowledge.* Harmondsworth: Penguin Books. First ed., Berkeley and Los Angeles: University of California Press, 1968.
   1973 *A Separate Reality: Further Conversations with Don Juan.* Harmondsworth: Penguin Books. First published, New York: Simon and Schuster, 1971.
   1982 *The Eagle's Gift.* Harmondsworth: Penguin Books.

Coomaraswamy, Ananda K.
1957 *The Dance of Shiva*. Rev. ed. New York: Noonday Press.

Davenport, Guy
1964 *Carmina Archilochi*. See Archilochus (1964).

Descartes, René
1649 *Les Passions de l'âme*. Amsterdam.

Diehl, Ernst, ed.
1952 *Anthologia Lyrica Graeca*, fasc. 3. Leipzig: Teubner.

Douglas, Mary
1975 "The Authenticity of Castaneda." In idem, *Implicit Meanings: Essays in Anthropology*, chap. 13. London: Routledge & Kegan Paul. Reprinted in de Mille 1980:25–31.

Dumézil, Georges
1948 *Mitra-Varuṇa: essai sur deux représentations indo-européennes de la souveraineté*. Second ed. Paris: Gallimard.

Durkheim, Emile
[1915] *The Elementary Forms of the Religious Life*. Trans. Joseph Ward Swain. London: George Allen & Unwin.

Durkheim, Emile, and Mauss, Marcel
1963 *Primitive Classification*. Trans. and ed. with an introduction by Rodney Needham. Chicago: University of Chicago Press.

Edmonds, J. M.
1931 *Elegy and Iambics*, vol. 2. Loeb Classical Library. London: William Heinemann; Cambridge: Harvard University Press.

Eliade, Mircea
1964 *Shamanism: Archaic Techniques of Ecstasy*. Trans. Willard R. Trask. New York: Bollingen Foundation.

Emerson, Ralph Waldo
1850 *Representative Men*. London: Chapman.

Feeley-Harnik, Gillian
1981 *The Lord's Table: Eucharist and Passover in Early Christianity*. Philadelphia: University of Pennsylvania Press.

Forisha, Barbara
1978 "Castaneda: Humanist and/or Mystic?" *Journal of Humanistic Psychology* 18:29–35.

Fürer-Haimendorf, Christoph von
    1939 *The Naked Nagas.* London: Methuen.

Gordon, Leonard H. D., ed.
    1970 *Taiwan: Studies in Chinese Local History.* New York: Columbia
          University Press.

Hawthorne, Audrey
    1967 *Art of the Kwakiutl Indians and Other Northwest Coast Tribes.* Van-
          couver: University of British Columbia; Seattle: University of
          Washington Press.

Herrigel, Eugen
    1948 *Zen in der Kunst des Bogenschiessens.* Konstanz: Weller.
    1953 *Zen in the Art of Archery.* Trans. R. F. C. Hull. Foreword by
          D. T. Suzuki. London: Routledge & Kegan Paul.
    1958 *Der Zen-Weg.* Comp. and ed. Hermann Tausend. München-
          Planegg: O. W. Barth.
    1960 *The Method of Zen.* Ed. Hermann Tausend. Trans. R. F. C. Hull.
          London and Henley: Routledge & Kegan Paul.

Herrigel, Gustie [Auguste Luise]
    1957 *Der Blumenweg.* München-Planegg: O. W. Barth.
    1958 *Zen in the Art of Flower Arrangement.* Trans. by R. F. C. Hull.
          Foreword by Daisetz T. Suzuki. London: Routledge & Kegan
          Paul.

Hopkins, Keith
    1980 "Brother-Sister Marriage in Roman Egypt." *Comparative Studies
          in Society and History* 22:303–54.

Hsieh, Chiao-min
    1964 *Taiwan—Ilha Formosa: A Geography in Perspective.* Washington,
          D.C.: Butterworth.

Hume, David
    1758 *Enquiries concerning the Human Understanding.* London.

Hussey, Edward L.
    1972 *The Presocratics.* London: Duckworth.

Johnson, Samuel
    1755 *A Dictionary of the English Language.* 2 vols. London.

[Kant, Immanuel]
    1766 *Träume eines Geistesehers, erläutert durch Träume der Metaphysik.* Riga.

Knox, Robert
    1681 *An Historical Relation of the Island of Ceylon in the East-Indies.* London: Richard Chiswell.
    1911 *An Historical Relation of Ceylon.* Ed. James Ryan. Glasgow: James MacLehose & Sons.

Kramrisch, Stella
    1981 *The Presence of Śiva.* Princeton: Princeton University Press.

Lalande, André, ed.
    1951 *Vocabulaire technique et critique de la philosophie.* Sixth ed. Paris: Presses Universitaires de France.

Lasserre, F., and Bonnard, A.
    1958 *Archiloque.* See Archilochus (1958).

Lévy-Bruhl, Lucien
    1904 *La Morale et la science des moeurs.* Second ed. Paris: Alcan.

Lichtenberg, Georg Christoph
    1968 *Schriften und Briefe,* vol. 1: *Sudelbücher.* Ed. Wolfgang Promies. Munich: Carl Hanser.
    1971 *Schriften und Briefe,* vol. 2: *Sudelbücher II, Materialhefte, Tagebücher.* Ed. Wolfgang Promies. Munich: Carl Hanser.

Lloyd, G. E. R.
    1964 "The Hot and the Cold, the Dry and the Wet in Greek Philosophy." *Journal of Hellenic Studies* 84:92–106.
    1973 "Right and Left in Greek Philosophy." In Needham, ed. (1973a), chap. 9.

Locke, John
    1690 *An Essay concerning Human Understanding.* London.

MacKay, George Leskie
    1896 *From Far Formosa: The Island, Its People and Missions.* Edinburgh and London: Oliphant, Anderson & Ferrier.

Malcolm, Norman
    1966 *Ludwig Wittgenstein: A Memoir.* London: Oxford University Press.

Malinowski, Bronislaw
    1929 *The Sexual Life of Savages.* London: Routledge & Kegan Paul.

Matilal, B. K.
    1975 "Mysticism and Reality: Ineffability." *Journal of Indian Philosophy*
          3:217–52.

Melville, Herman
    1857 *The Confidence-man: His Masquerade.* London.

Mille, Richard de
    1978 *Castaneda's Journey: The Power and the Allegory.* London: Sphere
          Books.
    1980 ed., *The Don Juan Papers: Further Castaneda Controversies.* Santa
          Barbara, Calif.: Ross-Erikson.

Moore, Sally Falk
    1958 *Power and Property in Inca Peru.* New York: Columbia University
          Press.

Morris, Ivan
    1971 *The Pillow Book of Sei Shōnagon.* Harmondsworth: Penguin
          Books.
    1979 *The World of the Shining Prince: Court Life in Ancient Japan.*
          Harmondsworth: Penguin Books.

Myerhoff, Barbara
    1974 *Peyote Hunt: The Sacred Journey of the Huichol Indians.* Ithaca,
          N.Y.: Cornell University Press.

Needham, Rodney
    1960 "The Left Hand of the Mugwe: An Analytical Note on the
          Structure of Meru Symbolism." *Africa* 30:20–33. Reprinted in
          Needham (1973a), chap. 7.
    1963 Introduction to: Durkheim and Mauss (1963): vii–xlviii.
    1972 *Belief, Language, and Experience.* Oxford: Basil Blackwell; Chi-
          cago: University of Chicago Press.
    1973a ed., *Right & Left: Essays on Dual Symbolic Classification.* Chi-
          cago and London: University of Chicago Press.
    1973b "Prospects and Impediments." *The Times Literary Supplement,*
          July 6:785–86.
    1974 *Remarks and Inventions: Skeptical Essays about Kinship.* London:
          Tavistock Publications; New York: Harper & Row.

1975 "Polythetic Classification: Convergence and Consequences." *Man*, n.s. 10:349–69. Reprinted in Needham (1983), chap. 3.

1976 "Skulls and Causality." *Man*, n.s. 11:71–88. Reprinted in Needham (1983), chap. 4.

1978 *Primordial Characters*. Charlottesville: University Press of Virginia.

1979 *Symbolic Classification*. Santa Monica, Calif.: Goodyear Publishing. Distributed by Random House, New York.

1980 *Reconnaissances*. Toronto: University of Toronto Press.

1981 *Circumstantial Deliveries*. Quantum Books. Berkeley and Los Angeles: University of California Press.

1983 *Against the Tranquility of Axioms*. Berkeley and Los Angeles: University of California Press.

Nijō
1983 *The Confessions of Lady Nijō*. Trans. Karen Brazell. London: Zenith Books.

Noel, Daniel C., ed.
1976 *Seeing Castaneda: Reactions to the "Don Juan" Writings of Carlos Castaneda*. New York: G. P. Putnam's Sons.

Oates, Joyce Carol
1976 Letter to Daniel C. Noel. In Noel (1976):69.

O'Flaherty, Wendy Doniger
1973 *Śiva: The Erotic Ascetic*. London: Oxford University Press.

Pascal, Blaise
1964 *Pensées*. Edition Brunschwicg. Introduction and notes by Ch.-M. des Granges. Paris: Garnier.

Patrick, Mary Mills
1899 *Sextus Empiricus and Greek Scepticism*. Cambridge, England: Deighton Bell.

Plotinus
1967 *Enneads, III. 1–9*. Trans. A. H. Armstrong. Loeb Classical Library. London: William Heinemann; Cambridge: Harvard University Press.

Promies, Wolfgang
1964 *Georg Christoph Lichtenberg, in Selbstzeugnissen und Bilddokumenten*. Reinbek bei Hamburg: Rowohlt.

Rankin, H. D.
1977 *Archilochus of Paros*. Park Ridge, N.J.: Noyes Press.

Rhees, Rush
1982 "Wittgenstein on Language and Ritual." In Brian McGuinness, ed., *Wittgenstein and His Times*: 69–107. Oxford: Basil Blackwell.

Richter, Gisela M. A.
1965 *The Portraits of the Greeks*. 3 vols. London: Phaidon Press.

Rose, Henry
1675 *A Philosophicall Essay for the Reunion of Languages*. Oxford.

Rudich, Norman, and Stassen, Manfred
1971 "Wittgenstein's Implied Anthropology: Remarks on Wittgenstein's Notes on Frazer." *History and Theory* 10:84–89.

Schulte Nordholt, H. G.
1971 *The Political System of the Atoni of Timor*. Verhandelingen van het Koninklijk Instituut voor Taal-, Land- en Volkenkunde 60. The Hague: Martinus Nijhoff.

Sebald, Hans
1980 "Roasting Rabbits in Tularemia." In de Mille (1980):34–38.

Sextus Empiricus
1955 *Outlines of Pyrrhonism*. Trans. with an introduction by R. G. Bury. Loeb Classical Library. London: William Heinemann; Cambridge: Harvard University Press.

Sigstedt, Cyriel Odhner
1952 *The Swedenborg Epic: The Life and Works of Emanuel Swedenborg*. New York: Bookman Associates.

Sukenick, Ronald
1976 "Upward and Juanward: The Possible Dream." In Noel (1976): 110–20.

Suzuki, D. T.
1956 *Zen Buddhism: Selected Writings*. Ed. William Barrett. Garden City, N.Y.: Doubleday.
1959 *Zen and Japanese Culture*. Bollingen Series 64. Princeton: Princeton University Press.
1971 *What Is Zen?* London: Buddhist Society.

Swedenborg, Emanuel
    1778 *A Treatise concerning Heaven and Hell.* London.
    1781 *True Christian Religion; containing the Universal Theology of the New Church.* 2 vols. London.
    1784 *Clavis Hieroglyphica Arcanorum Naturalium & Spiritualium, per Viam Repraesentationum et Correspondentiarum.* London.
    1875 *The Earths in the Universe, and their Inhabitants.* London: Swedenborg Society.
    1955 "A Hieroglyphic Key to Natural and Spiritual Arcana by Way of Representations and Correspondences." In *Psychological Transactions,* trans. and with a preface by Alfred Acton: 155–213. Philadelphia: Swedenborg Scientific Association. First published 1920.

Toksvig, Signe
    1949 *Emanuel Swedenborg, Scientist and Mystic.* London: Faber & Faber.

Waismann, Friedrich
    1968 *How I See Philosophy.* Ed. R. Harré. London: Macmillan; New York: St. Martin's Press.

Waite, Deborah
    1966 "Kwakiutl Transformation Masks." In Douglas Fraser, ed., *The Many Faces of Primitive Art*: 266–300. Englewood Cliffs: Prentice-Hall.

Waley, Arthur
    1938 *The Analects of Confucius.* London: George Allen & Unwin.
    1939 *Three Ways of Thought in Ancient China.* London: George Allen & Unwin.

Whitehead, Arthur North
    1958 *Symbolism: Its Meaning and Effect.* Cambridge: Cambridge University Press. First ed., Macmillan, 1927.

Wilkins, John
    1668 *An Essay towards a Real Character and a Philosophical Language.* London.

Wilson, Bryan R., ed.
    1970 *Rationality.* Oxford: Basil Blackwell.

Wittgenstein, Ludwig
    1958 *The Blue and Brown Books.* Oxford: Basil Blackwell.

1966   *Lectures and Conversations on Aesthetics, Psychology and Religious Belief.* Ed. Cyril Barrett. Oxford: Basil Blackwell.
1967a *Philosophical Investigations.* Trans. Elizabeth Anscombe. Third ed. Oxford: Basil Blackwell.
1967b "Bemerkungen über Frazers *The Golden Bough.*" *Synthese* 17:233–53.
1967c *Zettel.* Ed. G. E. M. Anscombe and G. H. von Wright. Trans. G. E. M. Anscombe. Oxford: Basil Blackwell.
1969   *On Certainty.* Ed. G. E. M. Anscombe and G. H. von Wright. Trans. Denis Paul and G. E. M. Anscombe. Oxford: Basil Blackwell.
1971   "Remarks on Frazer's 'The Golden Bough.'" Trans. A. C. Miles. Introductory note by Rush Rhees. *The Human World* 3:18–41.
1977a *Vermischte Bermerkungen.* Ed. George Henrik von Wright in co-operation with Heikki Nyman. Oxford: Basil Blackwell.
1977b "Remarques sur le rameau d'or de Frazer." Trans. Jean Lacoste. *Actes de la Recherche en Sciences Sociales* 16:35–42.
1979   *Remarks on Frazer's "Golden Bough"/Bemerkungen über Frazers "Golden Bough."* Ed. Rush Rhees. Trans. A. C. Miles, rev. by Rush Rhees. Retsford, Nottinghamshire: Brynmill Press.

Yarnold, Edward
1971   *The Awe-Inspiring Rites of Initiation: Baptismal Homilies of the Fourth Century.* Slough: St. Paul Publications.

Psalmanaazaar Bibliography

Although the story of Psalmanaazaar is relatively little known, certainly among social anthropologists, there exists a fairly extensive literature on him. Quite a number of the publications are derivative, however, and in recent years especially articles and other treatments have tended simply to record the authors' discovery of this curious personage. It is very desirable that a major critical biography shall in due course be undertaken, and it is in this hope that a separate and annotated bibliography of Psalmanaazaar is provided here. It comprises the sources consulted for chapter 5 above, and, whereas it is more ample than any previously published, it is not claimed to be complete. Editions cited in other publications on Psalmanaazaar but not seen have nevertheless been mentioned, and where particulars could be had from library catalogues these have been supplied. Such routine items as entries in modern works of reference have not been included.

Adams, Percy G.
  1962 *Travelers and Travel Liars, 1660–1800.* Berkeley and Los Angeles: University of California Press.
      Brief account (93–97); the author says of Psalmanaazaar's *Memoirs* that they "have always been considered truthful" (93).

Aikin, John, et al.
  1813 *General Biography; or, Lives, Critical and Historical . . .* , vol. 8. London.
      Entry "Psalmanazar, George" (371–73); "an extraordinary literary impostor" (371); *Description of Formosa* said to have been "commonly regarded as containing genuine information, though in fact replete with improbabilities and inconsistencies" (372); "As a literary character, he is not distinguished from other laborious compilers" (373); source of entry identified as the *Memoirs*; initialed "A." (presumably Aikin).

Amalvi, I. de
  1706 *Éclaircissemens nécessaires . . . par rapport à la conversion de M' George Psalmanazar, Japonais, dans son livre intitulé de l'isle Formosa.* The Hague.

Anon.

    n.d.   [ca. 1710] *An Enquiry into the Objections against George Psalmanaa-
zaar of Formosa, in which the Accounts of the People, and Language of
Formosa by Candidius, and the other European Authors, and the Letters from Geneva, and from Suffolk, about Psalmanaazaar, are proved
not to contradict his Accounts, with Accurate and Authentick Maps of
Formosa and the Isles adjacent, as far as Leuconia, China, and Japan.
With two other very Particular Descriptions of Formosa. To which is
added George Psalmanaazaar's Answer to Mons. D'Amalvy of Sluice.*
London.

        The Epistle Dedicatory concludes with "Your most obe-
dient, and, most devoted Servants"; the Bodleian copy is
inscribed "From yᵉ Authors." "We got all the printed Accounts we could hear of, and enquired of as many Trav-
ellers as we met with . . ."; "we put out publick Notice of
our Inquiry, and intreated, and as far as good Manners permitted, even challenged the World to send us what they
have to say against him" (3). Includes "A Short Description
of the Isle Formosa" by Johannes Albertus Lubomirski
(21–25); reproduces "Paper of Objections" received by the
bookseller in response to the authors' advertisement; the
objections are posed in the form of twenty questions heard
leveled against Psalmanaazaar's *Description*, the majority re-
lating to Christianity (26–29).

Anon.

    1711   "Advertisement." *The Spectator*, No. 14, Friday March 16 (two
pages, unnumbered; item on verso).

        "On the first of April will be performed at the Play-house
in the Hay-mauket [*sic*] an Opera call'd The Cruelty
of Atreus. N.B. The Scene wherein Thyestes eats his
own Children, is to be performed by the famous Mr.
Psalmanazar, lately arrived from Formosa: The whole Sup-
per being set to Kettle-drums."

Anon.

    1764a   "Some Account of the late learned George Psalmanazar, the
reputed Formosan and Convert to Christianity." *Annual Register*
("Characters"):66–71. London, 1792.

        Account based on the *Memoirs*, which are largely quoted:
"He seemed, through a long course of life, to abhor the imposture, yet contented himself with owning it to his most
intimate friends" (70).

Anon.
    1764b "Some Account of the late George Psalmanazar, from a History written by himself." *The Gentleman's Magazine* 34:503–8, 573–76, 623–29.

        Introductory note, in the November issue, alludes to Psalmanaazaar as one "who pretended to be a Native of Formosa, and published a fabulous Account of that Island"; articles abstracted "from a History written by himself, and just printed for the Benefit of his Executrix" (503).

Anon.
    1765a "Some Account of the late George Psalmanazar." *The Gentleman's Magazine* 35:9–14.

        Account based on the *Memoirs*, reported in the third person, concluded.

Anon.
    1765b "A Genuine Conversation held with Psalmanazar on his first coming to England, with the Sentiments of the People at that Time concerning him." *The Gentleman's Magazine* 35:78–81.

        Introductory note states that the information is "taken from some letters written almost immediately after the conversation happened." Letter headed "Sherdington, June, 1704" reports a dinner with Sir John Guise at Gloucester, where Psalmanaazaar was spoken of. Identical with Gwinnett and Thomas (1731), q.v.

Bayne-Powell, Rosamund
    1951 *Travellers in Eighteenth-century England.* London: John Murray.

        A few scattered allusions (100, 102, 106), followed by a brief account of Psalmanaazaar (191–94); shallow, sometimes inaccurate or suppositious; no original matter.

Boswell, James
    1934 *Boswell's Life of Johnson.* Ed. George Birkbeck Hill; rev. and enl. by L. F. Powell. 6 vols. Oxford: Clarendon Press.

        Appendix A, "George Psalmanazar" (3:443–49), by G. B. Hill. Excellent compendium.

Boucher de la Richarderie, G.
    1808 *Bibliothèque universelle des voyages*, vol. 5. Paris.

        "Isle de Formose.—Description de l'île de Formose, par Gaspard [*sic*] Psalmanazar" (289–91); based on 1704 edition of the *Description*; cites also a French edition of 1708 and a

German edition of 1716 (Frankfurt). Psalmanaazaar given
as authority for the eating of human flesh: "lui-même,
transporté à Londres, avoit tellement conservé ce goût
dépravé, qu'excité à manger de la chair d'une femme pen-
due, il le fit sans répugnance" (290).

Bowen, Emanuel
1747 *A Complete System of Geography: Being a Description of all the
Countries . . . of the Known World.* 2 vols. London.
Rejects the assumption that the *Description of Formosa* is a
true account; states that Psalmanaazaar "hath long since ingenuously owned the contrary" (2:251).

Bracey, Robert
1925 *Eighteenth Century Studies, and Other Papers.* Oxford: Basil
Blackwell.
Account of "George Psalmanazar, Impostor and Penitent"
(77–85). "It must be admitted that only a genius of the first
rank could thus have created an island, constructed a history, excogitated an alphabet, language and grammar, made
a new division of the year into twenty months, and evolved
an entirely new religion!" (81). Mentions a second edition
of the *Memoirs:* "London, Davis and Newbury, 1765."

Campbell, Wm., ed.
1896 *The Articles of Christian Instruction in Favorlang-Formosan . . .
with Psalmanazar's Dialogue between a Japanese and a Formosan.
. . .* London: Kegan Paul, Trench, Trübner.
The *Dialogue* is reprinted from the original printing of
1707, with the title page in facsimile (103–21).

Candidius, George
1704 "An Account of the Island of Formosa in the East-Indies." In *A
Collection of Voyages and Travels,* 1:526–33. London: Awnsham
and John Churchill.
Publication commonly referred to as "Churchill's Voyages"; the account by Candidius is a translation from "the
High-Dutch"; source and date not given; cf. Montanus
(1671).

Chevalley, A. D.
1936 *La Bête du Gévaudan.* Paris: Nouvelle Revue Française.
Not seen; reported to contain a part on Psalmanaazaar. Cf.
Winnet (1971).

D'Israeli, Isaac

    1824 *A Second Series of Curiosities of Literature.* 3 vols. London: John Murray.

        Psalmanaazaar treated in the chapter entitled "Literary Forgeries" (3:64–72); brief biography based on the *Memoirs*. "The life is tedious; but I have curiously traced the progress of the mind in an ingenious imposture, which is worth preservation" (64).

    1932 *Curiosities of Literature.* Selected and edited by Edwin Valentine Mitchell. New York and London: D. Appleton.

        "George Psalmanazar . . . exceeded in powers of deception any of the great impostors of learning. His Island of Formosa was an illusion eminently bold, and maintained with as much felicity as erudition; and great must have been that erudition which could form a pretended language and its grammar, and fertile the genius which could invent the history of an unknown people: it is said that the deception was only satisfactorily ascertained by his own penitential confession; he had defied and baffled the most learned" (103–4, complete entry; Psalmanaazaar is not in the index).

Farrer, J. A.

    1907 *Literary Forgeries.* Introduction by Andrew Lang. London: Longmans, Green.

        Chapter V, "Psalmanazar: The Famous Formosan" (82–97). "The secret of Psalmanazar's success lay in the fact that he not only tickled that love for the marvellous in the British people . . . but also pandered to the strong feeling against the Jesuits then prevalent in England" (91). Judges the *Description* to be "of far less interest than the *Memoirs*," which purports to be pure autobiography but unfolds "an amazing story of real life that puts a severe strain on belief" (94). Characterizes the *Description* none the less as a "triumphant fraud" (95). A fair, readable, and accurate sketch; serviceable as a general introduction to the character.

Gwinnett, Richard, and Thomas, Elizabeth

    1731 *Pylades and Corinna.* . . . London.

        "A Conversation between Psalmanaazaar the Formosan, and some Ladies, with several curious Particulars not in his Book" (Table of Contents, referring to p. 59; account continues to p. 66). Reports "a dinner with Sir John Guise, at Gloucester, who gave me [Gwinnett] some Account of the

famous Formosan Psalmanaazaar, whom he had seen lately
at London" (57–58). "He is thought by some to be a Counterfeit, and a Jesuit under the Character of a Japonese; the
Truth or Falsehood of which Supposition, time will discover" (58). The writer afterwards had an interview with
Psalmanaazaar, in the company of several gentlemen and
ladies, at Oxford. The report includes particulars of a number of topics including most prominently human sacrifice
and cannibalism; Psalmanaazaar claimed to have eaten part
of a black slave, whose flesh he found "tough and un-
savoury" because slaves worked so hard (61). "Psalmanaazar
is thought to be a fictitious name . . . ; certain it is, he
makes no brags of his family, and is not very easy in being
examined much about it" (79).

Hearne, Thomas
    1885 *Remarks and Collections*, vol. 1. Oxford: Clarendon Press.
            Entry of July 28, 1705, quoted in chap. 5 above. Entry of
            July 9, 1706, reads: "Mr. Topping of Xt. [Christ] Church
            . . . tells me y^t Salmanezzer, the famous Formosan, when
            he left Xt. Church (where he resided while in Oxoñ) left
            behind him a Book in MS^t. wherein a distinct Acct. was
            given of ye Consular and Imperial Coyns, by himself"
            (271). No trace of such a work survives in the college.

Johnson, Samuel
    1787 *Works*. Ed. J. Hawkins. London.
            "He [Johnson] was very well acquainted with Psalmanaazar
            [*sic*], the pretended Formosan. . . . He told many anecdotes
            of him, and said, he was supposed by his accent to have
            been a Gascon. He said, that Psalmanaazar spoke English
            with the city accent, and coarsely enough. He for some
            years spent his evenings at a publick house near Old-Street,
            where many persons went to talk with him; Johnson was
            asked whether he ever contradicted Psalmanaazar;—I should
            as soon, said he, have thought of contradicting a bishop;—
            so high did he hold his character in the latter part of his life.
            When he was asked whether he had ever mentioned For-
            mosa before him, he said, he was afraid to mention even
            China" (11:206–7).

Knowlson, James R.
1965 "George Psalmanaazaar: The Fake Formosan." *History Today* 15:871–76.
Suggests that Psalmanaazaar, in inventing his "Formosan" language, was influenced by works on universal and ideal languages, such as that by John Wilkins (1668); supplies no grounds to think so. Says that in the *Description* Psalmanaazaar added much that was taken from works of travel "or prose fiction"; does not provide evidence. Thin; no original case apart from the above.

Lee, Sidney
1921–22 "Compton, Henry." *Dictionary of National Biography* 4:899–903. London: Oxford University Press.
Contains nothing on Psalmanaazaar, but very useful on his first powerful protector.
1921–22 "Psalmanazar, George." *Dictionary of National Biography* 16:439–42.
Indispensable; the most informative and reliable single biography to date.

Le Fêvre-Deumier, J.
1895 *Célébrités anglaises . . . George Psalmanazar, etc.* Paris.
Not seen; Lee describes it as "a very slight sketch" (*Dictionary of National Biography* 16:442).

Maycock, A. L.
1934 "The Amazing Story of George Psalmanasar" [*sic*]. *Blackwood's Magazine* 235:797–808.
Well written narrative, based on the *Memoirs*, which are described as "a fascinating book, written throughout with a touching sincerity and alive with the readiest wit and keenest insight" (808); no new matter or original analysis.

Montanus [van Bergen or van den Berg], Arnoldus
1671 *Atlas Chinensis . . . English'd* [etc.] *by John Ogilby.* London.
Part "On Formosa" (9–39); cites Candidius (14) as authority who resided on the island in 1628. (Montanus is identified in A. J. van der Aa, *Biographisch Woordenboek der Nederlanden . . .* , vol. 12 [Haarlem, 1869]:1006–9.) Gives the Chinese name for Formosa as Paccande (9), which in the

form "Pac-Ando" as rendered by Psalmanaazaar (1704:145; cf. 1705a, 14 Object. 4 Answ.) was declared by a contemporary critic not to be Chinese, a detail which increases by its particularity the likelihood that Psalmanaazaar relied on Montanus.

Napier, Elizabeth R.
1979 "Swift's 'Trampling upon the Crucifix': A Parallel." *Notes and Queries* 26 (December):544–48.
1981 "Swift, Kaempfner, and Psalmanaazaar: Further Remarks on 'Trampling upon the Crucifix.'" *Notes and Queries* 28 (June):226.

Palmer, S. [actually Psalmanaazaar, George]
1732 *A General History of Printing*. London.
The preface expresses an obligation to the Earls of Pembroke and Oxford (v); the former was a patron of Psalmanaazaar until he lost confidence in him. A page added after Palmer's death concludes: "those who know Mr. Palmer will think it sufficient to say the subject is the Art of Printing, and he the author of it" (vii); the imputation to which this responds is not stated.

Piozzi, Hester Lynch
1786 *Anecdotes of the late Samuel Johnson, Ll.D., during the last Twenty Years of his Life*. London.
"When I asked Dr. Johnson, who was the *best* man he had ever known? 'Psalmanazar,' was the unexpected reply" (173). "Though there was much esteem however, there was I believe but little confidence between them; they conversed merely about general topics, religion and learning, of which both were undoubtedly stupendous examples" (174). Of his contributions to the *Universal History*: "all traces of the wit and the wanderer were probably worn out before he undertook the work." "His pious and patient endurance of a tedious illness, ending in an exemplary death, confirmed the strong impression his merit had made upon the mind of Mr. Johnson" (175).

Psalmanaazaar, George [pseud.]
1704 *An Historical and Geographical Description of Formosa, an Island subject to the Emperor of Japan, giving an Account of the Religion, Customs, Manners, &c. of the Inhabitants*. London: Printed for Dan. Brown, at the Black Swan.

1705a *An Historical and Geographical Description of Formosa, an Island subject to the Emperor of Japan.* Second ed., corr. London.

"The second Edition corrected, with many large and useful Additions, particularly a new Preface clearly answering every thing that has been objected against the Author and the Book" (title page). The new preface is described as "in Vindication of himself from the Reflections of a Jesuit lately come from *China*, with an account of what passed between them" (loc. cit.).

1705b *Description de l'île Formosa, . . . dressée sur les mémoires du sieur George Psalmanaazaar . . . par le sieur N.F.D.B.R.* Amsterdam.

Not seen; particulars from the catalogue of the Bibliothèque Nationale, Paris.

1707 *A Dialogue between a Japonese and a Formosan, about some Points of the Religion of the Time.* London.

Name of author given as "G. P—m—r." The preface announces the chief purpose of the work to be "to vindicate the Japonese" of the European charge of "being a People, much given to Superstition" (first page).

n.d. *L'Eclercisseur Eclercy, or an Answer to a Book entituled Eclercissements sur ce que, &c., by Isaack D'Amalvy, Minister of the French Church at Sluice.* In Anon., *Enquiry* [1710]: 55–78.

Answers objections attaching to Psalmanaazaar's conversion and baptism, and to points of theology. The publication date of 1710 is from the catalogue of the Bodleian Library, confirmed by the general catalogue of the British Library and assented to by Mr. Alan Sterenberg of the Reference Division of the latter institution.

1739 *Description dressée sur les mémoires du sieur George Psalmanaazaar, contenant une ample relation de l'isle Formosa. . . .* Paris: aux dépens de la Compagnie.

Not seen; particulars from catalogue of the Bibliothèque Nationale, Paris.

1753 *Essays on the Following Subjects: 1. On the Reality and Evidence of Miracles . . .* [etc.] London.

Author given as "An Obscure Layman in Town."

1764 *Memoirs of * * * *, commonly known by the Name of George Psalmanazar; a Reputed Native of Formosa.* Written by himself in order to be published after his death. London: Printed for the Executrix.

Second ed., London: Davis & Newbury, 1765 (Bracey 1925:85); Dublin, 1765 (British Library catalogue).

1926 *An Historical and Geographical Description of Formosa.* . . . The
      Library of Impostors, ed. N. M. Penzer, vol. 2. London: Robert
      Holden.
      A reprint of the 1704 edition.

Richardson, John
   1778 *A Dissertation on the Languages, Literature, and Manners of the East-
         ern Nations.* Second ed. Oxford: Clarendon Press.
         "In Europe, we have had many instances of the forgery of
         books, in matters of mere curiosity; and we have found their
         detection difficult" (26); footnote (f) refers to "the History
         of Formosa by the Jew Psalmanasar [*sic*]"; "Psalmanazar in-
         vented even a language, sufficiently original, copious, and
         regular, to impose upon men of very extensive learning"
         (237, n. f).

Sergeant, Philip W.
   n.d. [1925] *Liars and Fakers.* London: Hutchinson.
         "Psalmanazar the Formosan" (199–235). "Psalmanazar's
         writings . . . reveal no sense of humour." Date of his birth:
         "He makes several statements which cannot be reconciled
         with the date in his will and favour rather a date as late as
         1684. The point is only of importance in so far as, the later
         he was born, the more wonderful his imposture" (202).
         The *Enquiry* (Anon. 1710) "was obviously inspired by Psal-
         manazar himself, and was dedicated to Bishop Compton,
         who probably contributed to the expense of publication"
         (223); evidence to this effect does not appear.

Smollett, Tobias George
   1771 *The Expedition of Humphrey Clinker.* 3 vols. London.
         "Psalmanazar, after having drudged half a century in the lit-
         erary mill, in all the simplicity and abstinence of an Asiatic,
         subsists upon the charity of a few booksellers, just sufficient
         to keep him from the parish" (2:35, letter of J. Melford,
         headed London, June 10, to Sir Watkin Phillips, Jesus Col-
         lege, Oxon.).

[Swift, Jonathan]
   1729 *A Modest Proposal for Preventing the Children of Poor People from
         being a Burthen to their Parents or the Country and for making them
         Beneficial to the Publick.* Dublin.

"The want of Venison might well be supplied by the Bodies of young Lads and Maidens, not exceeding fourteen Years of Age, nor under Twelve. . . . But, in order to justify my friend, he confessed that this expedient was put into his head by the famous *Sallmanaazor*, a Native of the Island *Formosa*, who came from thence to London, above twenty Years ago, and in Conversation told my friend, that in his Country when any young Person happened to be put to Death, the Executioner sold the Carcass to *Persons of Quality*, as a prime Dainty, and that, in his Time, the Body of a plump Girl of fifteen, who was crucified for an attempt to Poison the Emperor, was sold to his Imperial Majesty's prime Minister of State, and other great Mandarins of the Court, in *Joints from the Gibbet*, at four hundred Crowns" (10).

Varenius, Bernhardus
   1649 *Descriptio Regni Iaponiae*. Amsterdam.

Walckenaer, Charles-Athanase
   1843 "Psalmanazar, George." *Biographie Universelle* (ed. Louis Gabriel Michaud), nouvelle édition, rev., 34:435–41.
      From the example of an incompetent Jesuit teacher at school, "Il vit qu'il était possible avec de l'audace de parler de beaucoup de choses sans les connaître" (436). ". . . Il eût été facile de s'assurer, par un examen attentif, que [la description] de Psalmanazar n'était qu'une fiction grossière" (439). Three French editions of the *Description*, in 1705, 1708, and 1712; two in German, 1712 and 1716 (440). "Dans toutes les biographies anglaises ou françaises que nous avons eu occasion de compulser, l'article de cet aventurier extraordinaire, de cet estimable et laborieux écrivain, est à la fois inexact et incomplet" (441).

Walpole, Horace
   1955 *Correspondence with William Mason*. Yale Edition of Horace Walpole's Correspondence, ed. W. S. Lewis, vol. 28. London: Oxford University Press; New Haven: Yale University Press.
      Letter to Mason, 17 February 1777: "Psalmanazar alone seems to have surpassed the genius of Chatterton" (282).

Whitehead, John
   1973 *This Solemn Mockery: The Art of Literary Forgery*. London: Arlington Books.

Chapter 3: "The History of Formosa" (36–43); account of
Psalmanaazaar. "His book [viz. the *Description*] is a very
convincing and clever piece of fiction writing" (39). Brief
narrative of Psalmanaazaar's life, based on the *Memoirs*, the
Enquiry [Anon. 1710], and Sergeant (1925).

Winnet, A. R.
1971 "George Psalmanazar." *The New Rambler: Journal of the Johnson
Society of London* 110:6–17.
Concerning the *Description*: ". . . the whole effect being
one of such verisimilitude as to deceive an unsuspecting
reader" (8). Among the motives of impostors, "an inability
to distinguish fact from reality, . . . of which there is no indication in Psalmanazar" (15–16). A summary made from
published sources including Bracey (1925) and Chevalley
(1936).

Index